P9-CNB-632

I'm trying to remember when I've read a more important book. With prophetic intensity, Yancey successfully nudges aside every other worthy—and not so worthy—agenda and restores "dispensing grace" as the central mission of the church. His thesis will alienate those whose Christianity centers on something else, and he invites all who thirst for grace to make it the bottom line of their lives. The message of this book has the power to reform the church, one relationship at a time.

—Dr. Larry Crabb
Psychologist, author,
Professor, Colorado Christian University

Philip Yancey is a writer's writer. His command and precision of language, textured narrative, sentence cadence, depth of insight, graceful style, and disarming self-disclosure make *What's So Amazing About Grace?* the crown jewel of all his books.

If you read the chapter "The Lovesick Father" and do not weep for joy, I suggest you check your pulse, get an electrocardiogram, or make an appointment with your mortician.

—Brennan Manning
Author of *Abba's Child*

As journalist, gadfly, and prophet rolled into one, Yancey's habit is to stick out his neck and say, "Look—see—change!" Yancey's treatment of the life of grace is vintage Yancey, and will give readers a salutary Christian shake-up.

—J. I. Packer
Professor, Regent College

This is a very important book about the most important subject in human history. There are huge amounts of sermon material here. Philip Yancey has written another brilliant award winner.

—Dr. Tony Campolo

This is beyond a doubt the very best book I have read from a Christian author in my life. . . .

Yancey might have written the "last best word" about the "last best word," namely, grace. A gifted writer with profound insights who can make the biblical text come alive, Yancey also has the ability to relate it to the world in which we all live today. Philip has seen much of that world, has reflected deeply on its needs, and has come back to the Bible and this beautiful gift of grace that needs to be continually offered. At a time when the actions of Christians holding extreme positions can inoculate many against the Gospel and the claims of Christ, Philip draws us back to the gift of grace, freely offered, needing to be humbly accepted, if we are to bear effective witness of God's love for us.

—Dr. Robert A. Seiple
President, World Vision

According to Philip Yancey, "Grace is, among other things, Christianity's best gift to the world—is free of charge to people who do not deserve it—sounds a startling note of liberation—and has no end to what it might pardon." Philip stretches the mind, touches the heart, and applies the grace of God to his writing theology applications and illustrations—the result being blessing, help, hope and joy for the reader. What a grand investment of time for those of us thirsty to "know" in reality the grace of our Lord Jesus Christ.

—Jill Briscoe

One of the most gifted writers of our day has put a telescope on the brilliant star of grace and finely focused on what a beautiful and powerful healing force followers of Jesus Christ could become. Empowered by love and forgiveness we could mount a revolution more glorious than all the political establishments the world has ever known.

—The Honorable Mark O. Hatfield

Evangelical Christians are big on salvation but often short on grace. Philip Yancey longs for the day when churches won't be regarded as clubs of righteous people or dens of political correctness, but rather as communities of sinners to which all other sinners are welcome.

What's So Amazing About Grace? is a marvelously important book.

—Jim Wallis
Editor-in-chief, *Sojourners*
author, *Who Speaks for God*?

Once more Philip Yancey has charmed us with amazing insight on an old but never outworn concept: *grace.* Page after page of this wonderful book has spoken to my soul and left a treasure of thought. This is great writing! Only those blind in spirit, hardened with hatred, will miss its significant message. Although Yancey never says it, he has written about the key to something many Christ-followers often talk and pray about: genuine *revival.*

—Gordon MacDonald

Philip Yancey is one of the most engaging and convicting writers in the Christian world. Once again he has produced a work with something in it to make everybody mad.

—Charles W. Colson
Prison Fellowship Ministry

PHILIP YANCEY

AUTHOR OF THE JESUS I NEVER KNEW

WHAT'S SO AMAZING ABOUT GRACE?

ZondervanPublishingHouse
Grand Rapids, Michigan

A Division of HarperCollins*Publishers*

What's So Amazing About Grace?
Copyright © 1997 by Philip D. Yancey

Requests for information should be addressed to:

ZondervanPublishingHouse
Grand Rapids, Michigan 49530

Library of Congress Cataloging-in-Publication Data

Yancey, Philip.
What's so amazing about grace? / Philip Yancey.
p. cm.
Includes bibliographical references.
ISBN: 0-310-21327-4
1. Grace (Theology) I. Title.
BT761.2.Y35 1997
234—dc21 97-21286
CIP

This edition printed on acid-free paper and meets the American National Standards Institute Z39.48 standard.

Interior design by Sherri L. Hoffman

Printed in the United States of America

99 00 01 02 03 04 05 06 /❖ DC/ 30 29 28 27 26 25 24 23 22 21 20 19

Contents

Acknowledgments

Reading a list of names in someone's acknowledgments page reminds me of the acceptance speeches on Oscars night, when actors and actresses thank everyone from their kindergarten nannies to their third-grade piano teachers.

I suppose I'm also grateful to my third-grade piano teacher, but I find that when I write a book, there are a few people who are not luxuries but necessities. The first draft and the final draft of this book are astonishingly different, thanks mainly to feedback from these people: Doug Frank, Harold Fickett, Tim Stafford, Scott Hoezee, and Hal Knight. I asked for their help because they all know something about writing and also something about grace, and their responses to me proved that. I am in their debt.

My colleagues at *Christianity Today,* especially Harold Myra, helped me with some very sensitive areas in the manuscript.

One poor fellow, John Sloan, gets paid to edit my manuscripts, and as a result he gave feedback on not just the first draft but all subsequent drafts as well. Editors do their work invisibly, but John's fine contributions are very visible to me as I read the final result.

Thanks also to Bob Hudson at Zondervan, who added the final editing touches.

A feeling of gratitude is wholly appropriate when my theme is grace. As I think of these my friends, I feel at once enriched and undeserving.

Come to think of it, I should also thank the apostle Paul who, in his magnificent letter to the Romans, taught me everything I know about grace and gave me the outline to this book as well. I describe "ungrace," attempt to fathom grace, deal with objections that arise during that process, and discuss how grace is lived out in a cold, flinty world—precisely the progression in Romans.

(I should also note that, though the stories in this book are true, in some cases I have changed names and places to protect confidentiality.)

What's So Amazing About Grace?

I know nothing, except what everyone knows—
if there when Grace dances, I should dance.

W. H. AUDEN

ONE

The Last Best Word

I told a story in my book *The Jesus I Never Knew*, a true story that long afterward continued to haunt me. I heard it from a friend who works with the down-and-out in Chicago:

> A prostitute came to me in wretched straits, homeless, sick, unable to buy food for her two-year-old daughter. Through sobs and tears, she told me she had been renting out her daughter—two years old!—to men interested in kinky sex. She made more renting out her daughter for an hour than she could earn on her own in a night. She had to do it, she said, to support her own drug habit. I could hardly bear hearing her sordid story. For one thing, it made me legally liable—I'm required to report cases of child abuse. I had no idea what to say to this woman.
>
> At last I asked if she had ever thought of going to a church for help. I will never forget the look of pure, naive shock that crossed her face. "Church!" she cried. "Why would I ever go there? I was already feeling terrible about myself. They'd just make me feel worse."

What struck me about my friend's story is that women much like this prostitute fled toward Jesus, not away from him. The worse a person felt about herself, the more likely she saw Jesus as a refuge. Has the church lost that gift? Evidently the down-and-out, who flocked to Jesus when he lived on earth, no longer feel welcome among his followers. What has happened?

The more I pondered this question, the more I felt drawn to one word as the key. All that follows uncoils from that one word.

As a writer, I play with words all day long. I toy with them, listen for their overtones, crack them open, and try to stuff my thoughts inside. I've found that words tend to spoil over the years, like old meat. Their meaning rots away. Consider the word "charity," for instance. When King James translators contemplated the highest form of love they settled on the word "charity" to convey it. Nowadays we hear the scornful protest, "I don't want your charity!"

Perhaps I keep circling back to *grace* because it is one grand theological word that has not spoiled. I call it "the last best word" because every English usage I can find retains some of the glory of the original. Like a vast aquifer, the word underlies our proud civilization, reminding us that good things come not from our own efforts, rather by the grace of God. Even now, despite our secular drift, taproots still stretch toward grace. Listen to how we use the word.

Many people "say grace" before meals, acknowledging daily bread as a gift from God. We are *grateful* for someone's kindness, *gratified* by good news, *congratulated* when successful, *gracious* in hosting friends. When a person's service pleases us, we leave a *gratuity*. In each of these uses I hear a pang of childlike delight in the undeserved.

A composer of music may add *grace notes* to the score. Though not essential to the melody—they are *gratuitous*—these notes add a flourish whose presence would be missed. When I first attempt a piano sonata by Beethoven or Schubert I play it through a few times without the grace notes. The sonata carries along, but oh what a difference it makes when I am able to add in the grace notes, which season the piece like savory spices.

In England, some uses hint loudly at the word's theological source. British subjects address royalty as "Your grace." Students at Oxford and Cambridge may "receive a grace" exempting them from certain academic requirements. Parliament declares an "act of grace" to pardon a criminal.

New York publishers also suggest the theological meaning with their policy of *gracing*. If I sign up for twelve issues of a magazine, I may receive a few extra copies even after my subscription has expired. These are "grace issues," sent free of charge (or, *gratis*) to tempt me to resubscribe. Credit cards, rental car agencies, and mortgage companies likewise extend to customers an undeserved "grace period."

I also learn about a word from its opposite. Newspapers speak of communism's "fall from grace," a phrase similarly applied to Jimmy Swaggart, Richard Nixon, and O. J. Simpson. We insult a person by pointing out the dearth of grace: "You *ingrate!*" we say, or worse, "You're a *disgrace!*" A truly despicable person has no "saving grace" about him. My favorite use of the root word *grace* occurs in the mellifluous phrase *persona non grata*: a person who offends the U.S. government by some act of treachery is officially proclaimed a "person without grace."

The many uses of the word in English convince me that *grace* is indeed amazing—truly our last best word. It contains the essence of the gospel as a drop of water can contain the image of the sun. The world thirsts for grace in ways it does not even recognize; little wonder the hymn "Amazing Grace" edged its way onto the Top Ten charts two hundred years after composition. For a society that seems adrift, without moorings, I know of no better place to drop an anchor of faith.

Like grace notes in music, though, the state of grace proves fleeting. The Berlin Wall falls in a night of euphoria; South African blacks queue up in long, exuberant lines to cast their first votes ever; Yitzhak Rabin and Yasser Arafat shake hands in the Rose Garden—for a moment, grace descends. And then Eastern Europe sullenly settles into the long task of rebuilding, South Africa tries to figure out how to run a country, Arafat dodges bullets and Rabin is felled by one. Like a dying star, grace dissipates in a final burst of pale light, and is then engulfed by the black hole of "ungrace."

"The great Christian revolutions," said H. Richard Niebuhr, "come not by the discovery of something that was not known before. They happen when somebody takes radically something that was always there." Oddly, I sometimes find a shortage of grace within the church, an institution founded to proclaim, in Paul's phrase, "the gospel of God's grace."

Author Stephen Brown notes that a veterinarian can learn a lot about a dog owner he has never met just by observing the dog. What does the world learn about God by watching us his followers on earth? Trace the roots of *grace*, or *charis* in Greek, and you will find a verb that means "I rejoice, I am glad." In my experience, rejoicing and gladness are not the first images that come to mind when people think of the church. They think of holier-than-thous. They think of church as a place to go after you have cleaned up your act, not before. They think of morality, not grace. "Church!" said the prostitute, "Why would I ever go there? I was already feeling terrible about myself. They'd just make me feel worse."

Such an attitude comes partly from a misconception, or bias, by outsiders. I have visited soup kitchens, homeless shelters, hospices, and prison ministries staffed by Christian volunteers generous with grace. And yet the prostitute's comment stings because she has found a weak spot in the church. Some of us seem so anxious about avoiding hell that we forget to celebrate our journey toward heaven. Others of us, rightly concerned about issues in a modern "culture war," neglect the church's mission as a haven of grace in this world of ungrace.

"Grace is everywhere," said the dying priest in Georges Bernanos's novel *Diary of a Country Priest*. Yes, but how easily we pass by, deaf to the euphony.

I attended a Bible college. Years later, when I was sitting next to the president of that school on an airplane, he asked me to assess my education. "Some good, some bad," I replied. "I met many godly people there. In fact, I met God there. Who can place a value on that? And yet I later realized that in four years I learned almost nothing about grace. It may be the most important word in the Bible, the heart of the gospel. How could I have missed it?"

I related our conversation in a subsequent chapel address and, in doing so, offended the faculty. Some suggested I not be invited back to speak. One gentle soul wrote to ask whether I should have phrased things differently. Shouldn't I have said that as a student I lacked the receptors to receive the grace that was all around me? Because I respect and love this man, I thought long and hard about his question. Ultimately, however, I concluded that I had experienced as much ungrace on the campus of a Bible college as I had anywhere else in life.

A counselor, David Seamands, summed up his career this way:

> Many years ago I was driven to the conclusion that the two major causes of most emotional problems among evangelical Christians are these: the failure to understand, receive, and live out God's unconditional grace and forgiveness; and the failure to give out that unconditional love, forgiveness, and grace to other people. . . . We read, we hear, we believe a good theology of grace. But that's not the way we live. The good news of the Gospel of grace has not penetrated the level of our emotions.

The world can do almost anything as well as or better than the church," says Gordon MacDonald. "You need not be a Christian to build houses, feed the hungry, or heal the sick. There is only one thing the world cannot do. It cannot offer grace." MacDonald has put his finger on the church's single most important contribution. Where else can the world go to find grace?

The Italian novelist Ignazio Silone wrote about a revolutionary hunted by the police. In order to hide him, his comrades dressed him in the garb of a priest and sent him to a remote village in the foothills of the Alps. Word got out, and soon a long line of peasants appeared at his door, full of stories of their sins and broken lives. The "priest" protested and tried to turn them away, to no avail. He had no recourse but to sit and listen to the stories of people starving for grace.

I sense, in fact, that is why any person goes to church: out of hunger for grace. The book *Growing Up Fundamentalist* tells of a reunion of students from a missionary academy in Japan. "With one or two exceptions, all had left the faith and come back," one of the students reported. "And those of us who had come back had one thing in common: we had all discovered grace. . . ."

As I look back on my own pilgrimage, marked by wanderings, detours, and dead ends, I see now that what pulled me along was my search for grace. I rejected the church for a time because I found so little grace there. I returned because I found grace nowhere else.

I have barely tasted of grace myself, have rendered less than I have received, and am in no wise an "expert" on grace. These are, in fact, the very reasons that impel me to write. I want to know more, to understand more, to experience more grace. I dare not—and the danger is very real—write an ungracious book about grace. Accept then, here at the beginning, that I write as a pilgrim qualified only by my craving for grace.

Grace does not offer an easy subject for a writer. To borrow E. B. White's comment about humor, "[Grace] can be dissected, as a frog, but the thing dies in the process, and the innards are discouraging to any but the pure scientific mind." I have just read a thirteen-page treatise on grace in the *New Catholic Encyclopedia*, which has cured me of any desire to dissect grace and display its innards. I do not want the thing to die. For this reason, I will rely more on stories than on syllogisms.

In sum, I would far rather convey grace than explain it.

PART I

How Sweet the Sound

Two

Babette's Feast: A Story

Karen Blixen, Danish by birth, married a baron and spent the years 1914–31 managing a coffee plantation in British East Africa (her *Out of Africa* tells of these years). After a divorce she returned to Denmark and began writing in English under the pseudonym Isak Dinesen. One of her stories, "Babette's Feast," became a cult classic after being made into a movie in the 1980s.

Dinesen set her story in Norway, but the Danish filmmakers changed the location to an impoverished fishing village on the coast of Denmark, a town of muddy streets and thatched-roof hovels. In this grim setting, a white-bearded Dean led a group of worshipers in an austere Lutheran sect.

What few worldly pleasures could tempt a peasant in Norre Vosburg, this sect renounced. All wore black. Their diet consisted of boiled cod and a gruel made from boiling bread in water fortified with a splash of ale. On the Sabbath, the group met together and sang songs about "Jerusalem, my happy home, name ever dear to me." They had fixed their compasses on the New Jerusalem, with life on earth tolerated as a way to get there.

The old Dean, a widower, had two teenage daughters: Martine, named for Martin Luther, and Philippa, named for

Luther's disciple Philip Melanchthon. Villagers used to attend the church just to feast their eyes on these two, whose radiant beauty could not be suppressed despite the sisters' best efforts.

Martine caught the eye of a dashing young cavalry officer. When she successfully resisted his advances—after all, who would care for her aging father?—he rode away to marry instead a lady-in-waiting to Queen Sophia.

Philippa possessed not only beauty but also the voice of a nightingale. When she sang about Jerusalem, shimmering visions of the heavenly city seemed to appear. And so it happened that Philippa made the acquaintance of the most famous operatic singer of the day, the Frenchman Achille Papin, who was spending some time on the coast for his health. As he walked the dirt paths of a backwater town, Papin heard to his astonishment a voice worthy of the Grand Opera of Paris.

Allow me to teach you to sing properly, he urged Philippa, and all of France will fall at your feet. Royalty will line up to meet you, and you will ride in a horse-drawn carriage to dine at the magnificent Café Anglais. Flattered, Philippa consented to a few lessons, but only a few. Singing about love made her nervous, the flutterings she felt inside troubled her further, and when an aria from *Don Giovanni* ended with her being held in Papin's embrace, his lips brushing hers, she knew beyond doubt that these new pleasures must be renounced. Her father wrote a note declining all future lessons, and Achille Papin returned to Paris, as disconsolate as if he'd misplaced a winning lottery ticket.

Fifteen years passed, and much changed in the village. The two sisters, now middle-aged spinsters, had attempted to carry on the mission of their deceased father, but without his stern leadership the sect splintered badly. One Brother bore a grudge against another concerning some business matter. Rumors spread about a thirty-year-old sexual affair involving two of the members. A pair of old ladies had not spoken to each other for a decade. Although the sect still met on the Sabbath and sang the old hymns, only a handful bothered to attend, and the music had lost its luster. Despite all these problems, the Dean's two daughters remained faithful, organizing the services and boiling bread for the toothless elders of the village.

One night, a night too rainy for anyone to venture on the muddy streets, the sisters heard a heavy thump at the door. When they opened it, a woman collapsed in a swoon. They revived her only to find she spoke no Danish. She handed them a letter from Achille Papin. At the sight of his name Philippa's face flushed, and her hand trembled as she read the letter of introduction. The woman's name was Babette, and she had lost her husband and son during the civil war in France. Her life in danger, she had to flee, and Papin had found her passage on a ship in hopes that this village might show her mercy. "Babette can cook," the letter read.

The sisters had no money to pay Babette and felt dubious about employing a maid in the first place. They distrusted her cooking—didn't the French eat horses and frogs? But through gestures and pleading, Babette softened their hearts. She would do any chores in exchange for room and board.

For the next twelve years Babette worked for the sisters. The first time Martine showed her how to split a cod and cook the gruel, Babette's eyebrow shot upward and her nose wrinkled a little, but she never once questioned her assignments. She fed the poor people of the town and took over all housekeeping chores. She even helped with Sabbath services. Everyone had to agree that Babette brought new life to the stagnant community.

Since Babette never referred to her past life in France, it came as a great surprise to Martine and Philippa when one day, after twelve years, she received her very first letter. Babette read it, looked up to see the sisters staring at her, and announced matter-of-factly that a wonderful thing had happened to her. Each year a friend in Paris had renewed Babette's number in the French lottery. This year, her ticket had won. Ten thousand francs!

The sisters pressed Babette's hands in congratulations, but inwardly their hearts sank. They knew that soon Babette would be leaving.

As it happened, Babette's winning the lottery coincided with the very time the sisters were discussing a celebration to honor the hundredth anniversary of their father's birth. Babette came to them with a request. In twelve years I have asked nothing of you, she began. They nodded. But now I have a request: I would like to prepare the meal for the anniversary service. I would like to cook you a real French dinner.

Although the sisters had grave misgivings about this plan, Babette was certainly right that she had asked no favors in twelve years. What choice had they but to agree?

When the money arrived from France, Babette went away briefly to make arrangements for the dinner. Over the next few weeks after her return, the residents of Norre Vosburg were treated to one amazing sight after another as boats docked to unload provisions for Babette's kitchen. Workmen pushed wheelbarrows loaded with crates of small birds. Cases of champagne—*champagne!*—and wine soon followed. The entire head of a cow, fresh vegetables, truffles, pheasants, ham, strange creatures that lived in the sea, a huge tortoise still alive and moving his snakelike head from side to side—all these ended up in the sisters' kitchen now firmly ruled by Babette.

Martine and Philippa, alarmed over this apparent witch's brew, explained their predicament to the members of the sect, now old and gray and only eleven in number. Everyone clucked in sympathy. After some discussion they agreed to eat the French meal, withholding comment about it lest Babette get the wrong idea. Tongues were meant for praise and thanksgiving, not for indulging in exotic tastes.

It snowed on December 15, the day of the dinner, brightening the dull village with a gloss of white. The sisters were pleased to learn that an unexpected guest would join them: ninety-year-old Miss Loewenhielm would be escorted by her nephew, the cavalry officer who had courted Martine long ago, now a general serving in the royal palace.

Babette had somehow scrounged enough china and crystal, and had decorated the room with candles and evergreens. Her table looked lovely. When the meal began all the villagers remembered their agreement and sat mute, like turtles around a pond. Only the general remarked on the food and drink. "Amontillado!" he exclaimed when he raised the first glass. "And the finest Amontillado that I have ever tasted." When he sipped the first spoonful of soup, the general could have sworn it was turtle soup, but how could such a thing be found on the coast of Jutland?

"Incredible!" said the general when he tasted the next course. "It is Blinis Demidoff!" All the other guests, their faces puckered with deep wrinkles, were eating the same rare delicacy without expression or comment. When the general rhapsodized about the champagne, a Veuve Cliquot 1860, Babette ordered her kitchen boy to keep the general's glass filled at all times. He alone seemed to appreciate what was set before him.

Although no one else spoke of the food or drink, gradually the banquet worked a magical effect on the churlish villagers. Their blood warmed. Their tongues loosened. They spoke of the old days when the Dean was alive and of Christmas the year the bay froze. The Brother who had cheated another on a business deal finally confessed, and the two women who had feuded found themselves conversing. A woman burped, and the Brother next to her said without thinking, "Hallelujah!"

The general, though, could speak of nothing but the meal. When the kitchen boy brought out the *coup de grâce* (that word, again), baby quail prepared *en Sarcophage*, the general exclaimed that he had seen such a dish in only one place in Europe, the famous Café Anglais in Paris, the restaurant once renowned for its woman chef.

Heady with wine, his senses sated, unable to contain himself, the general rose to make a speech. "Mercy and truth, my friends, have met together," he began. "Righteousness and bliss shall kiss one another." And then the general had to pause, "for he was in the habit of forming his speeches with care, conscious of his purpose, but here, in the midst of the Dean's simple congregation, it was as if the whole figure of General Loewenhielm, his breast covered with decorations, were but a mouthpiece for a message which meant to be brought forth." The general's message was grace.

Although the Brothers and Sisters of the sect did not fully comprehend the general's speech, at that moment "the vain illusions of this earth had dissolved before their eyes like smoke, and they had seen the universe as it really is." The little company broke up and went outside into a town coated with glistening snow under a sky ablaze with stars.

"Babette's Feast" ends with two scenes. Outside, the old-timers join hands around the fountain and lustily sing the old songs of faith. It is a communion scene: Babette's feast opened the gate and grace stole in. They felt, adds Isak Dinesen, "as if they had indeed had their sins washed white as wool, and in this regained innocent attire were gamboling like little lambs."

The final scene takes place inside, in the wreck of a kitchen piled high with unwashed dishes, greasy pots, shells, carapaces, gristly bones, broken crates, vegetable trimmings, and empty bottles. Babette sits amid the mess, looking as wasted as the night she arrived twelve years before. Suddenly the sisters realize that, in accordance with the vow, no one has spoken to Babette of the dinner.

"It was quite a nice dinner, Babette," Martine says tentatively.

Babette seems far away. After a time she says to them, "I was once cook at the Café Anglais."

"We will all remember this evening when you have gone back to Paris, Babette," Martine adds, as if not hearing her.

Babette tells them that she will not be going back to Paris. All her friends and relatives there have been killed or imprisoned. And, of course, it would be expensive to return to Paris.

"But what about the ten thousand francs?" the sisters ask.

Then Babette drops the bombshell. She has spent her winnings, every last franc of the ten thousand she won, on the feast they have just devoured. Don't be shocked, she tells them. That is what a proper dinner for twelve costs at the Café Anglais.

In the general's speech, Isak Dinesen leaves no doubt that she wrote "Babette's Feast" not simply as a story of a fine meal but as a parable of grace: a gift that costs everything for the giver and nothing for the recipient. This is what General Loewenhielm told the grim-faced parishioners gathered around him at Babette's table:

> We have all of us been told that grace is to be found in the universe. But in our human foolishness

> and shortsightedness we imagine divine grace to be finite. . . . But the moment comes when our eyes are opened, and we see and realize that grace is infinite. Grace, my friends, demands nothing from us but that we shall await it with confidence and acknowledge it in gratitude.

Twelve years before, Babette had landed among the graceless ones. Followers of Luther, they heard sermons on grace nearly every Sunday and the rest of the week tried to earn God's favor with their pieties and renunciations. Grace came to them in the form of a feast, Babette's feast, a meal of a lifetime lavished on those who had in no way earned it, who barely possessed the faculties to receive it. Grace came to Norre Vosburg as it always comes: free of charge, no strings attached, on the house.

O momentary grace of mortal men,
Which we more hunt for than the grace of God.

SHAKESPEARE, *RICHARD III*

Three

A World Without Grace

A friend of mine riding a bus to work overheard a conversation between the young woman sitting next to him and her neighbor across the aisle. The woman was reading Scott Peck's *The Road Less Traveled*, the book that has stayed on *The New York Times* Best-Sellers list longer than any other.

"What are you reading?" asked the neighbor.

"A book a friend gave me. She said it changed her life."

"Oh, yeah? What's it about?"

"I'm not sure. Some sort of guide to life. I haven't got very far yet." She began flipping through the book. "Here are the chapter titles: 'Discipline, Love, Grace, . . .'"

The man stopped her. "What's grace?"

"I don't know. I haven't got to Grace yet."

I think of that last line sometimes when I listen to reports on the evening news. A world marked by wars, violence, economic oppression, religious strife, lawsuits, and family breakdown clearly hasn't got to grace yet. "Ah, what a thing is man devoid of grace," sighed the poet George Herbert.

Unfortunately, I also think of that line from the bus conversation when I visit certain churches. Like fine wine poured into a jug of water, Jesus' wondrous message of grace gets diluted in the vessel of the church. "For the law was given through Moses; grace and truth came through Jesus Christ," wrote the apostle John. Christians have spent enormous energy over the years debating and decreeing truth; every church defends its particular version. But what about grace? How rare to find a church competing to "out-grace" its rivals.

Grace is Christianity's best gift to the world, a spiritual nova in our midst exerting a force stronger than vengeance, stronger than racism, stronger than hate. Sadly, to a world desperate for this grace the church sometimes presents one more form of ungrace. Too often we more resemble the grim folks who gather to eat boiled bread than those who have just partaken of Babette's feast.

I grew up in a church that drew sharp lines between "the age of Law" and "the age of Grace." While ignoring most moral prohibitions from the Old Testament, we had our own pecking order rivaling the Orthodox Jews'. At the top were smoking and drinking (this being the South, however, with its tobacco-dependent economy, some allowances were made for smoking). Movies ranked just below these vices, with many church members refusing even to attend *The Sound of Music.* Rock music, then in its infancy, was likewise regarded as an abomination, quite possibly demonic in origin.

Other proscriptions—wearing makeup and jewelry, reading the Sunday paper, playing or watching sports on Sunday, mixed swimming (curiously termed "mixed bathing"), skirt length for girls, hair length for boys—were heeded or not heeded depending on a person's level of spirituality. I grew up with the strong impression that a person became spiritual by attending to these gray-area rules. For the life of me, I could not figure out much difference between the dispensations of Law and Grace.

My visits to other churches have convinced me that this ladder-like approach to spirituality is nearly universal. Catholics, Mennonites, Churches of Christ, Lutherans, and Southern Baptists all have their own custom agenda of legalism. You gain the church's, and presumably God's, approval by following the prescribed pattern.

Later, when I began writing about the problem of pain, I met another form of ungrace. Some readers objected to my sympathy toward those who suffer. People suffer because they deserve it, they told me. God is punishing them. I have many such letters in my files, modern restatements of the "proverbs of ashes" from Job's friends.

In his book *Guilt and Grace*, the Swiss doctor Paul Tournier, a man of deep personal faith, admits, "I cannot study this very serious problem of guilt with you without raising the very obvious and tragic fact that religion—my own as well as that of all believers—can crush instead of liberate."

Tournier tells of patients who come to him: a man harboring guilt over an old sin, a woman who cannot put out of her mind an abortion that took place ten years before. What the patients truly seek, says Tournier, is grace. Yet in some churches they encounter shame, the threat of punishment, and a sense of judgment. In short, when they look in the church for grace, they often find ungrace.

A divorced woman recently told me of standing in the sanctuary of her church with her 15-year-old daughter when the pastor's wife approached. "I hear you are divorcing. What I can't understand is that if you love Jesus and he loves Jesus, why are you doing that?" The pastor's wife had never really spoken to my friend before, and her brusque rebuke in the daughter's presence stunned my friend. "The pain of it was that my husband and I both did love Jesus, but the marriage was broken beyond mending. If she had just put her arms around me and said, 'I'm so sorry. . .' "

Mark Twain used to talk about people who were "good in the worst sense of the word," a phrase that, for many, captures the reputation of Christians today. Recently I have been asking a question of strangers—for example, seatmates on an airplane—when I strike up a conversation. "When I say the words 'evangelical Christian' what comes to mind?" In reply, mostly I hear political descriptions: of strident pro-life activists, or gay-rights opponents, or proposals for censoring the Internet. I hear references to the Moral Majority, an organization disbanded years ago. Not once—*not once*—have I heard a description redolent of grace. Apparently that is not the aroma Christians give off in the world.

H. L. Mencken described a Puritan as a person with a haunting fear that someone, somewhere is happy; today, many people would apply the same caricature to evangelicals or fundamentalists. Where does this reputation of uptight joylessness come from? A column by humorist Erma Bombeck provides a clue:

> In church the other Sunday I was intent on a small child who was turning around smiling at everyone. He wasn't gurgling, spitting, humming, kicking, tearing the hymnals, or rummaging through his mother's handbag. He was just smiling. Finally, his mother jerked him about and in a stage whisper that could be heard in a little theatre off Broadway said, "Stop that grinning! You're in church!" With that, she gave him a belt and as the tears rolled down his cheeks added, "That's better," and returned to her prayers....
>
> Suddenly I was angry. It occurred to me the entire world is in tears, and if you're not, then you'd better get with it. I wanted to grab this child with the tear-stained face close to me and tell him about my God. The happy God. The smiling God. The God who had to have a sense of humor to have created the likes of us.... By tradition, one wears faith with the solemnity of a mourner, the gravity of a mask of tragedy, and the dedication of a Rotary badge.
>
> What a fool, I thought. Here was a woman sitting next to the only light left in our civilization—the only hope, our only miracle—our only promise of infinity. If he couldn't smile in church, where was there left to go?

These characterizations of Christians are surely incomplete, for I know many Christians who embody grace. Yet somehow throughout history the church has managed to gain a reputation for its ungrace. As a little English girl prayed, "O God, make the bad people good, and the good people nice."

William James, perhaps the leading American philosopher of the last century, had a sympathetic view of the church, as expressed in his classic study, *The Varieties of Religious Experience.* Still, he struggled to understand the pettiness of Christians who persecuted Quakers for not tipping their hats and who vigorously debated the morality of dyeing clothes. He wrote of the asceticism of a French country priest who decided "that he should never smell a flower, never drink when parched with thirst, never drive away a fly, never show disgust before a repugnant object, never complain of anything that had to do with his personal comfort, never sit down, never lean upon his elbows when he was kneeling."

The renowned mystic St. John of the Cross advised believers to mortify all joy and hope, to turn "not to what most pleases, but to what disgusts," and to "despise yourself, and wish that others should despise you." St. Bernard habitually covered his eyes to avoid the beauty of Swiss lakes.

Nowadays legalism has changed its focus. In a thoroughly secular culture, the church is more likely to show ungrace through a spirit of moral superiority or a fierce attitude toward opponents in the "culture wars."

The church also communicates ungrace through its lack of unity. Mark Twain used to say he put a dog and cat in a cage together as an experiment, to see if they could get along. They did, so he put in a bird, pig, and goat. They, too, got along fine after a few adjustments. Then he put in a Baptist, Presbyterian, and Catholic; soon there was not a living thing left.

More seriously, the modern Jewish intellectual Anthony Hecht writes:

> Over the years I not only grew to know it [my faith] better but became increasingly acquainted with the convictions of my Christian neighbors. Many of these were good people whom I admire, and from whom I learned goodness itself, among other things. And there was much in Christian doctrine that seemed appealing as well. But few things struck me with more force than the profound and unappeasable hostility of Protestants and Catholics toward one another.

I have been picking on Christians because I am one, and see no reason to pretend we are better than we are. I fight the tentacular grip of ungrace in my own life. Although I may not perpetuate the strictness of my upbringing, I battle daily against pride, judgmentalism, and a feeling that I must somehow earn God's approval. In the words of Helmut

Thielicke, ". . . the devil succeeds in laying his cuckoo eggs in a pious nest. . . . The sulphurous stench of hell is as nothing compared with the evil odor emitted by divine grace gone putrid."

In truth, though, a virulent strain of ungrace shows up in all religions. I have heard eyewitness accounts of the recently revived Sun Dance ritual, in which young Lakota warriors fasten eagle claws to their nipples and, straining against a rope attached to a sacred pole, fling themselves outward until the claws rip through their flesh. Then they enter a sweat lodge and pile high red-hot rocks until the temperature becomes unbearable, all in an attempt to atone for sins.

I have watched devout peasants crawl on bloody knees across cobblestone streets in Costa Rica and Hindu peasants offer sacrifices to the gods of smallpox and poisonous snakes in India. I have visited Islamic countries where "morals police" patrol the sidewalks with clubs, looking for women whose clothing offends them or who dare to drive a car.

In a dark irony, the humanists who rebel against religion often manage to invent worse forms of ungrace. At modern universities, activists for "liberal" causes—feminism, the environment, multiculturalism—may demonstrate a harsh spirit of ungrace. I know of no legalism more all-encompassing than that of Soviet communism, which set up a web of spies to report any false thinking, misuse of words, or disrespect for communist ideals. Solzhenitsyn, for example, spent his years in the Gulag as punishment for a careless remark he made about Stalin in a personal letter. And I know of no Inquisition more severe than that carried out by the Red Guards in China, complete with dunce caps and staged displays of public contrition.

Even the best humanists devise systems of ungrace to replace those rejected in religion. Benjamin Franklin settled on thirteen virtues, including Silence ("Speak not but what may benefit others or yourself; avoid trifling conversation"), Frugality ("Make no expense but to do good to others or yourself; that is, waste nothing"), Industry ("Lose no time; be always employed in something useful; cut off all unnecessary actions"), and Tranquillity ("Be not disturbed at trifles or at accidents common or unavoidable"). He set up a book with a page for each virtue, lining a column in which to record "defects." Choosing a different virtue to work on each week, he daily noted every mistake, starting over every thirteen weeks in order to cycle through the list four times a year. For many decades Franklin carried his little book with him, striving for a clean thirteen-week cycle. As he made progress, he found himself struggling with yet another defect:

> There is perhaps no one of natural passions so hard to subdue as *pride.* Disguise it. Struggle with it. Stifle it. Mortify it as much as one pleases. It is still alive, and will every now and then peep out and show itself. . . . Even if I could conceive that I had completely overcome it, I should probably be proud of my humility.

Could such vigorous efforts, in all its forms, betray a deep longing for grace? We live in an atmosphere choked with the fumes of ungrace. Grace comes from outside, as a gift and not an achievement. How easily it vanishes from our dog-eat-dog, survival-of-the-fittest, look-out-for-number-one world.

Guilt exposes a longing for grace. An organization in Los Angeles operates the Apology Sound-Off Line, a telephone service that gives callers an opportunity to confess their wrongs for the price of a phone call. People who no longer believe in priests now trust their sins to an answering machine. Two hundred anonymous callers contact the service each day, leaving sixty-second messages. Adultery is a common confession. Some callers confess to criminal acts: rape, child sexual abuse, and even murder. A recovering alcoholic left the message, "I would like to apologize to all the people I hurt in my eighteen years as an addict." The phone rings on. "I just want to say I'm sorry," sobs a young woman. She says she just caused an automobile accident in which five people died. "I wish I could bring them back."

A colleague once caught the agnostic actor W. C. Fields in his dressing room reading a Bible. Embarrassed, Fields snapped the book shut and explained, "Just looking for loopholes." Probably, he was looking for grace.

Lewis Smedes, a professor in psychology at Fuller Theological Seminary, wrote an entire book drawing connections between shame and grace (titled, appropriately, *Shame and Grace*). For him, "Guilt was not my problem as I felt it. What I felt most was a glob of unworthiness that I could not tie down to any concrete sins I was guilty of. What I needed more than pardon was a sense that God accepted me, owned me, held me, affirmed me, and would never let go of me even if he was not too much impressed with what he had on his hands."

Smedes goes on to say that he has identified three common sources of crippling shame: secular culture, graceless religion, and unaccepting parents. Secular culture tells us a person must look good, feel good, and make good. Graceless religion tells us we must follow the letter of the rules, and failure will bring eternal rejection. Unaccepting parents—"Aren't you ashamed of yourself!"—convince us we will never meet their approval.

Like city-dwellers who no longer notice the polluted air, we breathe in the atmosphere of ungrace unawares. As early as preschool and kindergarten we are tested and evaluated before being slotted into an "advanced," "normal," or "slow" track. From then on we receive grades denoting performance in math, science, reading, and even "social skills" and "citizenship." Test papers come back with errors—not correct answers—highlighted. All this helps prepare us for the real world with its relentless ranking, a grown-up version of the playground game "king of the hill."

The military practices ungrace in its purest form. Assigned a title, uniform, salary, and code of behavior, every soldier knows exactly where he or she stands in relation to every other: you salute and obey superiors, you give orders to inferiors. Corporations are more subtle—barely. Ford grades employees on a scale of 1 (clerks and secretaries) to 27 (chairman of the board). You must reach at least Grade 9 to qualify for an outside parking place; Grade 13 brings with it such perks as a window, plants, and an intercom system; Grade 16 offices come equipped with private bathrooms.

Every institution, it seems, runs on ungrace and its insistence that we *earn* our way. Justice departments, airline frequent-flyer programs, and mortgage companies cannot operate by grace. Government hardly knows the word. A sports franchise rewards those who complete passes, throw strikes, or make baskets, and has no place for those who fail. *Fortune* magazine annually lists the five hundred richest people; no one knows the names of the five hundred poorest.

The disease anorexia is a direct product of ungrace: hold up the ideal of beautiful, skinny models, and teenage girls will starve themselves to death in an attempt to reach that ideal. A peculiar offshoot of modern Western civilization, anorexia has no known history and rarely occurs in places like modern Africa (where plumpness, not thinness, is admired).

All this takes place in the United States, a supposedly egalitarian society. Other societies have refined the art of ungrace through rigid social systems based on class, race, or caste. South Africa used to assign every citizen to one of four racial categories: white, black, colored, and Asian (when Japanese investors objected, the government invented a new category, "honorary white people"). India's caste system was so labyrinthine that in the 1930s the British discovered a new caste they had not encountered in three centuries of presence there: assigned the role of washing clothes for the Untouchables, these poor creatures believed they would contaminate higher castes by sight, so they emerged only at night and avoided all contact with other people.

The New York Times recently ran a series on crime in modern Japan. Why is it, they asked, that for every 100,000 citizens the United States imprisons 519 whereas Japan only imprisons 37? In search of answers, the *Times* reporter interviewed a Japanese man who had just served a sentence for murder. In the fifteen years he spent in prison, he did not receive a single visitor. After his release, his wife and son met with him, only to tell him never to return to their village. His three daughters, now married, refuse to see him. "I have four grandchildren, I think," the man said sadly; he has never even seen pictures of them. Japanese society has found a way to harness the power of ungrace. A culture that values "saving face" has no room for those who bring disgrace.

Even families, which link individuals by the accident of birth, not performance, breathe in the polluted fumes of ungrace. A story by Ernest Hemingway reveals this truth. A Spanish father decides to reconcile with his son who had run away to Madrid. Now remorseful, the father takes out this ad in the *El Liberal* newspaper: "PACO MEET ME AT HOTEL MONTANA NOON TUESDAY ALL IS FORGIVEN PAPA." Paco is a common name in Spain, and when the father goes to the square he finds eight hundred young men named Paco waiting for their fathers.

Hemingway knew about the ungrace of families. His devout parents—Hemingway's grandparents had attended evangelical Wheaton College—detested Hemingway's libertine life, and after a time his mother refused to allow him in her presence. One year for his birthday, she mailed him a cake along with the gun his father had used to kill himself. Another year she wrote him a letter explaining that a mother's life is like a bank. "Every child that is born to her enters the world with a large and prosperous bank account, seemingly inexhaustible." The child, she continued, makes withdrawals but no deposits during all the early years. Later, when the child grows up, it is his responsibility to replenish the supply he has drawn down. Hemingway's mother then proceeded to spell out all the specific ways in which Ernest should be making "deposits to keep the account in good standing": flowers, fruit or candy, a surreptitious paying of Mother's bills, and above all a determination to stop "neglecting your duties to God and your Saviour, Jesus Christ." Hemingway never got over his hatred for his mother or for her Saviour.

Occasionally a grace note sounds, high, lilting, ethereal, to interrupt the monotonous background growl of ungrace.

One day I stuck my hand in a pants pocket at a factory-outlet store and found a twenty-dollar bill. I had no way to trace the original owner, and the store manager said I should keep it. For the first time ever I purchased a pair of pants (thirteen dollars) and walked out with a net profit. I relive the experience every time I put on the pants, and tell it to my friends whenever the subject of bargains comes up.

Another day, I climbed a fourteen-thousand-foot mountain, the first one I had ever attempted. It was a brutal and exhausting hike, and when I finally descended to flat ground I felt I had earned the right to a steak dinner and a week's pass from aerobic activities. As my car rounded a bend on the way back to town, I came upon a pristine Alpine lake guarded by bright-green aspen trees behind which arced the most vivid rainbow I had ever seen. I pulled to the side of the road and stared a long time, in silence.

On a trip to Rome, my wife and I followed a friend's advice to visit St. Peter's early in the morning. "Take a bus before dawn to the bridge adorned with all the Bernini statues," the friend instructed. "Wait there for sunrise, then dash to St. Peter's a few blocks away. Early in the morning, you'll find only nuns, pilgrims, and priests there." The sun rose in a clear sky that morning, tinting the Tiber red and casting rays the color of marmalade on Bernini's exquisite angel statues. Following orders, we tore ourselves from the scene and power-walked to St. Peter's. Rome was just beginning to wake up. Sure enough, we were the only tourists; our footsteps on the marble floor echoed loudly in the basilica. We admired the Pietà, the altar, and the various monuments, then climbed an outside stairway to reach a balcony at the base of the huge dome designed by Michelangelo. Just then I noticed a line of two hundred people stretched across the square. "Perfect timing," I said to my wife, thinking them tourists. They were not tourists, however, but a choir of pilgrims from Germany. They filed in, gathered in a semicircle directly beneath us, and began singing hymns. As their voices rose, reverberating around the dome and blending together in multi-part harmony, Michelangelo's half-sphere became not just a work of architectural grandeur but a temple of celestial music. The sound set our cells vibrating. It took on substance, as if we could lean on it, or swim in it, as if the hymns and not the balcony were supporting us.

Surely it has theological significance that unearned gifts and unexpected pleasures bring the most joy. Grace billows up. Or, as the bumper sticker says, "Grace Happens."

For many, romantic love is the closest experience of pure grace. Someone at last feels that I—*I!*—am the most desirable, attractive, companionable creature on the planet. Someone lies awake at night thinking of *me*. Someone forgives me before I ask, thinks of me when she gets dressed, orders her life around mine. Someone loves me just the way I am. For this reason, I think, modern writers like John Updike and Walker Percy, who have strong Christian sensibilities, may choose a sexual affair as a symbol of grace in their novels. They are speaking the language our culture understands: grace as a rumor, not a doctrine.

And then along comes a movie like *Forrest Gump*, about a kid with a low IQ who speaks in platitudes handed down from his mother. This dimwit rescues his buddies in Vietnam, remains faithful to his girl Jenny despite her infidelity, stays true to himself and his child, and lives as though he genuinely does not know he is the butt of every joke. A magical scene of a feather opens and ends the movie—a note of grace so light no one knows where it might land. *Forrest Gump* was to recent times what *The Idiot* was to Dostoevsky's era, and it provoked similar reactions. Many thought it naive, ridiculous, manipulative. Others, however, saw in it a rumor of grace that made a sharp relief against the violent ungrace of *Pulp Fiction* and *Natural Born Killers.* As a result, *Forrest Gump* became the most successful movie of its time. The world starves for grace.

Peter Greave wrote a memoir of his life with leprosy, a disease he contracted while stationed in India. He returned to England, half-blind and partially paralyzed, to live on a compound run by a group of Anglican sisters. Unable to work, an outcast from society, he turned bitter. He thought of suicide. He made elaborate plans to escape the compound, but always backed out because he had nowhere to go. One morning, uncharacteristically, he got up very early and strolled the grounds. Hearing a buzzing noise, he followed it to the chapel, where sisters were praying for the patients whose names were written on its walls. Among the names, he found his own. Somehow that experience of connection, of linking, changed the course of his life. He felt wanted. He felt graced.

Religious faith—for all its problems, despite its maddening tendency to replicate ungrace—lives on because we sense the numinous beauty of a gift undeserved that comes at unexpected moments from Outside. Refusing to believe that our lives of guilt and shame lead to nothing but annihilation, we hope against hope for another place run by different rules. We grow up hungry for love, and in ways so deep as to remain unexpressed we long for our Maker to love us.

Grace did not come to me initially in the forms or the words of faith. I grew up in a church that often used the word but meant something else. Grace, like many religious words, had been leached of meaning so that I could no longer trust it.

I first experienced grace through music. At the Bible college I was attending, I was viewed as a deviant. People would publicly pray for me and ask me if I needed exorcism. I felt harassed, disordered, confused. Doors to the dormitory were locked at night, but fortunately I lived on the first floor. I would climb out the window of my room and sneak into the chapel, which contained a nine-foot Steinway grand piano. In a chapel dark but for a small light by which to read music, I would sit for an hour or so each night and play Beethoven's sonatas, Chopin's preludes, and Schubert's impromptus. My own fingers pressed a kind of tactile order onto the world. My mind was confused, my body was confused, the world was confused—but here I sensed a hidden world of beauty, grace, and wonder light as a cloud and startling as a butterfly wing.

Something similar happened in the world of nature. To get away from the crush of ideas and people, I would take long walks in the pine forests splashed with dogwood. I followed the zigzag paths of dragonflies along the river, watched flocks of birds wheeling overhead, and picked apart logs to find the iridescent beetles inside. I liked the sure, inevitable way of nature giving form and place to all living things. I saw evidence that the world contains grandeur, great goodness, and, yes, traces of joy.

About the same time, I fell in love. It felt exactly like a fall, a head-over-heels tumble into a state of unbearable lightness. The earth tilted on its axis. I did not believe in romantic love at the time, thinking it a human construct, an invention of fourteenth-century Italian poets. I was as unprepared for love as I had been for goodness and beauty. Suddenly, my heart seemed swollen, too large for my chest.

I was experiencing "common grace," to use the theologians' term. It is a terrible thing, I found, to be grateful and have no one to thank, to be awed and have no one to worship. Gradually, very gradually, I came back to the cast-off faith of my childhood. I had experienced the "drippings of grace," C. S. Lewis's term for what awakens deep longing for "a scent of a flower we have not found, the echo of a tune we have not heard, news from a country we have never yet visited."

Grace is everywhere, like lenses that go unnoticed because you are looking through them. Eventually God gave me eyes to notice the grace around me. I became a writer, I feel certain, in an attempt to reclaim words that had been tarnished by graceless Christians. In my first job, with a Christian magazine, I worked for a kind and wise employer, Harold Myra, who let me work out my faith at my own speed, with no pretense.

For some of my first books I teamed with Dr. Paul Brand, who had spent much of his life in a hot, arid region of South India serving leprosy patients, many of whom belonged to the Untouchable caste. In this most unlikely soil, Brand experienced and conveyed the grace of God. From people such as him, I learned grace by being graced.

I had one last skin to molt on my way toward growth in grace. I came to see that the image of God I had been raised with was woefully incomplete. I came to know a God who is, in the words of the psalmist, "a compassionate and gracious God, slow to anger, abounding in love and faithfulness."

Grace comes free of charge to people who do not deserve it and I am one of those people. I think back to who I was—resentful, wound tight with anger, a single hardened link in a long chain of ungrace learned from family and church. Now I am trying in my own small way to pipe the tune of grace. I do so because I know, more surely than I know anything, that any pang of healing or forgiveness or goodness I have ever felt comes solely from the grace of God. I yearn for the church to become a nourishing culture of that grace.

It is to the prodigals . . . that the memory of their Father's house comes back. If the son had lived economically he would never have thought of returning.

SIMONE WEIL

Four

Lovesick Father

During a British conference on comparative religions, experts from around the world debated what, if any, belief was unique to the Christian faith. They began eliminating possibilities. Incarnation? Other religions had different versions of gods appearing in human form. Resurrection? Again, other religions had accounts of return from death. The debate went on for some time until C. S. Lewis wandered into the room. "What's the rumpus about?" he asked, and heard in reply that his colleagues were discussing Christianity's unique contribution among world religions. Lewis responded, "Oh, that's easy. It's grace."

After some discussion, the conferees had to agree. The notion of God's love coming to us free of charge, no strings attached, seems to go against every instinct of humanity. The Buddhist eight-fold path, the Hindu doctrine of *karma*, the Jewish covenant, and Muslim code of law—each of these offers a way to earn approval. Only Christianity dares to make God's love unconditional.

Aware of our inbuilt resistance to grace, Jesus talked about it often. He described a world suffused with God's grace: where the sun shines on people good and bad; where birds gather seeds gratis, neither plowing nor harvesting to earn them; where untended wildflowers burst into bloom on the rocky hillsides. Like a visitor from a foreign country who notices what the natives overlook, Jesus saw grace everywhere. Yet he never analyzed or defined grace, and almost never used the word. Instead, he communicated grace through stories we know as parables—which I will take the liberty of transposing into a modern setting.

A vagrant lives near the Fulton Fish Market on the lower east side of Manhattan. The slimy smell of fish carcasses and entrails nearly overpowers him, and he hates the trucks that noisily arrive before sunrise. But midtown gets crowded, and the cops harass him there. Down by the wharves nobody bothers with a grizzled man who keeps to himself and sleeps on a loading dock behind a Dumpster.

Early one morning when the workers are slinging eel and halibut off the trucks, yelling to each other in Italian, the vagrant rouses himself and pokes through the Dumpsters behind the tourist restaurants. An early start guarantees good pickings: last night's uneaten garlic bread and French fries, nibbled pizza, a wedge of cheesecake. He eats what he can stomach and stuffs the rest in a brown paper sack. The bottles and cans he stashes in plastic bags in his rusty shopping cart.

The morning sun, pale through harbor fog, finally makes it over the buildings by the wharf. When he sees the ticket from last week's lottery lying in a pile of wilted lettuce, he almost lets it go. But by force of habit he picks it up and jams it in his pocket. In the old days, when luck was better, he used to buy one ticket a week, never more. It's past noon when he remembers the ticket stub and holds it up to the newspaper box to compare the numbers. Three numbers match, the fourth, the fifth—all seven! It can't be true. Things like that don't happen to him. Bums don't win the New York Lottery.

But it is true. Later that day he is squinting into the bright lights as television crews present the newest media darling, the unshaven, baggy-pants vagrant who will receive $243,000 per year for the next twenty years. A chic-looking woman wearing a leather miniskirt shoves a microphone in his face and asks, "How do you feel?" He stares back dazed, and catches a whiff of her perfume. It has been a long time, a very long time, since anyone has asked him that question.

He feels like a man who has been to the edge of starvation and back, and is beginning to fathom that he'll never feel hunger again.

An entrepreneur in Los Angeles decides to cash in on the boom in adventure travel. Not all Americans sleep in Holiday Inns and eat at McDonald's when traveling overseas; some prefer to stray from the beaten path. He gets the idea of touring the Seven Wonders of the Ancient World.

Most of the ancient wonders, he finds, have left no trace. But there is a move underway to restore the Hanging Gardens of Babylon, and after a lot of legwork the entrepreneur lines up a charter plane, a bus, accommodations, and a guide who promises to let tourists work alongside the professional archeologists. Just the kind of thing adventure tourists love. He orders up an expensive series of television ads and schedules them during golf tournaments, when well-heeled tourists might be watching.

To finance his dream the entrepreneur has arranged a million-dollar loan from a venture capitalist, calculating that after the fourth trip he can cover operating expenses and start paying back the loan.

One thing he has not calculated, however: two weeks before his inaugural trip, Saddam Hussein invades Kuwait and the State Department bans all travel to Iraq, which happens to be the site of the ancient Hanging Gardens of Babylon.

He agonizes for three weeks over how to break the news to the venture capitalist. He visits banks and gets nowhere. He investigates a home-equity loan, which would net him only two hundred thousand dollars, one-fifth of what he needs. Finally, he puts together a plan that commits him to repay five thousand dollars a month the rest of his life. He draws up a contract, and even as he does so, the folly sinks in. Five thousand a month will not even cover the interest on a million-dollar loan. Besides, where will he get the five thousand a month? But the alternative, bankruptcy, would ruin his credit. He visits his backer's office on Sunset Boulevard, nervously fumbles through an apology, and then pulls out the paperwork for his ridiculous repayment plan. He breaks out in sweat in the air-conditioned office.

The venture capitalist holds up a hand to interrupt him. "Wait. What nonsense are you talking about? Repayment?" He laughs. "Don't be silly. I'm a speculator. I win some, I lose some. I knew your plan had risks. It was a good idea, though, and it's hardly your fault that a war broke out. Just forget it." He takes the contract, rips it in two, and tosses it in the paper shredder.

One of Jesus' stories about grace made it into three different Gospels, in slightly different versions. My favorite version, though, appeared in another source entirely: the *Boston Globe*'s account in June 1990 of a most unusual wedding banquet.

Accompanied by her fiancé, a woman went to the Hyatt Hotel in downtown Boston and ordered the meal. The two of them pored over the menu, made selections of china and silver, and pointed to pictures of the flower arrangements they liked. They both had expensive taste, and the bill came to thirteen thousand dollars. After leaving a check for half that amount as down payment, the couple went home to flip through books of wedding announcements.

The day the announcements were supposed to hit the mailbox, the potential groom got cold feet. "I'm just not sure," he said. "It's a big commitment. Let's think about this a little longer."

When his angry fiancée returned to the Hyatt to cancel the banquet, the Events Manager could not have been more understanding. "The same thing happened to me, Honey," she said, and told the story of her own broken engagement. But about the refund, she had bad news. "The contract is binding. You're only entitled to thirteen hundred dollars back. You have two options: to forfeit the rest of the down payment, or go ahead with the banquet. I'm sorry. Really, I am."

It seemed crazy, but the more the jilted bride thought about it, the more she liked the idea of going ahead with the party—not a wedding banquet, mind you, but a big blowout. Ten years before, this same woman had been living in a homeless shelter. She had got back on her feet, found a good job, and set aside a sizable nest egg. Now she had the wild notion of using her savings to treat the down-and-outs of Boston to a night on the town.

And so it was that in June of 1990 the Hyatt Hotel in downtown Boston hosted a party such as it had never seen before. The hostess changed the menu to boneless chicken—"in honor of the groom," she said—and sent invitations to rescue missions and homeless shelters. That warm summer night, people who were used to peeling half-gnawed pizza off the cardboard dined instead on chicken cordon bleu. Hyatt waiters in tuxedos served *hors d'oeuvres* to senior citizens propped up by crutches and aluminum walkers. Bag ladies, vagrants, and addicts took one night off from the hard life on the sidewalks outside and instead sipped champagne, ate chocolate wedding cake, and danced to big-band melodies late into the night.

A young girl grows up on a cherry orchard just above Traverse City, Michigan. Her parents, a bit old-fashioned, tend to overreact to her nose ring, the music she listens to, and the length of her skirts. They ground her a few times, and she seethes inside. "I hate you!" she screams at her father when he knocks on the door of her room after an argument, and that night she acts on a plan she has mentally rehearsed scores of times. She runs away.

She has visited Detroit only once before, on a bus trip with her church youth group to watch the Tigers play. Because newspapers in Traverse City report in lurid detail the gangs, the drugs, and the violence in downtown Detroit, she concludes that is probably the last place her parents will look for her. California, maybe, or Florida, but not Detroit.

Her second day there she meets a man who drives the biggest car she's ever seen. He offers her a ride, buys her lunch, arranges a place for her to stay. He gives her some pills that make her feel better than she's ever felt before. She was right all along, she decides: her parents were keeping her from all the fun.

The good life continues for a month, two months, a year. The man with the big car—she calls him "Boss"—teaches her a few things that men like. Since she's underage, men pay a premium for her. She lives in a penthouse, and orders room service whenever she wants. Occasionally she thinks about the folks back home, but their lives now seem so boring and provincial that she can hardly believe she grew up there.

She has a brief scare when she sees her picture printed on the back of a milk carton with the headline "Have you seen this child?" But by now she has blond hair, and with all the makeup and body-piercing jewelry she wears, nobody would mistake her for a child. Besides, most of her friends are runaways, and nobody squeals in Detroit.

After a year the first sallow signs of illness appear, and it amazes her how fast the boss turns mean. "These days, we can't mess around," he growls, and before she knows it she's out on the street without a penny to her name. She still turns a couple of tricks a night, but they don't pay much, and all the money goes to support her habit. When winter blows in she finds herself sleeping on metal grates outside the big department stores. "Sleeping" is the wrong word—a teenage girl at night in downtown Detroit can never relax her guard. Dark bands circle her eyes. Her cough worsens.

One night as she lies awake listening for footsteps, all of a sudden everything about her life looks different. She no longer feels like a woman of the world. She feels like a little girl, lost in a cold and frightening city. She begins to whimper. Her pockets are empty and she's hungry. She needs a fix. She pulls her legs tight underneath her and shivers under the newspapers she's piled atop her coat. Something jolts a synapse of memory and a single image fills her mind: of May in Traverse City, when a million cherry trees bloom at once, with her golden retriever dashing through the rows and rows of blossomy trees in chase of a tennis ball.

God, why did I leave, she says to herself, and pain stabs at her heart. *My dog back home eats better than I do now.* She's sobbing, and she knows in a flash that more than anything else in the world she wants to go home.

Three straight phone calls, three straight connections with the answering machine. She hangs up without leaving a message the first two times, but the third time she says, "Dad, Mom, it's me. I was wondering about maybe coming home. I'm catching a bus up your way, and it'll get there about midnight tomorrow. If you're not there, well, I guess I'll just stay on the bus until it hits Canada."

It takes about seven hours for a bus to make all the stops between Detroit and Traverse City, and during that time she realizes the flaws in her plan. What if her parents are out of town and miss the message? Shouldn't she have waited another day or so until she could talk to them? And even if they are home, they probably wrote her off as dead long ago. She should have given them some time to overcome the shock.

Her thoughts bounce back and forth between those worries and the speech she is preparing for her father. "Dad, I'm sorry. I know I was wrong. It's not your fault; it's all mine. Dad, can you forgive me?" She says the words over and over, her throat tightening even as she rehearses them. She hasn't apologized to anyone in years.

The bus has been driving with lights on since Bay City. Tiny snowflakes hit the pavement rubbed worn by thousands of tires, and the asphalt steams. She's forgotten how dark it gets at night out here. A deer darts across the road and the bus swerves. Every so often, a billboard. A sign posting the mileage to Traverse City. *Oh, God.*

When the bus finally rolls into the station, its air brakes hissing in protest, the driver announces in a crackly voice over the microphone, "Fifteen minutes, folks. That's all we have here." Fifteen minutes to decide her life. She checks herself in a compact mirror, smoothes her hair, and licks the lipstick off her teeth. She looks at the tobacco stains on her fingertips, and wonders if her parents will notice. If they're there.

She walks into the terminal not knowing what to expect. Not one of the thousand scenes that have played out in her mind prepare her for what she sees. There, in the concrete-walls-and-plastic-chairs bus terminal in Traverse City, Michigan, stands a group of forty brothers and sisters and great-aunts and uncles and cousins and a grandmother and great-grandmother to boot. They're all wearing goofy party hats and blowing noise-makers, and taped across the entire wall of the terminal is a computer-generated banner that reads "Welcome home!"

Out of the crowd of well-wishers breaks her dad. She stares out through the tears quivering in her eyes like hot mercury and begins the memorized speech, "Dad, I'm sorry. I know . . ."

He interrupts her. "Hush, child. We've got no time for that. No time for apologies. You'll be late for the party. A banquet's waiting for you at home."

We are accustomed to finding a catch in every promise, but Jesus' stories of extravagant grace include no catch, no loophole disqualifying us from God's love. Each has at its core an ending too good to be true—or so good that it must be true.

How different are these stories from my own childhood notions about God: a God who forgives, yes, but reluctantly, after making the penitent squirm. I imagined God as a distant thundering figure who prefers fear and respect to love. Jesus tells instead of a father publicly humiliating himself by rushing out to embrace a son who has squandered half the family fortune. There is no solemn lecture, "I hope you've learned your lesson!" Instead, Jesus tells of the father's exhilaration—"This my son was dead, and is alive again; he was lost, and is found"—and then adds the buoyant phrase, "they began to make merry."

What blocks forgiveness is not God's reticence—"But while he was still a long way off, his father saw him and was filled with compassion for him"—but ours. God's arms are always extended; we are the ones who turn away.

I have meditated enough on Jesus' stories of grace to let their meaning filter through. Still, each time I confront their astonishing message I realize how thickly the veil of ungrace obscures my view of God. A housewife jumping up and down in glee over the discovery of a lost coin is not what naturally comes to mind when I think of God. Yet that is the image Jesus insisted upon.

The story of the Prodigal Son, after all, appears in a string of three stories by Jesus—the lost sheep, the lost coin, the lost son—all of which seem to make the same point. Each underscores the loser's sense of loss, tells of the thrill of rediscovery, and ends with a scene of jubilation. Jesus says in effect, "Do you want to know what it feels like to be God? When one of those two-legged humans pays attention to me, it feels like I just reclaimed my most valuable possession, which I had given up for lost." To God himself, it feels like the discovery of a lifetime.

Strangely, rediscovery may strike a deeper chord than discovery. To lose, and then find, a Mont Blanc pen makes the owner happier than the day she got it in the first place. Once, in the days before computers,

I lost four chapters of a book I was writing when I left my only copy in a motel room drawer. For two weeks the motel insisted that cleaning personnel had thrown the stack of papers away. I was inconsolable. How could I summon the energy to start all over when for months I had worked at polishing and improving those four chapters? I would never find the same words. Then one day a cleaning woman who spoke little English called to tell me she had not thrown the chapters away after all. Believe me, I felt far more joy over the chapters that were found than I had ever felt in the process of writing them.

That experience gives me a small foretaste of what it must feel like for a parent to get a phone call from the FBI reporting that the daughter abducted six months ago has been located at last, alive. Or for a wife to get a visit from the Army with a spokesman apologizing about the mix-up; her husband had not been aboard the wrecked helicopter after all. And those images give a mere glimpse of what it must feel like for the Maker of the Universe to get another member of his family back. In Jesus' words, "In the same way, I tell you, there is rejoicing in the presence of the angels of God over one sinner who repents."

Grace is shockingly personal. As Henri Nouwen points out, "God rejoices. Not because the problems of the world have been solved, not because all human pain and suffering have come to an end, nor because thousands of people have been converted and are now praising him for his goodness. No, God rejoices because *one* of his children who was lost has been found."

If I focus on the ethics of the individual characters in the parables—the vagrant of Fulton Street, the businessman who lost a million dollars, the motley crew at the Boston banquet, the teenage prostitute from Traverse City—I come away with a very strange message indeed. Obviously, Jesus did not give the parables to teach us how to live. He gave them, I believe, to correct our notions about who God is and who God loves.

In the Academy of Fine Arts in Venice there hangs a painting by Paolo Veronese, a painting that got him in trouble with the Inquisition.

The painting depicts Jesus at a banquet with his disciples, complete with Roman soldiers playing in one corner, a man with a bloody nose on the other side, stray dogs roaming around, a few drunks, and also midgets, blackamoors, and anachronistic Huns. Called before the Inquisition to explain these irreverences, Veronese defended his painting by showing from the Gospels that these were the very kinds of people Jesus mingled with. Scandalized, the Inquisitors made him change the title of the painting and make the scene secular rather than religious.

In doing so, of course, the Inquisitors replicated the attitude of the Pharisees in Jesus' day. They too were scandalized by the tax collectors, half-breeds, foreigners, and women of ill repute who hung out with Jesus. They too had trouble swallowing the notion that these are the people God loves. At the very moment Jesus was captivating the crowd with his parables of grace, Pharisees stood at the edges of the crowd muttering and grinding their teeth. In the story of the Prodigal Son, provocatively, Jesus brought in the older brother to voice proper outrage at his father for rewarding irresponsible behavior. What kind of "family values" would his father communicate by throwing a party for such a renegade? What kind of virtue would that encourage?*

The gospel is not at all what we would come up with on our own. I, for one, would expect to honor the virtuous over the profligate. I would expect to have to clean up my act before even applying for an audience with a Holy God. But Jesus told of God ignoring a fancy religious teacher and turning instead to an ordinary sinner who pleads, "God, have mercy." Throughout the Bible, in fact, God shows a marked preference for "real" people over "good" people. In Jesus' own words, "There will be more rejoicing in heaven over one sinner who repents than over ninety-nine righteous persons who do not need to repent."

In one of his last acts before death, Jesus forgave a thief dangling on a cross, knowing full well the thief had converted out of plain fear. That

*The contemporary preacher Fred Craddock once tinkered with details of the parable to make just this point. In a sermon, he had the father slip the ring and robe on the *elder* brother, then kill the fatted calf in honor of his years of faithfulness and obedience. A woman in the back of the sanctuary yelled out, "That's the way it *should* have been written!"

thief would never study the Bible, never attend synagogue or church, and never make amends to all those he had wronged. He simply said "Jesus, remember me," and Jesus promised, "Today you will be with me in paradise." It was another shocking reminder that grace does not depend on what we have done for God but rather what God has done for us.

Ask people what they must do to get to heaven and most reply, "Be good." Jesus' stories contradict that answer. All we must do is cry, "Help!" God welcomes home anyone who will have him and, in fact, has made the first move already. Most experts—doctors, lawyers, marriage counselors—set a high value on themselves and wait for clients to come to them. Not God. As Søren Kierkegaard put it,

> When it is a question of a sinner He does not merely stand still, open his arms and say, "Come hither"; no, He stands there and waits, as the father of the lost son waited, rather He does not stand and wait, He goes forth to seek, as the shepherd sought the lost sheep, as the woman sought the lost coin. He goes—yet no, He has gone, but infinitely farther than any shepherd or any woman, He went, in sooth, the infinitely long way from being God to becoming man, and that way He went in search of sinners.

Kierkegaard puts his finger on perhaps the most important aspect of Jesus' parables. They were not merely pleasant stories to hold listeners' attention or literary vessels to hold theological truth. They were, in fact, the template of Jesus' life on earth. He was the shepherd who left the safety of the fold for the dark and dangerous night outside. To his banquets he welcomed tax collectors and reprobates and whores. He came for the sick and not the well, for the unrighteous and not the righteous. And to those who betrayed him—especially the disciples, who forsook him at his time of greatest need—he responded like a lovesick father.

Theologian Karl Barth, after writing thousands of pages in his *Church Dogmatics*, arrived at this simple definition of God: "the One who loves."

Not long ago I heard from a pastor friend who was battling with his fifteen-year-old daughter. He knew she was using birth control, and several nights she had not bothered to come home at all. The parents had tried various forms of punishment, to no avail. The daughter lied to them, deceived them, and found a way to turn the tables on them: "It's your fault for being so strict!"

My friend told me, "I remember standing before the plate-glass window in my living room, staring out into the darkness, waiting for her to come home. I felt such rage. I wanted to be like the father of the Prodigal Son, yet I was furious with my daughter for the way she would manipulate us and twist the knife to hurt us. And of course, she was hurting herself more than anyone. I understood then the passages in the prophets expressing God's anger. The people knew how to wound him, and God cried out in pain.

"And yet I must tell you, when my daughter came home that night, or rather the next morning, I wanted nothing in the world so much as to take her in my arms, to love her, to tell her I wanted the best for her. I was a helpless, lovesick father."

Now, when I think about God, I hold up that image of the lovesick father, which is miles away from the stern monarch I used to envision. I think of my friend standing in front of the plate-glass window gazing achingly into the darkness. I think of Jesus' depiction of the Waiting Father, heartsick, abused, yet wanting above all else to forgive and begin anew, to announce with joy, "This my son was dead, and is alive again; he was lost, and is found."

Mozart's *Requiem* contains a wonderful line that has become my prayer, one I pray with increasing confidence: "Remember, merciful Jesu, That I am the cause of your journey." I think he remembers.

Except for the point, the still point,
There would be no dance, and there is only the dance.

T. S. ELIOT

FIVE

The New Math of Grace

When a column of mine titled "The Atrocious Mathematics of the Gospel" appeared in *Christianity Today* magazine, I soon learned that not everyone appreciates satire. Response letters scorched the inside of my mailbox. "Philip Yancey, you do not walk with God or with Jesus!" wrote one irate reader; "This column is blasphemy." Another condemned my "antichristian, intellectualized philosophies." Yet another reader labeled me "satanic." "Are there not enough review editors on your staff to weed out such sophomoric tripe?" he asked the editor.

Feeling chastened, and unaccustomed to being regarded as blasphemous, antichristian, and satanic, I went back and puzzled over that column. What had gone wrong? I had taken four stories, one from each of the Gospels, and with tongue obviously in cheek—or so I thought—pointed out the absurdity of the mathematics involved.

Luke tells of a shepherd who left his flock of ninety-nine and plunged into the darkness to search for one lost sheep. A noble deed, to be sure, but reflect for a moment on the underlying arithmetic. Jesus says the shepherd left the ninety-nine sheep "in the country," which presumably means vulnerable to rustlers, wolves, or a feral desire to bolt free. How would the shepherd feel if he returned with the one lost lamb slung across his shoulders only to find twenty-three others now missing?

In a scene recounted in John, a woman named Mary took a *pint*—worth a year's wages!—of exotic perfume and poured it on Jesus' feet. Think of the wastefulness. Would not an ounce of perfume accomplish the same purpose? Even Judas could see the absurdity: the treasure now running in fragrant rivulets across the dirt floor could have been sold to help the poor.

Mark records yet a third scene. After watching a widow drop two puny coins in the temple collection bucket, Jesus belittled more hefty contributions. "I tell you the truth," he remarked, "this poor widow has put more into the treasury than all the others." I hope he said those words softly, for major donors would not appreciate the comparison.

The fourth story, from Matthew, involves a parable I have heard few sermons preached on, with good reason. Jesus told of a farmer who hired people to work his vineyards. Some clocked in at sunrise, some at morning coffee break, some at lunchtime, some at afternoon coffee break, and some an hour before quitting time. Everybody seemed content until payroll time, when the stalwarts who had worked twelve hours under a blazing sun learned that the sweatless upstarts who had put in barely an hour would receive exactly the same pay. The boss's action contradicted everything known about employee motivation and fair compensation. It was atrocious economics, plain and simple.

Besides learning a lesson about satire with that column, I also learned an important lesson about grace. Perhaps the word "atrocious" was ill-chosen, but surely grace sounds a shrill note of *unfairness*. Why should a widow's pennies count more than a rich man's millions? And what employer would pay Johnny-come-latelies the same as his trusted regulars?

Not long after writing the column, I attended *Amadeus* (Latin for "beloved of God"), a play that shows a composer in the eighteenth century seeking to understand the mind of God. The devout Antonio Salieri has the earnest desire, but not the aptitude, to create immortal music of praise. It infuriates him that God has instead lavished the greatest gift of musical genius ever known on an impish preadolescent named Wolfgang Amadeus Mozart.

While watching the performance, I realized I was seeing the flip side of a problem that had long troubled me. The play was posing the same question as the biblical book of Job, only inverted. The author of Job ponders why God would "punish" the most righteous man on the face of the earth; the author of *Amadeus* ponders why God would "reward" an undeserving brat. The problem of pain meets its match in the scandal of grace. A line from the play expresses the scandal: "What use, after all, is man if not to teach God his lessons?"

Why would God choose Jacob the conniver over dutiful Esau? Why confer supernatural powers of strength on a Mozartian delinquent named Samson? Why groom a runty shepherd boy, David, to be Israel's king? And why bestow a sublime gift of wisdom on Solomon, the fruit of that king's adulterous liaison? Indeed, in each of these Old Testament stories the scandal of grace rumbles under the surface until finally, in Jesus' parables, it bursts forth in a dramatic upheaval to reshape the moral landscape.

Jesus' parable of the workers and their grossly unfair paychecks confronts this scandal head-on. In a contemporary Jewish version of this story, the workers hired late in the afternoon work so hard that the employer, impressed, decides to award them a full day's wages. Not so in Jesus' version, which notes that the last crop of workers have been idly standing around in the marketplace, something only lazy, shiftless workers would do during harvest season. Moreover, these laggards do nothing to distinguish themselves, and the other workers are shocked by the pay they receive. What employer in his right mind would pay the same amount for one hour's work as for twelve!

Jesus' story makes no economic sense, and that was his intent. He was giving us a parable about grace, which cannot be calculated like a day's wages. Grace is not about finishing last or first; it is about not counting. We receive grace as a gift from God, not as something we toil to earn, a point that Jesus made clearly through the employer's response:

> Friend, I am not being unfair to you. Didn't you agree to work for a denarius? Take your pay and go. I want to give the man who was hired last the same as I gave you. Don't I have the right to do what I want with my own money? Or are you envious because I am generous?

Are you, Salieri, envious because I am so generous to Mozart? Are you, Saul, envious because I am so generous to David? Are you Pharisees envious because I open the gate to Gentiles so late in the game? That I honor the prayer of a tax collector above a Pharisee's, that I accept a thief's last-minute confession and welcome him to Paradise—does this arouse your envy? Do you begrudge my leaving the obedient flock to seek the stray or my serving a fatted calf to the no-good prodigal?

The employer in Jesus' story did not cheat the full-day workers by paying everyone for one hour's work instead of twelve. No, the full-day workers got what they were promised. Their discontent arose from the scandalous mathematics of grace. They could not accept that their employer had the right to do what he wanted with his money when it meant paying scoundrels twelve times what they deserved.

Significantly, many Christians who study this parable identify with the employees who put in a full day's work, rather than the add-ons at the end of the day. We like to think of ourselves as responsible workers, and the employer's strange behavior baffles us as it did the original hearers. We risk missing the story's point: that God dispenses gifts, not wages. None of us gets paid according to merit, for none of us comes close to satisfying God's requirements for a perfect life. If paid on the basis of fairness, we would all end up in hell.

In the words of Robert Farrar Capon, "If the world could have been saved by good bookkeeping, it would have been saved by Moses, not Jesus." Grace cannot be reduced to generally accepted accounting principles. In the bottom-line realm of ungrace, some workers deserve more than others; in the realm of grace the word *deserve* does not even apply.

Frederick Buechner says,

> People are prepared for everything except for the fact that beyond the darkness of their blindness there is a great light. They are prepared to go on breaking their backs plowing the same old field until the cows come home without seeing, until they stub their toes on it, that there is a treasure buried in that field rich enough to buy Texas. They are prepared for a God who strikes hard bargains but not for a God who gives as much for an hour's work as for a day's. They are prepared for a mustard-seed kingdom of God no bigger than the eye of a newt but not for the great banyan it becomes with birds in its branches singing

Mozart. They are prepared for the potluck supper at First Presbyterian but not for the marriage supper of the lamb. . . .

By my reckoning Judas and Peter stand out as the most mathematical of the disciples. Judas must have shown some facility with numbers or the others would not have elected him treasurer. Peter was a stickler for detail, always trying to pin down Jesus' precise meaning. Also, the Gospels record that when Jesus engineered a miraculous catch of fish, Peter hauled in 153 big ones. Who but a mathematician would have bothered to count the squirming pile?

It was altogether in character, then, for the scrupulous apostle Peter to pursue some mathematical formula of grace. "How many times shall I forgive my brother when he sins against me?" he asked Jesus. "Up to seven times?" Peter was erring on the side of magnanimity, for the rabbis in his day had suggested three as the maximum number of times one might be expected to forgive.

"Not seven times, but seventy-seven times," replied Jesus in a flash. Some manuscripts have "seventy times seven," but it hardly matters whether Jesus said 77 or 490: forgiveness, he implied, is not the kind of thing you count on an abacus.

Peter's question prompted another of Jesus' trenchant stories, about a servant who has somehow piled up a debt of several million dollars. The fact that realistically no servant could accumulate a debt so huge underscores Jesus' point: confiscating the man's family, children, and all his property would not make a dent in repaying the debt. It is unforgivable. Nevertheless the king, touched with pity, abruptly cancels the debt and lets the servant off scot-free.

Suddenly, the plot twists. The servant who has just been forgiven seizes a colleague who owes him a few dollars and begins to choke him. "Pay back what you owe me!" he demands, and throws the man into jail. In a word, the greedy servant is an *ingrate.*

Why Jesus draws the parable with such exaggerated strokes comes clear when he reveals that the king represents God. This above all should determine our attitude toward others: a humble awareness that God has already forgiven us a debt so mountainous that beside it any person's wrongs against us shrink to the size of anthills. How can we *not* forgive each other in light of all God has forgiven us?

As C. S. Lewis put it, "To be a Christian means to forgive the inexcusable, because God has forgiven the inexcusable in you." Lewis himself fathomed the depths of God's forgiveness in a flash of revelation as he repeated the phrase in the Apostle's Creed, "I believe in the forgiveness of sins," on St. Mark's Day. His sins were gone, forgiven! "This truth appeared in my mind in so clear a light that I perceived that never before (and that after many confessions and absolutions) had I believed it with my whole heart."

The more I reflect on Jesus' parables, the more tempted I am to reclaim the word "atrocious" to describe the mathematics of the gospel. I believe Jesus gave us these stories about grace in order to call us to step completely outside our tit-for-tat world of ungrace and enter into God's realm of infinite grace. As Miroslav Volf puts it, "the economy of undeserved grace has primacy over the economy of moral deserts."

From nursery school onward we are taught how to succeed in the world of ungrace. The early bird gets the worm. No pain, no gain. There is no such thing as a free lunch. Demand your rights. Get what you pay for. I know these rules well because I live by them. I work for what I earn; I like to win; I insist on my rights. I want people to get what they deserve—nothing more, nothing less.

Yet if I care to listen, I hear a loud whisper from the gospel that I did not get what I deserved. I deserved punishment and got forgiveness. I deserved wrath and got love. I deserved debtor's prison and got instead a clean credit history. I deserved stern lectures and crawl-on-your-knees repentance; I got a banquet—Babette's feast—spread for me.

In a manner of speaking, grace solves a dilemma for God. You do not have to read far in the Bible to detect an underlying tension in how God feels about humanity. On the one hand, God loves us; on the other hand, our behavior repulses him. God yearns to see in people something of his own image reflected; at best he sees shattered fragments of that image. Still, God cannot—or will not—give up.

A passage from Isaiah is often cited as proof of God's remoteness and power:

"For my thoughts are not your thoughts,
neither are your ways my ways,"
declares the LORD.
"As the heavens are higher than the earth,
so are my ways higher than your ways
and my thoughts than your thoughts."

In context, though, God is actually describing his eagerness to forgive. The same God who created the heavens and the earth has the power to bridge the great chasm that separates him from his creatures. He will reconcile, he will forgive, no matter what obstacles his prodigal children put in the way. As the prophet Micah says, "You do not stay angry forever but delight to show mercy."

Sometimes God's conflicting emotions tug against each other in the very same scene. In the book of Hosea, for example, God wavers between tender reminiscences of his people and solemn threats of judgment. "Swords will flash in their cities," he warns darkly, and then almost in midsentence a cry of love escapes:

How can I give you up, Ephraim?
How can I hand you over, Israel? . . .
My heart is changed within me;
all my compassion is aroused.

"I will not carry out my fierce anger," God concludes at last. "For I am God, and not man—the Holy One among you." Once again God reserves the right to alter the rules of retribution. Although Israel has fully earned his rebuff, they will not get what they deserve. *I am God, and not man. . . . Don't I have the right to do what I want with my own money?* God will go to any preposterous length to get his family back.

In an astonishing acted-out parable, God asks the prophet Hosea to marry a woman named Gomer in order to illustrate his love for Israel. Gomer bears three children for Hosea, then abandons the family to live with another man. For a time she works as a prostitute, and it is during this period that God gives the shocking command to Hosea, "Go, show your love to your wife again, though she is loved by another and is an adulteress. Love her as the LORD loves the Israelites, though they turn to other gods. . . ."

In Hosea, the scandal of grace became an actual, talk-of-the-town scandal. What goes through a man's mind when his wife treats him as Gomer treated Hosea? He wanted to kill her, he wanted to forgive her. He wanted divorce, he wanted reconciliation. She shamed him, she melted him. Absurdly, against all odds, the irresistible power of love won out. Hosea the cuckold, joke of the community, welcomed his wife back home.

Gomer did not get fairness, or even justice; she got grace. Every time I read their story—or read God's speeches that begin with sternness and dissolve into tears—I marvel at a God who allows himself to endure such humiliation only to come back for more. "How can I give you up, Ephraim? How can I hand you over, Israel?" Substitute your own name for Ephraim and Israel. At the heart of the gospel is a God who deliberately surrenders to the wild, irresistible power of love.

Centuries later an apostle would explain God's response in more analytical terms: "But where sin increased, grace increased all the more." Paul knew better than anyone who has ever lived that grace comes undeserved, at God's initiative and not our own. Knocked flat on the ground on the way to Damascus, he never recovered from the impact of grace: the word appears no later than the second sentence in every one of his letters. As Frederick Buechner says, "Grace is the best he can wish them because grace is the best he himself ever received."

Paul harped on grace because he knew what could happen if we believe we have earned God's love. In the dark times, if perhaps we badly fail God, or if for no good reason we simply feel unloved, we would stand on shaky ground. We would fear that God might stop loving us when he discovers the real truth about us. Paul—"the chief of sinners" he once called himself—knew beyond doubt that God loves people because of who God is, not because of who we are.

Aware of the apparent scandal of grace, Paul took pains to explain how God has made peace with human beings. Grace baffles us because it goes against the intuition everyone has that, in the face of injustice, some price must be paid. A murderer cannot simply go free. A child abuser cannot shrug and say, "I just felt like it." Anticipating these objections, Paul stressed that a price has been paid—by God himself. God gave up his own Son rather than give up on humanity.

Like Babette's feast, grace costs nothing for the recipients but everything for the giver. God's grace is not a grandfatherly display of "niceness," for it cost the exorbitant price of Calvary. "There is only one real law—the law of the universe," said Dorothy Sayers. "It may be fulfilled either by way of judgment or by the way of grace, but it *must* be fulfilled one way or the other." By accepting the judgment in his own body, Jesus fulfilled that law, and God found a way to forgive.

In the movie *The Last Emperor*, the young child anointed as the last emperor of China lives a magical life of luxury with a thousand eunuch servants at his command. "What happens when you do wrong?" his brother asks. "When I do wrong, someone else is punished," the boy emperor replies. To demonstrate, he breaks a jar, and one of the servants is beaten. In Christian theology, Jesus reversed that ancient pattern: when the servants erred, the King was punished. Grace is free only because the giver himself has borne the cost.

When the renowned theologian Karl Barth visited the University of Chicago, students and scholars crowded around him. At a press conference, one asked, "Dr. Barth, what is the most profound truth you have learned in your studies?" Without hesitation he replied, "Jesus loves me, this I know, for the Bible tells me so." I agree with Karl Barth. Why, then, do I so often act as if I am trying to earn that love? Why do I have such trouble accepting it?

As Dr. Bob Smith and Bill Wilson, the founders of Alcoholics Anonymous, first devised their twelve-step program, they went to Bill D., a prominent attorney who had flunked out of eight separate detox programs in six months. Strapped in a hospital bed as punishment for attacking two nurses, Bill D. had no choice but to listen to his visitors, who shared their own stories of addiction and the recent hope they had discovered through belief in a Higher Power.

As soon as they mentioned their Higher Power, Bill D. shook his head sadly. "No, no," he said. "It's too late for me. I still believe in God all right, but I know mighty well that He doesn't believe in me any more."

Bill D. expressed what many of us feel at times. Weighed down by repeated failures, lost hope, a sense of unworthiness, we pull around ourselves a shell that makes us almost impervious to grace. Like foster children who choose again and again to return to abusive families, we turn stubbornly away from grace.

I know how I respond to rejection letters from magazine editors and to critical letters from readers. I know how high my spirits soar when a larger than expected royalty check arrives, and how low they sink when the check is small. I know that my self-image at the end of the day depends largely on what kind of messages I have received from other people. Am I liked? Am I loved? I await the answers from my friends, my neighbors, my family—like a starving man, I await the answers.

Occasionally, all too occasionally, I sense the truth of grace. There are times when I study the parables and grasp that they are about *me.* I am the sheep the shepherd has left the flock to find, the prodigal for whom the father scans the horizon, the servant whose debt has been forgiven. I am the beloved one of God.

Not long ago I received in the mail a postcard from a friend that had on it only six words, "I am the one Jesus loves." I smiled when I saw the return address, for my strange friend excels at these pious slogans. When I called him, though, he told me the slogan came from the author and speaker Brennan Manning. At a seminar, Manning referred to Jesus' closest friend on earth, the disciple named John, identified in the Gospels as "the one Jesus loved." Manning said, "If John were to be asked, 'What is your primary identity in life?' he would not reply, 'I am a disciple, an apostle, an evangelist, an author of one of the four Gospels,' but rather, 'I am the one Jesus loves.'"

What would it mean, I ask myself, if I too came to the place where I saw my primary identity in life as "the one Jesus loves"? How differently would I view myself at the end of a day?

Sociologists have a theory of the looking-glass self: you become what the most important person in your life (wife, father, boss, etc.) thinks you are. How would my life change if I truly believed the Bible's astounding words about God's love for me, if I looked in the mirror and saw what God sees?

Brennan Manning tells the story of an Irish priest who, on a walking tour of a rural parish, sees an old peasant kneeling by the side of the road, praying. Impressed, the priest says to the man, "You must be very close to God." The peasant looks up from his prayers, thinks a moment, and then smiles, "Yes, he's very fond of me."

God exists outside of time, the theologians tell us. God created time as an artist chooses a medium to work with, and is unbound by it. He sees the future and the past in a kind of eternal present. If right about this property of God, the theologians have helped explain how God can possibly call "beloved" a person as inconstant, fickle, and temperamental as I am. When God looks upon my life graph, he sees not jagged swerves toward good and bad but rather a steady line of good: the goodness of God's Son captured in a moment of time and applied for all eternity.

As the seventeenth-century poet John Donne put it,

> For in the Book of Life, the name of Mary Magdalen was as soon recorded, for all her incontinency, as the name of the blessed Virgin, for all her integrity; and the name of St. Paul, who drew his sword against Christ, as soon as St. Peter, who drew his in defence of him: for the Book of Life was not written successively, word after word, line after line, but delivered as a Print, all together.

I grew up with the image of a mathematical God who weighed my good and bad deeds on a set of scales and always found me wanting. Somehow I missed the God of the Gospels, a God of mercy and generosity who keeps finding ways to shatter the relentless laws of ungrace. God tears up the mathematical tables and introduces the new math of *grace*, the most surprising, twisting, unexpected-ending word in the English language.

Grace makes its appearance in so many forms that I have trouble defining it. I am ready, though, to attempt something like a definition of grace in relation to God. *Grace means there is nothing we can do to make God love us more*—no amount of spiritual calisthenics and renunciations, no amount of knowledge gained from seminaries and divinity schools, no amount of crusading on behalf of righteous causes. *And grace means there is nothing we can do to make God love us less*—no amount of racism or pride or pornography or adultery or even murder. Grace means that God already loves us as much as an infinite God can possibly love.

There is a simple cure for people who doubt God's love and question God's grace: to turn to the Bible and examine the kind of people God loves. Jacob, who dared take God on in a wrestling match and ever after bore a wound from that struggle, became the eponym for God's people, the "children of Israel." The Bible tells of a murderer and adulterer who gained a reputation as the greatest king of the Old Testament, a "man after God's own heart." And of a church being led by a disciple who cursed and swore that he had never known Jesus. And of a missionary being recruited from the ranks of the Christian-torturers. I get mailings from Amnesty International, and as I look at their photos of men and women who have been beaten and cattle-prodded and jabbed and spit on and electrocuted, I ask myself, "What kind of human being could do that to another human being?" Then I read the book of Acts and meet the kind of person who could do such a thing—now an apostle of grace, a servant of Jesus Christ, the greatest missionary history has ever known. If God can love that kind of person, maybe, just maybe, he can love the likes of me.

I cannot moderate my definition of grace, because the Bible forces me to make it as sweeping as possible. God is "the God of all grace," in the apostle Peter's words. And grace means there is nothing I can do to make God love me more, and nothing I can do to make God love me less. It means that I, even I who deserve the opposite, am invited to take my place at the table in God's family.

By instinct I feel I must *do something* in order to be accepted. Grace sounds a startling note of contradiction, of liberation, and every day I must pray anew for the ability to hear its message.

Eugene Peterson draws a contrast between Augustine and Pelagius, two fourth-century theological opponents. Pelagius was urbane, courteous, convincing, and liked by everyone. Augustine squandered away his youth in immorality, had a strange relationship with his mother, and made many enemies. Yet Augustine started from God's grace and got it right, whereas Pelagius started from human effort and got it wrong. Augustine passionately pursued God; Pelagius methodically worked to please God. Peterson goes on to say that Christians tend to be Augustinian in theory but Pelagian in practice. They work obsessively to please other people and even God.

Each year in spring, I fall victim to what the sports announcers diagnose as "March Madness." I cannot resist the temptation to tune in to the final basketball game, in which the sole survivors of a sixty-four-team tournament meet for the NCAA championship. That most important game always seems to come down to one eighteen-year-old kid standing on a freethrow line with one second left on the clock.

He dribbles nervously. If he misses these two foul shots, he knows, he will be the goat of his campus, the goat of his state. Twenty years from now he'll be in counseling, reliving this moment. If he makes these shots, he'll be a hero. His picture will be on the front page. He could probably run for governor.

He takes another dribble and the other team calls time, to rattle him. He stands on the sideline, weighing his entire future. Everything depends on him. His teammates pat him encouragingly, but say nothing.

One year, I remember, I left the room to answer a phone call just as the kid was setting himself to shoot. Worry lines creased his forehead. He was biting his lower lip. His left leg quivered at the knee. Twenty thousand fans were yelling, waving banners and handkerchiefs to distract him.

The phone call took longer than expected, and when I returned I saw a new sight. This same kid, his hair drenched with Gatorade, was now riding atop the shoulders of his teammates, cutting the cords of a basketball net. He had not a care in the world. His grin filled the entire screen.

Those two freeze-frames—the same kid crouching at the free throw line and then celebrating on his friends' shoulders—came to symbolize for me the difference between ungrace and grace.

The world runs by ungrace. Everything depends on what I do. I have to make the shot.

Jesus' kingdom calls us to another way, one that depends not on our performance but his own. We do not have to achieve but merely follow. He has already earned for us the costly victory of God's acceptance.

When I think of those two images a troubling question enters my mind: Which of those two scenes most resembles my spiritual life?

PART II

Breaking the Cycle of Ungrace

Six

Unbroken Chain: A Story

In 1898 Daisy was born into a working-class Chicago family, the eighth child of ten. The father barely earned enough to feed them all, and after he took up drinking, money got much scarcer. Daisy, closing in on her hundredth birthday as I write this, shudders when she talks about those days. Her father was a "mean drunk," she says. Daisy used to cower in the corner, sobbing, as he kicked her baby brother and sister across the linoleum floor. She hated him with all her heart.

One day the father declared that he wanted his wife out of the house by noon. All ten kids crowded around their mother, clinging to her skirt and crying, "No, don't go!" But their father did not back down. Holding on to her brothers and sisters for support, Daisy watched through the bay window as her mother walked down the sidewalk, shoulders adroop, a suitcase in each hand, growing smaller and smaller until finally she disappeared from view.

Some of the children eventually rejoined their mother, and some went to live with other relatives. It fell to Daisy to stay with her father. She grew up with a hard knot of bitterness inside her, a tumor of hatred over what he had done to the family. All the kids dropped out of school early in order to take jobs or join the Army, and then one by one they moved away to other towns. They got married, started families, and tried to put the past behind them. The father vanished—no one knew where and no one cared.

Many years later, to everyone's surprise, the father resurfaced. He had guttered out, he said. Drunk and cold, he had wandered into a Salvation Army rescue mission one night. To earn a meal ticket he first had to attend a worship service. When the speaker asked if anyone wanted to accept Jesus, he thought it only polite to go forward along with some of the other drunks. He was more surprised than anybody when the "sinner's prayer" actually worked. The demons inside him quieted down. He sobered up. He began studying the Bible and praying. For the first time in his life he felt loved and accepted. He felt clean.

And now, he told his children, he was looking them up one by one to ask for forgiveness. He couldn't defend anything that had happened. He couldn't make it right. But he was sorry, more sorry than they could possibly imagine.

The children, now middle-aged and with families of their own, were initially skeptical. Some doubted his sincerity, expecting him to fall off the wagon at any moment. Others figured he would soon ask for money. Neither happened, and in time the father won them over, all except Daisy.

Long ago Daisy had vowed never to speak to her father—"that man" she called him—again. Her father's reappearance rattled her badly, and old memories of his drunken rages came flooding back as she lay in bed at night. "He can't undo all that just by saying 'I'm sorry,'" Daisy insisted. She wanted no part of him.

The father may have given up drinking, but alcohol had damaged his liver beyond repair. He got very sick, and for the last five years of his life he lived with one of his daughters, Daisy's sister. They lived, in fact, eight houses down the street from Daisy, on the very same row-house block. Keeping her vow, Daisy never once stopped in to visit her dying father, even though she passed by his house whenever she went grocery shopping or caught a bus.

Daisy did consent to let her own children visit their grandfather. Nearing the end, the father saw a little girl come to his door and step inside. "Oh, Daisy, Daisy, you've come to me at last," he cried, gathering her in his arms. The adults in the room didn't have the heart to tell him the girl was not Daisy, but her daughter Margaret. He was hallucinating grace.

All her life Daisy determined to be unlike her father, and indeed she never touched a drop of alcohol. Yet she ruled her own family with a milder form of the tyranny she had grown up under. She would lie on a couch with a rubber ice pack on her head and scream at the kids to "Shut up!"

"Why did I ever have you stupid kids anyway?" she would yell. "You've ruined my life!" The Great Depression had hit, and each child was one more mouth to feed. She had six in all, rearing them in the two-bedroom row house she lives in to this day. In such close quarters, they seemed always underfoot. Some nights she gave them all whippings just to make a point: she knew they'd done wrong even if she hadn't caught them.

Hard as steel, Daisy never apologized and never forgave. Her daughter Margaret remembers as a child coming in tears to apologize for something she'd done. Daisy responded with a parental Catch-22: "You can't possibly be sorry! If you were really sorry, you wouldn't have done it in the first place."

I have heard many such stories of ungrace from Margaret, whom I know well. All her life she determined to be different from her mother, Daisy. But Margaret's life had its own tragedies, some large and some small, and as her four children entered their teenage years she felt she was losing control of them. She too wanted to lie on the couch with an ice pack and scream, "Shut up!" She too wanted to whip them just to make a point or maybe to release some of the tension coiled inside her.

Her son Michael, who turned sixteen in the 1960s, especially got under her skin. He listened to rock and roll, wore "granny glasses," let his hair grow long. Margaret kicked him out of the house when she caught him smoking pot, and he moved into a hippie commune. She continued to threaten and scold him. She reported him to a judge. She wrote him out of her will. She tried everything she could think of, and nothing got through to Michael. The words she flung up against him fell back, useless, until finally one day in a fit of anger she said, "I never want to see you again as long as I live." That was twenty-six years ago and she has not seen him since.

Michael is also my close friend. Several times during those twenty-six years I have attempted some sort of reconciliation between the two, and each time I confront again the terrible power of ungrace. When I asked Margaret if she regretted anything she had said to her son, if she'd like to take anything back, she turned on me in a flash of hot rage as if I were Michael himself. "I don't know why God didn't take him long ago, for all the things he's done!" she said, with a wild, scary look in her eye.

Her brazen fury caught me off guard. I stared at her for a minute: her hands clenched, her face florid, tiny muscles twitching around her eyes. "Do you mean you wish your own son was dead?" I asked at last. She never answered.

Michael emerged from the sixties mellower, his mind dulled by LSD. He moved to Hawaii, lived with a woman, left her, tried another, left her, and then got married. "Sue is the real thing," he told me when I visited him once. "This one will last."

It did not last. I remember a phone conversation with Michael, interrupted by the annoying technological feature known as "call waiting." The line clicked and Michael said, "Excuse me a second," then left me holding a silent phone receiver for at least four minutes. He apologized when he came back on. His mood had darkened. "It was Sue," he said. "We're settling some of the last financial issues of the divorce."

"I didn't know you still had contact with Sue," I said, making conversation.

"I don't!" he cut in, using almost the same tone I had heard from his mother, Margaret. "I hope I never see her again as long as I live!"

We both stayed silent for a long time. We had just been talking about Margaret, and although I said nothing it seemed to me that Michael had recognized in his own voice the tone of his mother, which was actually the tone of her mother, tracing all the way back to what happened in a Chicago row house nearly a century ago.

Like a spiritual defect encoded in the family DNA, ungrace gets passed on in an unbroken chain.

Ungrace does its work quietly and lethally, like a poisonous, undetectable gas. A father dies unforgiven. A mother who once carried a child in her own body does not speak to that child for half its life. The toxin steals on, from generation to generation.

Margaret is a devout Christian who studies the Bible every day, and once I spoke to her about the parable of the Prodigal Son. "What do you do with that parable?" I asked. "Do you hear its message of forgiveness?"

She had obviously thought about the matter, for without hesitation she replied that the parable appears in Luke 15 as the third in a series of three: lost coin, lost sheep, lost son. She said the whole point of the Prodigal Son is to demonstrate how human beings differ from inanimate objects (coins) and from animals (sheep). "People have free will," she said. "They have to be morally responsible. That boy had to come crawling back on his knees. He had to repent. That was Jesus' point."

That was not Jesus' point, Margaret. All three stories emphasize the *finder's* joy. True, the prodigal returned home of his own free will, but clearly the central focus of the story is the father's outrageous love: "But while he was still a long way off, his father saw him and was filled with compassion for him; he ran to his son, threw his arms around him and kissed him." When the son tries to repent, the father interrupts his prepared speech in order to get the celebration under way.

A missionary in Lebanon once read this parable to a group of villagers who lived in a culture very similar to the one Jesus described and who had never heard the story. "What do you notice?" he asked.

Two details of the story stood out to the villagers. First, by claiming his inheritance early, the son was saying to his father, "I wish you were dead!" The villagers could not imagine a patriarch taking such an insult or agreeing to the son's demand. Second, they noticed that the father *ran* to greet his long-lost son. In the Middle East, a man of stature walks with slow and stately dignity; never does he run. In Jesus' story the father runs, and Jesus' audience no doubt gasped at this detail.

Grace is unfair, which is one of the hardest things about it. It is unreasonable to expect a woman to forgive the terrible things her father did to her just because he apologizes many years later, and totally unfair to ask that a mother overlook the many offenses her teenage son committed. Grace, however, is not about fairness.

What is true of families is true also of tribes, races, and nations.

He who cannot forgive another breaks the bridge over which he must pass himself.

George Herbert

SEVEN

An Unnatural Act

I have told the story of one family that spans a century of ungrace. In world history similar stories span many centuries, with far worse consequences. If you ask a bomb-throwing teenager in Northern Ireland or a machete-wielding soldier in Rwanda or a sniper in the former Yugoslavia why they are killing, they may not even know. Ireland is still seeking revenge for atrocities Oliver Cromwell committed in the seventeenth century; Rwanda and Burundi are carrying on tribal feuds that extend long past anyone's memory; Yugoslavia is avenging memories from World War II and trying to prevent a replay of what happened six centuries ago.

Ungrace plays like the background static of life for families, nations, and institutions. It is, sadly, our natural human state.

I once shared a meal with two scientists who had just emerged from the glass-enclosed biosphere near Tucson, Arizona. Four men and four women had volunteered for the two-year isolation experiment. All were accomplished scientists, all had undergone psychological testing and preparation, and all had entered the biosphere fully briefed on the rigors they would face while sealed off from the outside world. The scientists told me that within a matter of months the eight "bionauts" had split into two groups of four, and during the final months of the experiment these two groups refused to speak to each other. Eight people lived in a bubble split in half by an invisible wall of ungrace.

Frank Reed, an American citizen held hostage in Lebanon, disclosed upon his release that he had not spoken to one of his fellow hostages for several months following some minor dispute. Most of that time, the two feuding hostages had been chained together.

Ungrace causes cracks to fissure open between mother and daughter, father and son, brother and sister, between scientists, and prisoners, and tribes, and races. Left alone, cracks widen, and for the resulting chasms of ungrace there is only one remedy: the frail rope-bridge of forgiveness.

In the heat of an argument my wife came up with an acute theological formulation. We were discussing my shortcomings in a rather spirited way when she said, "I think it's pretty amazing that I forgive you for some of the dastardly things you've done!"

Since I'm writing about forgiveness, not sin, I will omit the juicy details of those dastardly things. What struck me about her comment, rather, was its sharp insight into the nature of forgiveness. It is no sweet platonic ideal to be dispersed in the world like air-freshener sprayed from a can. Forgiveness is achingly difficult, and long after you've forgiven, the wound—my dastardly deeds—lives on in memory. Forgiveness is an unnatural act, and my wife was protesting its blatant unfairness.

A story from Genesis captures much the same sentiment. When I was a child listening to the story in Sunday school, I could not understand the loops and twists in the account of Joseph's reconciliation with his brothers. One moment Joseph acted harshly, throwing his brothers in jail; the next moment he seemed overcome with sorrow, leaving the room to blubber like a drunk. He played tricks on his brothers, hiding money in their grain sacks, seizing one as a hostage, accusing another of stealing his silver cup. For months, maybe years, these intrigues dragged on until finally Joseph could restrain himself no longer. He summoned his brothers and dramatically forgave them.

I now see that story as a realistic depiction of the unnatural act of forgiveness. The brothers Joseph struggled to forgive were the very ones who had bullied him, had cooked up schemes to murder him, had sold him into slavery. Because of them he had spent the best years of his youth moldering in an Egyptian dungeon. Though he went on to triumph over adversity and though with all his heart he now wanted to forgive these brothers, he could not bring himself to that point, not yet. The wound still hurt too much.

I view Genesis 42–45 as Joseph's way of saying, "I think it's pretty amazing that I forgive you for the dastardly things you've done!" When grace finally broke through to Joseph, the sound of his grief and love echoed throughout the palace. *What is that wail? Is the king's minister sick?* No, Joseph's health was fine. It was the sound of a man forgiving.

Behind every act of forgiveness lies a wound of betrayal, and the pain of being betrayed does not easily fade away. Leo Tolstoy thought he was getting his marriage off on the right foot when he asked his teenage fiancée to read his diaries, which spelled out in lurid detail all of his sexual dalliances. He wanted to keep no secrets from Sonya, to begin marriage with a clean slate, forgiven. Instead, Tolstoy's confession sowed the seeds for a marriage that would be held together by vines of hatred, not love.

"When he kisses me I'm always thinking, 'I'm not the first woman he has loved,'" wrote Sonya Tolstoy in her own diary. Some of his adolescent flings she could forgive, but not his affair with Axinya, a peasant woman who continued to work on the Tolstoy estate.

"One of these days I shall kill myself with jealousy," Sonya wrote after seeing the three-year-old son of the peasant woman, the spitting image of her husband. "If I could kill him [Tolstoy] and create a new person exactly the same as he is now, I would do so happily."

Another diary entry dates from January 14, 1909. "He relishes that peasant wench with her strong female body and her sunburnt legs, she allures him just as powerfully now as she did all those years ago . . ." Sonya wrote those words when Axinya was a shriveled crone of eighty. For half a century jealousy and unforgiveness had blinded her, in the process destroying all love for her husband.

Against such malignant power, what chance stands the Christian response? Forgiveness as an unnatural act—Sonya Tolstoy, Joseph, and my wife express this truth as if by instinct.

I and the public know
What all school children learn,
Those to whom evil is done
Do evil in return.

W. H. Auden, who wrote those lines, understood that the law of nature admits no forgiveness. Do squirrels forgive cats for chasing them up trees or dolphins forgive sharks for eating their playmates? It's a dog-eat-dog world out there, not dog-forgive-dog. As for the human species, our major institutions—financial, political, even athletic—run on the same unrelenting principle. An umpire never announces, "You were really out, but because of your exemplary spirit I'll call you safe." Or what nation responds to its belligerent neighbors with the proclamation, "You are right, we violated your borders. Will you please forgive us?"

The very taste of forgiveness seems somehow wrong. Even when we have committed a wrong, we want to earn our way back into the injured party's good graces. We prefer to crawl on our knees, to wallow, to do penance, to kill a lamb—and religion often obliges us. When the Holy Roman Emperor Henry IV decided to seek the pardon of Pope Gregory VII in 1077, he stood barefoot for three days in the snow outside the papal quarters in Italy. Probably, Henry went away with a self-satisfied feeling, wearing frostbite scars as the stigmata of forgiveness.

"Despite a hundred sermons on forgiveness, we do not forgive easily, nor find ourselves easily forgiven. Forgiveness, we discover, is always harder than the sermons make it out to be," writes Elizabeth O'Connor. We nurse sores, go to elaborate lengths to rationalize our behavior, perpetuate family feuds, punish ourselves, punish others—all to avoid this most unnatural act.

On a visit to Bath, England, I saw a more natural response to being wronged. In the Roman ruins there, archeologists have uncovered various "curses" written in Latin and inscribed on tin or bronze placards. Centuries ago, users of the baths tossed in these prayers as an offering to the gods of the bath, much as moderns toss coins into fountains for good luck. One asked for a goddess's help in blood vengeance against whoever stole his six coins. Another read, "Docimedes has lost two gloves. He asks that the person who has stolen them should lose his mind and his eyes in the temple where she appoints."

As I looked at the Latin inscriptions and read their translations, it struck me that these prayers made good sense. Why not employ divine power to assist us with human justice here on earth? Many of the Psalms express the same sentiment, imploring God to help avenge some wrong. "Lord, if you can't make me thin, then make my friends look fat," humorist Erma Bombeck once prayed. What could be more human?

Instead, in a stunning reversal, Jesus instructed us to pray, "Forgive us our trespasses, as we forgive those who trespass against us." At the center of the Lord's Prayer, which Jesus taught us to recite, lurks the unnatural act of forgiveness. Roman bathers urged their gods to abet human justice; Jesus hinged God's forgiveness on our willingness to forgive unjust acts.

Charles Williams has said of the Lord's Prayer, "No word in English carries a greater possibility of terror than the little word 'as' in that clause." What makes the "as" so terrifying? The fact that Jesus plainly links our forgiven-ness by the Father with our forgiving-ness of fellow human beings. Jesus' next remark could not be more explicit: "If you do not forgive men their sins, your Father will not forgive your sins."

It is one thing to get caught up in a cycle of ungrace with a spouse or business partner, and another thing entirely to get caught in such a cycle with Almighty God. Yet the Lord's Prayer pulls those two together: As we can allow ourselves to let go, to break the cycle, to start over, God can allow himself to let go, break the cycle, start over.

John Dryden wrote of the sobering effect of this truth. "More libels have been written against me, than almost any man now living," he protested, and prepared to lash out against his enemies. But "this consideration has often made me tremble when I was saying our Saviour's prayer; for the plain condition of the forgiveness which we beg is the pardoning of others the offences which they have done to us; for which reason I have many times avoided the commission of that fault, even when I have been notoriously provoked."

Dryden was right to tremble. In a world that runs by the laws of ungrace, Jesus requires—no, demands—a response of forgiveness. So urgent is the need for forgiveness that it takes precedence over "religious" duties: "Therefore, if you are offering your gift at the altar and there remember that your brother has something against you, leave your gift there in front of the altar. First go and be reconciled to your brother; then come and offer your gift."

Jesus concluded his parable of the unforgiving servant with a scene of the master turning over the servant to jailers to be tortured. "This is how my heavenly Father will treat each of you unless you forgive your brother from your heart," Jesus said. I fervently wish these words were not in the Bible, but there they are, from the lips of Christ himself. God has granted us a terrible agency: by denying forgiveness to others, we are in effect determining them unworthy of God's forgiveness, and thus so are we. In some mysterious way, divine forgiveness depends on us.

Shakespeare put it succinctly in *Merchant of Venice*: "How shalt thou hope for mercy, rendering none?"

Tony Campolo sometimes asks students at secular universities what they know about Jesus. Can they recall anything Jesus said? By clear consensus they reply, "Love your enemies."* More than any other teaching of Christ, that one stands out to an unbeliever. Such an attitude is unnatural, perhaps downright suicidal. It's hard enough to forgive your rotten brothers, as Joseph did, but your enemies? The gang of thugs down the block? Iraqis? The drug dealers poisoning our nation?

Most ethicists would agree instead with the philosopher Immanuel Kant, who argued that a person should be forgiven only if he deserves it. But the very word *forgive* contains the word "give" (just as the word *pardon* contains *donum*, or gift). Like grace, forgiveness has about it the maddening quality of being undeserved, unmerited, unfair.

---

*L. Gregory Jones observes, "Such a call to love one's enemies is startling in its frank acknowledgment that faithful Christians will have enemies. While Christ decisively defeated sin and evil through his cross and resurrection, the influence of sin and evil have not fully come to an end. So in at least one sense, we still live on *this* side of the fullness of Easter."

Why would God require of us an unnatural act that defies every primal instinct? What makes forgiveness so important that it becomes central to our faith? From my experience as an often-forgiven, sometimes-forgiving person, I can suggest several reasons. The first is theological. (The other, more pragmatic reasons, I will save for the next chapter.)

Theologically, the Gospels give a straightforward answer to why God asks us to forgive: because that is what God is like. When Jesus first gave the command, "Love your enemies," he added this rationale: "... that you may be sons of your Father in heaven. He causes his sun to rise on the evil and the good, and sends rain on the righteous and the unrighteous."

Anyone, said Jesus, can love friends and family: "Do not even pagans do that?" Sons and daughters of the Father are called to a higher law, in order to resemble the forgiving Father. We are called to be like God, to bear God's family likeness.

Wrestling with the command to "love your enemies" while being persecuted under Nazi Germany, Dietrich Bonhoeffer finally concluded that it was this very quality of the "peculiar ... the extraordinary, the unusual" that sets a Christian apart from others. Even as he worked to undermine the regime, he followed Jesus' command to "Pray for those who persecute you." Bonhoeffer wrote,

> Through the medium of prayer we go to our enemy, stand by his side, and plead for him to God. Jesus does not promise that when we bless our enemies and do good to them they will not despitefully use and persecute us. They certainly will. But not even that can hurt or overcome us, so long as we pray for them.... We are doing vicariously for them what they cannot do for themselves.

Why did Bonhoeffer strive to love his enemies and pray for his persecutors? He had only one answer: "God loves his enemies—that is the glory of his love, as every follower of Jesus knows." If God forgave our debts, how can we not do the same?

Again the parable of the unforgiving servant comes to mind. The servant had every right to resent the few dollars his colleague owed him.

By the laws of Roman justice, he had the right to throw the colleague into prison. Jesus did not dispute the servant's personal loss but, rather, set that loss against a master [God] who had already forgiven the servant several million dollars. Only the experience of being forgiven makes it possible for us to forgive.

I had a friend (now dead) who worked on the staff of Wheaton College for many years, during the course of which he heard several thousand chapel messages. In time most of these faded into a forgettable blur, but a few stood out. In particular he loved retelling the story of Sam Moffat, a professor at Princeton Seminary who had served as a missionary in China. Moffat told the Wheaton students a gripping tale of his flight from Communist pursuers. They seized his house and all his possessions, burned the missionary compound, and killed some of his closest friends. Moffat's own family barely escaped. When he left China, Moffat took with him a deep resentment against the followers of Chairman Mao, a resentment that metastasized inside him. Finally, he told the Wheaton students, he faced a singular crisis of faith. "I realized," said Moffat, "that if I have no forgiveness for the Communists, then I have no message at all."

The gospel of grace begins and ends with forgiveness. And people write songs with titles like "Amazing Grace" for one reason: grace is the only force in the universe powerful enough to break the chains that enslave generations. Grace alone melts ungrace.

One weekend I sat with ten Jews, ten Christians, and ten Muslims in a kind of encounter group led by author and psychiatrist M. Scott Peck, who hoped the weekend might lead to some sort of community, or at least the beginnings of reconciliation on a small scale. It did not. Fistfights almost broke out among these educated, sophisticated people. The Jews talked about all the horrible things done to them by Christians. The Muslims talked about all the horrible things done to them by Jews. We Christians tried to talk about our own problems, but they paled in contrast to stories of the Holocaust and the plight of Palestinian refugees, and so mainly we sat on the sidelines and listened to the other two groups recount the injustices of history.

At one point an articulate Jewish woman, who had been active in prior attempts at reconciliation with Arabs, turned to the Christians and said, "I believe we Jews have a lot to learn from you Christians about forgiveness. I see no other way around some of the logjams. And yet it seems so unfair, to forgive injustice. I am caught between forgiveness and justice."

I thought back to that weekend when I came across these words from Helmut Thielicke, a German who lived through the horrors of Nazism:

> This business of forgiving is by no means a simple thing. . . . We say, "Very well, if the other fellow is sorry and begs my pardon, I will forgive him, then I'll give in." We make of forgiveness a law of reciprocity. And this never works. For then both of us say to ourselves, "The other fellow has to make the first move." And then I watch like a hawk to see whether the other person will flash a signal to me with his eyes or whether I can detect some small hint between the lines of his letter which shows that he is sorry. I am always on the point of forgiving . . . but I never forgive. I am far too just.

The only remedy, Thielicke concluded, was his realization that God had forgiven his sins and given him another chance—the lesson of the parable of the unforgiving servant. Breaking the cycle of ungrace means *taking the initiative*. Instead of waiting for his neighbor to make the first move, Thielicke must do so, defying the natural law of retribution and fairness. He did this only when he realized that God's initiative lay at the heart of the gospel he had been preaching but not practicing.

At the center of Jesus' parables of grace stands a God who takes the initiative toward us: a lovesick father who runs to meet the prodigal, a king who cancels a debt too large for any servant to reimburse, an employer who pays eleventh-hour workers the same as the first-hour crew, a banquet-giver who goes out to the highways and byways in search of undeserving guests.

God shattered the inexorable law of sin and retribution by invading earth, absorbing the worst we had to offer, crucifixion, and then fashioning from that cruel deed the remedy for the human condition. Calvary broke up the logjam between justice and forgiveness. By accepting onto his innocent self all the severe demands of justice, Jesus broke forever the chain of ungrace.

Like Helmut Thielicke, all too often I drift back into a tit-for-tat struggle that slams the door on forgiveness. *Why should I make the first move? I was the one wronged.* So I make no move, and cracks in the relationship appear, then widen. In time a chasm yawns open that seems impossible to cross. I feel sad, but seldom do I accept the blame. Instead, I justify myself and point out the small gestures I made toward reconciliation. I keep a mental accounting of those attempts so as to defend myself if I am ever blamed for the rift. I flee from the risk of grace to the security of ungrace.

Henri Nouwen, who defines forgiveness as "love practiced among people who love poorly," describes the process at work:

> I have often said, "I forgive you," but even as I said these words my heart remained angry or resentful. I still wanted to hear the story that tells me that I was right after all; I still wanted to hear apologies and excuses; I still wanted the satisfaction of receiving some praise in return—if only the praise for being so forgiving!
>
> But God's forgiveness is unconditional; it comes from a heart that does not demand anything for itself, a heart that is completely empty of self-seeking. It is this divine forgiveness that I have to practice in my daily life. It calls me to keep stepping over all my arguments that say forgiveness is unwise, unhealthy, and impractical. It challenges me to step over all my needs for gratitude and compliments. Finally, it demands of me that I step over that wounded part of my heart that feels hurt and wronged and that wants to stay in control and put a few conditions between me and the one whom I am asked to forgive.

One day I discovered this admonition from the apostle Paul tucked in among many other admonitions in Romans 12. Hate evil, Be joyful, Live in harmony, Do not be conceited—the list goes on and on. Then appears this verse, "Do not take revenge, my friends, but leave room for God's wrath, for it is written: 'It is mine to avenge; I will repay,' says the Lord."

At last I understood: in the final analysis, forgiveness is an act of faith. By forgiving another, I am trusting that God is a better justice-maker than I am. By forgiving, I release my own right to get even and leave all issues of fairness for God to work out. I leave in God's hands the scales that must balance justice and mercy.

When Joseph finally came to the place of forgiving his brothers, the hurt did not disappear, but the burden of being their judge fell away. Though wrong does not disappear when I forgive, it loses its grip on me and is taken over by God, who knows what to do. Such a decision involves risk, of course: the risk that God may not deal with the person as I would want. (The prophet Jonah, for instance, resented God for being more merciful than the Ninevites deserved.)

I never find forgiveness easy, and rarely do I find it completely satisfying. Nagging injustices remain, and the wounds still cause pain. I have to approach God again and again, yielding to him the residue of what I thought I had committed to him long ago. I do so because the Gospels make clear the connection: God forgives my debts as I forgive my debtors. The reverse is also true: Only by living in the stream of God's grace will I find the strength to respond with grace toward others.

A cease-fire between human beings depends upon a cease-fire with God.

In the deserts of the heart
Let the healing fountain start,
In the prison of his days
Teach the free man how to praise.

W. H. Auden

EIGHT

Why Forgive?

I participated in a lively discussion on the topic of forgiveness the week Jeffrey Dahmer died in prison. Dahmer, a mass murderer, had abused and then killed seventeen young men, cannibalizing them and storing body parts in his refrigerator. His arrest caused a shake-up in the Milwaukee police department when it became known that officers had ignored the desperate pleas of a Vietnamese teenager who tried to escape by running, naked and bleeding, from Dahmer's apartment. That boy too became Dahmer's victim, one of eleven corpses found in his apartment.

In November of 1994, Dahmer himself was murdered, beaten to death with a broom handle wielded by a fellow prisoner. Television news reports that day included interviews with the grieving relatives of Dahmer's victims, most of whom said they regretted Dahmer's murder only because it ended his life too soon. He should have had to suffer by being forced to live longer and think about the terrible things he had done.

One network showed a television program taped a few weeks before Dahmer's death. The interviewer asked him how he could possibly do the things he had been convicted of. At the time he didn't believe in God, Dahmer said, and so he felt accountable to no one. He began with petty crimes, experimented with small acts of cruelty, and then just kept going, further and further. Nothing restrained him.

Dahmer then told of his recent religious conversion. He had been baptized in the prison whirlpool and was spending all his time reading religious material given him by a local Church of Christ minister. The camera switched to an interview with the prison chaplain, who affirmed that Dahmer had indeed repented and was now one of his most faithful worshipers.

The discussion in my small group tended to divide between those who had watched only the news programs on Dahmer's death and those who had also watched the interview with Dahmer. The former group saw Dahmer as a monster, and any reports of a jailhouse conversion they dismissed out-of-hand. The relatives' anguished faces had made a deep impression. One person said candidly, "Crimes that bad can never be forgiven. He couldn't be sincere."

Those who had seen the interview with Dahmer were not so sure. They agreed his crimes were heinous beyond belief. Yet he had seemed contrite, even humble. The conversation turned to the question, "Is anyone ever beyond forgiveness?" No one left the evening feeling entirely comfortable with the answers.

The scandal of forgiveness confronts anyone who agrees to a moral cease-fire just because someone says, "I'm sorry." When I feel wronged, I can contrive a hundred reasons against forgiveness. *He needs to learn a lesson. I don't want to encourage irresponsible behavior. I'll let her stew for a while; it will do her good. She needs to learn that actions have consequences. I was the wronged party—it's not up to me to make the first move. How can I forgive if he's not even sorry?* I marshal my arguments until something happens to wear down my resistance. When I finally soften to the point of granting forgiveness, it seems a capitulation, a leap from hard logic to mushy sentiment.

Why do I ever make such a leap? I have already mentioned one factor that motivates me as a Christian: I am commanded to, as the child of a Father who forgives. But Christians have no monopoly on forgiveness. Why do any of us, Christian or unbeliever alike, choose this unnatural act? I can identify at least three pragmatic reasons, and the more I ponder these reasons for forgiveness, the more I recognize in them a logic that seems not only "hard" but foundational.

First, forgiveness alone can halt the cycle of blame and pain, breaking the chain of ungrace. In the New Testament the most common Greek word for forgiveness means, literally, to release, to hurl away, to free yourself.

I readily admit that forgiveness is unfair. Hinduism, with its doctrine of *karma*, provides a far more satisfying sense of fairness. Hindu scholars have calculated with mathematical precision how long it may take for one person's justice to work itself out: for punishment to balance out all my wrongs in this life and future lives, 6,800,000 incarnations should suffice.

Marriage gives a glimpse of the karma process at work. Two stubborn people live together, get on each other's nerves, and perpetuate the power struggle through an emotional tug-of-war. "I can't believe you forgot your own mother's birthday," says one.

"Wait a minute, aren't you supposed to be in charge of the calendar?"

"Don't try to pass the blame to me—she's your mother."

"Yes, but I told you just last week to remind me. Why didn't you?"

"You're crazy—it's your own mother. Can't you keep track of your own mother's birthday?"

"Why should I? It's your job to remind me."

The inane dialogue bleats on and on through, say, 6,800,000 cycles until at last one of the partners says, "Stop! I'll break the chain." And the only way to do so is forgiveness: *I'm sorry. Will you forgive me?*

The word *resentment* expresses what happens if the cycle goes uninterrupted. It means, literally, "to feel again": resentment clings to the past, relives it over and over, picks each fresh scab so that the wound never heals. This pattern doubtless began with the very first couple on earth. "Think of all the squabbles Adam and Eve must have had in the course of their nine hundred years," wrote Martin Luther. "Eve would say, 'You ate the apple,' and Adam would retort, 'You gave it to me.'"

Two novels by Nobel laureates illustrate the pattern in a modern setting. In *Love in the Time of Cholera*, Gabriel García Márquez portrays a marriage that disintegrates over a bar of soap. It was the wife's job to keep the house in order, including provision of towels, toilet paper, and soap in the bathroom. One day she forgot to replace the soap, an oversight that her husband mentioned in an exaggerated way ("I've been bathing for almost a week without any soap"), and that she vigorously denied. Although it turned out that she had indeed forgotten, her pride was at stake and she would not back down. For the next seven months they slept in separate rooms and ate in silence.

"Even when they were old and placid," writes Márquez, "they were very careful about bringing it up, for the barely healed wounds could begin to bleed again as if they had been inflicted only yesterday." How can a bar of soap ruin a marriage? Because neither partner would say, "Stop. This cannot go on. I'm sorry. Forgive me."

The Knot of Vipers by François Mauriac tells a similar story of an old man who spends the last decades—decades!—of his marriage sleeping down the hall from his wife. A rift had opened thirty years before over whether the husband showed enough concern when their five-year-old daughter fell ill. Now, neither husband nor wife is willing to take the first step. Every night he waits for her to approach him, but she never appears. Every night she lies awake waiting for him to approach her, and he never appears. Neither will break the cycle that began years before. Neither will forgive.

In her memoir of a truly dysfunctional family, *The Liar's Club*, Mary Karr tells of a Texas uncle who remained married to his wife but did not speak to her for forty years after a fight over how much money she spent on sugar. One day he took out a lumber saw and sawed their house exactly in half. He nailed up planks to cover the raw sides and moved one of the halves behind a copse of scruffy pine trees on the same acre of ground. There the two, husband and wife, lived out the rest of their days in separate half-houses.

Forgiveness offers a way out. It does not settle all questions of blame and fairness—often it pointedly evades those questions—but it does allow a relationship to start over, to begin anew. In that way, said Solzhenitsyn, we differ from all animals. Not our capacity to think, but our capacity to repent and to forgive makes us different. Only humans can perform that most unnatural act, which transcends the relentless law of nature.

If we do not transcend nature, we remain bound to the people we cannot forgive, held in their vise grip. This principle applies even when one party is wholly innocent and the other wholly to blame, for the innocent party will bear the wound until he or she can find a way to release it—and forgiveness is the only way. Oscar Hijuelos wrote a poignant novel, *Mr. Ives' Christmas,* about a man who is throttled by bitterness until somehow he finds it within himself to forgive the Latino criminal who murdered his son. Although Ives himself did nothing wrong, for decades the murder has kept him an emotional prisoner.

Sometimes I let my mind wander and imagine a world with no forgiveness. What would happen if every child bore grudges against his or her parents, and every family passed down feuds to future generations? I told of one family—Daisy, Margaret, Michael—and the virus of ungrace that afflicts them all. I know, respect, and enjoy each member of that family, separately. Yet even though they share almost the same genetic code, today they cannot sit in the same room together. All of them have protested to me their innocence—but innocents too suffer the results of ungrace. "I never want to see you again as long as I live!" Margaret yelled at her son. She got her wish, and now she suffers from it every day. I can see the pain in the narrowing of her eyes and the tensing of her jaw every time I say the word, "Michael."

I let my imagination run further, to a world in which every former colony harbors grudges against its former imperial power, and every race hates every other race, and every tribe battles its rivals as if all of history's grievances amass behind every contact of nation, race, and tribe. I get depressed when I imagine such a scene because it seems so close to history as it now exists. As the Jewish philosopher Hannah Arendt said, the only remedy for the inevitability of history is forgiveness; otherwise, we remain trapped in the "predicament of irreversibility."

Not to forgive imprisons me in the past and locks out all potential for change. I thus yield control to another, my enemy, and doom myself to suffer the consequences of the wrong. I once heard an immigrant rabbi make an astonishing statement. "Before coming to America, I had to forgive Adolf Hitler," he said. "I did not want to bring Hitler inside me to my new country."

We forgive not merely to fulfill some higher law of morality; we do it for ourselves. As Lewis Smedes points out, "The first and often the only person to be healed by forgiveness is the person who does the forgiveness...

When we genuinely forgive, we set a prisoner free and then discover that the prisoner we set free was us."

For the biblical Joseph, who had borne a well-deserved grudge against his brothers, forgiveness spilled out in the form of tears and groans. These, like childbirth's, were harbingers of liberation, and through them Joseph gained at last his freedom. He named his son Manasseh, "one who causes to be forgotten."

The only thing harder than forgiveness is the alternative.

The second great power of forgiveness is that it can loosen the stranglehold of guilt in the perpetrator.

Guilt does its corrosive work even when consciously repressed. In 1993 a Ku Klux Klansman named Henry Alexander made a confession to his wife. In 1957 he and several other Klansmen had pulled a black truck driver from his cab, marched him to a deserted bridge high above a swift river, and made him jump, screaming, to his death. Alexander was charged with the crime in 1976—it took nearly twenty years to bring him to trial—pled innocent and was acquitted by a white jury. For thirty-six years he insisted on his innocence, until the day in 1993 when he confessed the truth to his wife. "I don't even know what God has planned for me. I don't even know how to pray for myself," he told her. A few days later, he died.

Alexander's wife wrote a letter of apology to the black man's widow, a letter subsequently printed in *The New York Times.* "Henry lived a lie all his life, and he made me live it too," she wrote. For all those years she had believed her husband's protestations of innocence. He showed no outward sign of remorse until the last days of his life, too late to attempt public restitution. Yet he could not carry the terrible secret of guilt to his grave. After thirty-six years of fierce denial, he still needed the release only forgiveness could provide.

Another member of the Ku Klux Klan, the Grand Dragon Larry Trapp of Lincoln, Nebraska, made national headlines in 1992 when he renounced his hatred, tore down his Nazi flags, and destroyed his many cartons of hate literature. As Kathryn Watterson recounts in the book *Not by the Sword*, Trapp had been won over by the forgiving love of a Jewish cantor and his family. Though Trapp had sent them vile pamphlets mocking big-nosed Jews and denying the Holocaust, though he had threatened violence in phone calls made to their home, though he had targeted their synagogue for bombing, the cantor's family consistently responded with compassion and concern. Diabetic since childhood, Trapp was confined to a wheelchair and rapidly going blind; the cantor's family invited Trapp into their home to care for him. "They showed me such love that I couldn't help but love them back," Trapp later said. He spent his last months of life seeking forgiveness from Jewish groups, the NAACP, and the many individuals he had hated.

In recent years audiences worldwide have watched a drama of forgiveness played out onstage in the musical version of *Les Misérables*. The musical follows its original source, Victor Hugo's sprawling novel, in telling the story of Jean Valjean, a French prisoner hounded and ultimately transformed by forgiveness.

Sentenced to a nineteen-year term of hard labor for the crime of stealing bread, Jean Valjean gradually hardened into a tough convict. No one could beat him in a fistfight. No one could break his will. At last Valjean earned his release. Convicts in those days had to carry identity cards, however, and no innkeeper would let a dangerous felon spend the night. For four days he wandered the village roads, seeking shelter against the weather, until finally a kindly bishop had mercy on him.

That night Jean Valjean lay still in an overcomfortable bed until the bishop and his sister drifted off to sleep. He rose from his bed, rummaged through the cupboard for the family silver, and crept off into the darkness.

The next morning three policemen knocked on the bishop's door, with Valjean in tow. They had caught the convict in flight with the purloined silver, and were ready to put the scoundrel in chains for life.

The bishop responded in a way that no one, especially Jean Valjean, expected.

> "So here you are!" he cried to Valjean. "I'm delighted to see you. Had you forgotten that I gave you the candlesticks as well?

They're silver like the rest, and worth a good 200 francs. Did you forget to take them?"

Jean Valjean's eyes had widened. He was now staring at the old man with an expression no words can convey.

Valjean was no thief, the bishop assured the gendarmes. "This silver was my gift to him."

When the gendarmes withdrew, the bishop gave the candlesticks to his guest, now speechless and trembling. "Do not forget, do not ever forget," said the bishop, "that you have promised me to use the money to make yourself an honest man."

The power of the bishop's act, defying every human instinct for revenge, changed Jean Valjean's life forever. A naked encounter with forgiveness—especially since he had never repented—melted the granite defenses of his soul. He kept the candlesticks as a precious memento of grace and dedicated himself from then on to helping others in need.

Hugo's novel stands, in fact, as a two-edged parable of forgiveness. A detective named Javert, who knows no law but justice, stalks Jean Valjean mercilessly over the next two decades. As Valjean is transformed by forgiveness, the detective is consumed by a thirst for retribution. When Valjean saves Javert's life—the prey showing grace to his pursuer—the detective senses his black-and-white world beginning to crumble. Unable to cope with a grace that goes against all instinct, and finding within himself no corresponding forgiveness, Javert jumps off a bridge into the Seine River.

Magnanimous forgiveness, such as that offered Valjean by the bishop, allows the possibility of transformation in the guilty party. Lewis Smedes details this process of "spiritual surgery":

> When you forgive someone, you slice away the wrong from the person who did it. You disengage that person from his hurtful act. You recreate him. At one moment you identify him ineradicably as the person who did you wrong. The next moment you change that identity. He is remade in your memory.

> You think of him now not as the person who hurt you, but a person who needs you. You feel him now not as the person who alienated you, but as the person who belongs to you. Once you branded him as a person powerful in evil, but now you see him as a person weak in his needs. You recreated your past by recreating the person whose wrong made your past painful.

Smedes adds many cautions. Forgiveness is not the same as pardon, he advises: you may forgive one who wronged you and still insist on a just punishment for that wrong. If you can bring yourself to the point of forgiveness, though, you will release its healing power both in you and in the person who wronged you.

A friend of mine who works in the inner city questions whether forgiveness of those who have not repented makes sense. This man daily sees the results of evil from child abuse, drugs, violence, and prostitution. "If I know something is wrong and 'forgive' without addressing the wrong, what am I doing?" he asks. "I am potentially enabling rather than freeing."

My friend has told me stories of the people he works with, and I agree that some of them seem beyond the pale of forgiveness. Yet I cannot forget the stirring scene of the bishop forgiving Jean Valjean, who had admitted no wrong. Forgiveness has its own extraordinary power which reaches beyond law and beyond justice. Before *Les Misérables* I read *The Count of Monte Cristo*, a novel by Hugo's compatriot Alexandre Dumas, which tells the story of a wronged man working exquisite revenge on the four men who had framed him. Dumas's novel appealed to my sense of justice; Hugo's awakened in me a sense of grace.

Justice has a good and righteous and rational kind of power. The power of grace is different: unworldly, transforming, supernatural. Reginald Denny, the truck driver assaulted during the riots in South Central Los Angeles, demonstrated this power of grace. The entire nation watched the helicopter video of two men smashing his truck window with a brick, hauling him from a cab, then beating him with a broken bottle and kicking him until the side of his face caved in. In court, his tormentors were belligerent and unrepentant, yielding no ground. With worldwide media looking on, Reginald Denny, his face still swollen and misshapen, shook off the protests of his lawyers, made his way over to the mothers of the two defendants, hugged them, and told them he forgave them. The mothers embraced Denny, one declaring, "I love you."

I do not know what effect that scene had on the surly defendants, sitting in handcuffs not far away. But I do know that forgiveness, and only forgiveness, can begin the thaw in the guilty party. And I also know what effect it has on me when a fellow worker, or my wife, comes to me without prompting and offers forgiveness for some wrong I am too proud and stubborn to confess.

Forgiveness—undeserved, unearned—can cut the cords and let the oppressive burden of guilt roll away. The New Testament shows a resurrected Jesus leading Peter by the hand through a three-fold ritual of forgiveness. Peter need not go through life with the guilty, hangdog look of one who has betrayed the Son of God. Oh, no. On the backs of such transformed sinners Christ would build his church.

Forgiveness breaks the cycle of blame and loosens the stranglehold of guilt. It accomplishes these two things through a remarkable linkage, placing the forgiver on the same side as the party who did the wrong. Through it we realize we are not as different from the wrongdoer as we would like to think. "I also am other than what I imagine myself to be. To know this is forgiveness," said Simone Weil.

At the beginning of this chapter I mentioned a small group discussion on forgiveness revolving around the case of Jeffrey Dahmer. Like many such discussions, it kept drifting away from personal illustrations, toward the abstract and theoretical. We discussed other horrific crimes, and Bosnia, and the Holocaust. Almost by accident, the word "divorce" came up, and to our surprise Rebecca spoke up.

Rebecca is a quiet woman, and in weeks of meeting together she had rarely opened her mouth. At the mention of divorce, though, she proceeded to tell her own story. She had married a pastor who had some renown as a retreat leader. It became apparent, however, that her husband had a dark side. He dabbled in pornography, and on his trips to other cities he solicited prostitutes. Sometimes he asked Rebecca for forgiveness, sometimes he did not. In time, he left her for another woman, Julianne.

Rebecca told us how painful it was for her, a pastor's wife, to suffer this humiliation. Some church members who had respected her husband treated her as if his sexual straying had been her fault. Devastated, she found herself pulling away from human contact, unable to trust another person. She could never put her husband out of mind because they had children and she had to make regular contact with him in order to arrange his visitation privileges.

Rebecca had the increasing sense that unless she forgave her former husband, a hard lump of revenge would be passed on to their children. For months she prayed. At first her prayers seemed as vengeful as some of the Psalms: she asked God to give her ex-husband "what he deserved." Finally she came to the place of letting God, not herself, determine "what he deserved."

One night Rebecca called her ex-husband and said, in a shaky, strained voice, "I want you to know that I forgive you for what you've done to me. And I forgive Julianne too." He laughed off her apology, unwilling to admit he had done anything wrong. Despite his rebuff, that conversation helped Rebecca get past her bitter feelings.

A few years later Rebecca got a hysterical phone call from Julianne, the woman who had "stolen" her husband. She had been attending a ministerial conference with him in Minneapolis, and he had left the hotel room to go for a walk. A few hours passed, then Julianne heard from the police: her husband had been picked up for soliciting a prostitute.

On the phone with Rebecca, Julianne was sobbing. "I never believed you," she said. "I kept telling myself that even if what you said was true, he had changed. And now this. I feel so ashamed, and hurt, and guilty. I have no one on earth who can understand. Then I remembered the night when you said you forgave us. I thought maybe you could understand what I'm going through. It's a terrible thing to ask, I know, but could I come talk to you?"

Somehow Rebecca found the courage to invite Julianne over that same evening. They sat in her living room, cried together, shared stories of betrayal, and in the end prayed together. Julianne now points to that night as the time when she became a Christian.

Our group was hushed as Rebecca told her story. She was describing forgiveness not in the abstract, but in a nearly incomprehensible scene of human linkage: husband-stealer and abandoned wife kneeling side by side on a living-room floor, praying.

"For a long time, I had felt foolish about forgiving my husband," Rebecca told us. "But that night I realized the fruit of forgiveness. Julianne was right. I could understand what she was going through. And because I had been there too, I could be on her side, instead of her enemy. We both had been betrayed by the same man. Now it was up to me to teach her how to overcome the hatred and revenge and guilt she was feeling."

In *The Art of Forgiving*, Lewis Smedes makes the striking observation that the Bible portrays God going through progressive stages when he forgives, much as we humans do. First, God rediscovers the humanity of the person who wronged him, by removing the barrier created by sin. Second, God surrenders his right to get even, choosing instead to bear the cost in his own body. Finally, God revises his feelings toward us, finding a way to "justify" us so that when he looks upon us he sees his own adopted children, with his divine image restored.

It occurred to me, as I thought about Smedes's insights, that the gracious miracle of God's forgiveness was made possible because of the linkage that occurred when God came to earth in Christ. Somehow God had to come to terms with these creatures he desperately wanted to love—but how? Experientially, God did not know what it was like to be tempted to sin, to have a trying day. On earth, living among us, he learned what it was like. He put himself on our side.

The book of Hebrews makes explicit this mystery of incarnation: "We do not have a high priest who is unable to sympathize with our weaknesses, but we have one who has been tempted in every way, just as we are—yet was without sin." Second Corinthians goes even further:

"God made him who had no sin to be sin for us." You cannot get any more explicit than that. God bridged the gap; he took our side all the way. And because he did, Hebrews affirms, Jesus can present our case to the Father. He has been here. He understands.

From the Gospels' accounts, it seems forgiveness was not easy for God, either. "If it is possible, may this cup be taken from me," Jesus prayed, contemplating the cost, and the sweat rolled off him like drops of blood. There was no other way. Finally, in one of his last statements before dying, he said, "Forgive them"—all of them, the Roman soldiers, the religious leaders, his disciples who had fled in darkness, you, me—"forgive them, for they do not know what they are doing." Only by becoming a human being could the Son of God truly say, "They do not know what they are doing." Having lived among us, he now understood.

In the nightmare of the dark
All the dogs of Europe bark,
And the living nations wait,
Each sequestered in its hate.

W. H. Auden

Nine

Getting Even

In the midst of the recent war in the former Yugoslavia, I picked up a book I had read several years before: *The Sunflower* by Simon Wiesenthal. It recounts a small incident that took place during this century's most successful "ethnic cleansing" campaign, an incident that does much to explain what propelled Wiesenthal to become the foremost hunter of Nazis and a relentless public voice against hate crimes. The book centers on forgiveness, and I turned to it for insight into what role forgiveness might play globally—in, say, the moral quagmire that once was Yugoslavia.

In 1944 Wiesenthal was a young Polish prisoner of the Nazis. He had looked on, helpless, as Nazi soldiers killed his grandmother on the stairway of her home and as they forced his mother into a freight car crammed with elderly Jewish women. Altogether, eighty-nine of his Jewish relatives would die at the hands of the Nazis. Wiesenthal himself tried without success to commit suicide when first captured.

One bright, sunny day as Wiesenthal's prison detail was cleaning rubbish out of a hospital for German casualties, a nurse approached him. "Are you a Jew?" she asked hesitantly, then signaled him to accompany her. Apprehensive, Wiesenthal followed her up a stairway and down a hallway until they reached a dark, musty room where a lone soldier lay swathed in bandages. White gauze covered the man's face, with openings cut out for mouth, nose, and ears.

The nurse disappeared, closing the door behind her to leave the young prisoner alone with the spectral figure. The wounded man was an SS officer, and he had summoned Wiesenthal for a deathbed confession.

"My name is Karl," said a raspy voice that came from somewhere within the bandages. "I must tell you of this horrible deed—tell you because you are a Jew."

Karl began his story by reminiscing about his Catholic upbringing and his childhood faith, which he had lost while in the Hitler Youth Corps. He later volunteered for the SS and served with distinction and had only recently returned, badly wounded, from the Russian front.

Three times as Karl tried to tell his story, Wiesenthal pulled away as if to leave. Each time the officer reached out to grab his arm with a white, nearly bloodless hand. He begged him to listen to what he had just experienced in the Ukraine.

In the town of Dnyepropetrovsk, abandoned by the retreating Russians, Karl's unit stumbled onto booby traps that killed thirty of their soldiers. As an act of revenge the SS rounded up three hundred Jews, herded them into a three-story house, doused it with gasoline, and fired grenades at it. Karl and his men encircled the house, their guns drawn to shoot anyone who tried to escape.

"The screams from the house were horrible," he said, reliving the moment. "I saw a man with a small child in his arms. His clothes were alight. By his side stood a woman, doubtless the mother of the child. With his free hand the man covered the child's eyes, then he jumped into the street. Seconds later the mother followed. Then from the other windows fell burning bodies. We shot . . . Oh God!"

All this time Simon Wiesenthal sat in silence, letting the German soldier speak. Karl went on to describe other atrocities, but he kept circling back to the scene of that young boy with black hair and dark eyes, falling from a building, target practice for the SS rifles. "I am left here with my guilt," he concluded at last:

> In the last hours of my life you are with me. I do not know who you are, I know only that you are a Jew and that is enough.
>
> I know that what I have told you is terrible. In the long nights while I have been waiting for death, time and time again I have longed to talk about it to a Jew and beg forgiveness from him. Only I didn't know whether there were any Jews left . . . I

know what I am asking is almost too much for you, but without your answer I cannot die in peace.

Simon Wiesenthal, an architect in his early twenties, now a prisoner dressed in a shabby uniform marked with the yellow Star of David, felt the immense crushing burden of his race bear down on him. He stared out the window at the sunlit courtyard. He looked at the eyeless heap of bandages lying in the bed. He watched a bluebottle fly buzzing the dying man's body, attracted by the smell.

"At last I made up my mind," Wiesenthal writes, "and without a word I left the room."

The Sunflower takes forgiveness out of the theoretical and thrusts it in the midst of living history. I chose to reread the book because the dilemma Wiesenthal faced had so many parallels with moral dilemmas that are still tearing the world apart in places like Yugoslavia, Rwanda, and the Middle East.

The first half of Wiesenthal's book tells the story I have just summarized. The next half records reactions to that story from such luminaries as Abraham Heschel, Martin Marty, Cynthia Ozick, Gabriel Marcel, Jacques Maritain, Herbert Marcuse, and Primo Levi. In the end, Wiesenthal turned to them for advice on whether he had done right.

The SS officer Karl soon died, unforgiven by a Jew, but Simon Wiesenthal lived on to be liberated from a death camp by American troops. The scene in the hospital room haunted him like a ghost. After the war Wiesenthal visited the officer's mother in Stuttgart, hoping somehow to exorcise the memory of that day. Instead, the visit only made the officer more human, for the mother spoke tenderly of her son's pious youth. Wiesenthal could not bear to tell her how her son ended up.

Over the years, Wiesenthal asked many rabbis and priests what he should have done. Finally, more than twenty years after the war had ended, he wrote down the story and sent it to the brightest ethical minds he knew: Jew and Gentile, Catholic, Protestant, and irreligious. "What would you have done in my place?" he asked them.

Of the thirty-two men and women who responded, only six said that Wiesenthal had erred in not forgiving the German. Two Christians pointed to Wiesenthal's lingering discomfort as a twinge of conscience that could only be stilled by forgiveness. One of them, a black man who had served in the French Resistance, said, "I can understand your refusal to forgive. This is entirely in accordance with the spirit of the Bible, with the spirit of the Old Law. But there is the New Law, that of Christ as expressed in the Gospels. As a Christian, I think you should have forgiven."

A few others waffled, but most of the respondents agreed Simon Wiesenthal had done the right thing. What moral or legal authority had he to forgive crimes done to someone else? they asked. One writer quoted the poet Dryden, "Forgiveness, to the injured doth belong."

A few of the Jewish respondents said that the enormity of Nazi crimes had exceeded all possibility of forgiveness. Herbert Gold, an American author and professor, declared, "The guilt for this horror lies so heavily on the Germans of that time that no personal reaction to it is unjustifiable." Said another, "The millions of innocent people who were tortured and slaughtered would have to come back to life before I could forgive." Novelist Cynthia Ozick was fierce: "Let the SS man die unshriven. Let him go to hell." A Christian writer confessed, "I think I would strangle him in his bed."

A few commentators questioned the whole notion of forgiveness. One professor disdained forgiveness as an act of sensual pleasure, the sort of thing lovers do after a spat before climbing back into bed. It has no place, she said, in a world of genocide and Holocaust. Forgive, and the whole business might easily repeat itself.

When I first read *The Sunflower*, ten years before, I was taken aback by the near unanimity of the responses. I expected more of the Christian theologians to speak of mercy. But this time as I reread the eloquent replies to Wiesenthal's question I was struck by the terrible, crystalline logic of unforgiveness. In a world of unspeakable atrocity, forgiveness indeed seems unjust, unfair, irrational. Individuals and families must learn to forgive, yes, but how do such high-minded principles apply in a case like Nazi Germany? As the philosopher Herbert Marcuse put it, "One cannot, and should not go around happily killing and torturing and then, when the moment has come, simply ask, and receive, forgiveness."

Is it too much to expect that the high ethical ideals of the gospel—of which forgiveness lies at the core—might transpose into the brutal world of politics and international diplomacy? In such a world what chance stands something as ethereal as forgiveness? These questions nagged at me as I reread Wiesenthal's story while listening to the unremitting bad news from the former Yugoslavia.

My Jewish friends have spoken with admiration of the Christian emphasis on forgiveness. I have presented it as our strongest weapon to disarm the counterforce of ungrace. And yet as the great Jewish scholar Joseph Klausner pointed out early in this century, the Christians' very insistence on such ideals leaves us vulnerable to a devastating critique. "The religion has stood for what is highest ethically and ideally," writes Klausner, "while the political and social life has remained at the other extreme of barbarity and paganism."

Klausner claims that the failures of Christian history prove his point that Jesus taught an impractical ethic that will not work in the real world. He mentions the Spanish Inquisition, which "was not thought to be incompatible with Christianity." A contemporary critic might add to his list Yugoslavia, Rwanda, and yes, even Nazi Germany, for all three of these conflicts took place in so-called Christian nations.

Does the Christian emphasis on love, grace, and forgiveness have any relevance outside quarreling families or church encounter groups? In a world where force matters most, a lofty ideal like forgiveness may seem as insubstantial as vapor. Stalin understood this principle all too well when he scoffed at the moral authority of the church: "How many divisions has the Pope?"

To be honest, I do not know how I would have responded in Simon Wiesenthal's place. Can we, should we forgive crimes of which we are not the victims? Karl the SS officer repented, making his case clearer, but what of the stony faces lined up, almost smirking, at the trials in Nuremberg and Stuttgart? Martin Marty, one of the Christian respondents in

Wiesenthal's book, wrote these lines, with which I am tempted to agree: "I can only respond with silence. Non-Jews and perhaps especially Christians should not give advice about Holocaust experience to its heirs for the next two thousand years. And then we shall have nothing to say."

Still, I must admit that as I read the eloquent voices in support of unforgiveness, I could not help wondering which carries a higher cost, forgiveness or unforgiveness. Herbert Gold judged that "no personal reaction to it [German guilt] is unjustifiable." Oh? What about the revenge execution of all surviving Germans—would that be justifiable?

The strongest argument in favor of grace is the alternative, a world of ungrace. The strongest argument for forgiveness is the alternative, a permanent state of unforgiveness. I grant that the Holocaust creates special conditions. What of other, more contemporary examples? As I write this, nearly two million Hutu refugees sit idly in refugee camps on the borders of Rwanda, refusing all entreaties to go home. Shouting through bullhorns, their leaders warn them not to trust Tutsi promises that "all is forgiven." They will murder you, say the Hutu leaders. They will seek revenge for the five hundred thousand murders we committed on the Tutsis.

Also as I write this, American soldiers are helping hold together the four separate nations that formed along the fault lines of a Yugoslavia riven by war. Like most Americans, I find everything about the Balkan region baffling, unpronounceable, and perverse. After rereading *The Sunflower*, though, I began to see the Balkans as merely the latest stage setting for a recurring motif of history. Where unforgiveness reigns, as essayist Lance Morrow has pointed out, a Newtonian law comes into play: For every atrocity there must be an equal and opposite atrocity.

The Serbs, of course, are everybody's whipping boy for what happened to Yugoslavia. (Note the language used to describe them in *Time* magazine's supposedly objective news section: "What has happened in Bosnia is just squalor and barbarism—the filthy work of liars and cynics manipulating tribal prejudices, using atrocity propaganda and old blood feuds to accomplish the unclean political result of 'ethnic cleansing.'") Caught up in righteous—and wholly appropriate—revulsion over Serbian atrocities, the world overlooks one fact: the Serbs are simply following the terrible logic of unforgiveness.

Nazi Germany, the very same regime that eliminated eighty-nine members of Simon Wiesenthal's family and that provoked such harsh words from refined people like Cynthia Ozick and Herbert Marcuse, included the Serbs in their "ethnic cleansing" campaign during World War II. True, in the 1990s the Serbs killed tens of thousands—but during Nazi occupation of Balkan territory in the 1940s, the Germans and Croats killed hundreds of thousands of Serbs, Gypsies, and Jews. Historical memory lives on: in the recent war German neo-Nazis enlisted to fight alongside the Croats, and units of the Croatian Army brazenly flew swastika flags and the old Croatian Fascist symbol.

"Never again," the rallying cry of Holocaust survivors, is also what inspired the Serbs to defy the United Nations and virtually the entire world. Never again will they let Croats rule over territory populated by Serbs. Never again will they let Muslims, either: the last war they fought with Muslims led to five centuries of Turkish rule (in historical perspective, a period more than twice as long as the United States has even existed).

In the logic of unforgiveness, not to strike against the enemy would betray ancestors and the sacrifices they made. There is one major flaw in the law of revenge, however: it never settles the score. The Turks got revenge in 1389, at the Battle of Kosovo; the Croats got it in the 1940s; now it's our turn, say the Serbs. Yet one day, as the Serbs surely know, the descendants of today's raped and mutilated victims will arise to seek vengeance on the avengers. The trapdoor has been opened, and wild bats flap about.

In the words of Lewis Smedes:

> Vengeance is a passion to get even. It is a hot desire to give back as much pain as someone gave you. . . . The problem with revenge is that it never gets what it wants; it never evens the score. Fairness never comes. The chain reaction set off by every act of vengeance always takes its unhindered course. It ties both the injured and the injurer to an escalator of pain. Both are stuck on the escalator as long as parity is demanded, and the escalator never stops, never lets anyone off.

Forgiveness may be unfair—it is, by definition—but at least it provides a way to halt the juggernaut of retribution. Today, as I write, violence is either breaking out or smoldering just under the surface between China and Taiwan, India and Pakistan, Russia and Chechnya, Great Britain and Ireland, and especially between Jews and Arabs in the Middle East. Each of these disputes traces back decades, centuries, or, in the case of the Jews and Arabs, millennia. Each side strives to overcome an injustice from the past, to right a perceived wrong.

Theologian Romano Guardini offers this diagnosis of the fatal flaw in the search for revenge: "As long as you are tangled in wrong and revenge, blow and counterblow, aggression and defense, you will be constantly drawn into fresh wrong.... Only forgiveness frees us from the injustice of others." If everyone followed the "eye for an eye" principle of justice, observed Gandhi, eventually the whole world would go blind.

We have many vivid demonstrations of the law of unforgiveness. In Shakespeare's and Sophocles' historical tragedies, bodies litter the stage. Macbeth, Richard III, Titus Andronicus, and Elektra must kill and kill and kill until they have their revenge, then live in fear lest some enemies have survived to seek counterrevenge.

Francis Ford Coppola's *Godfather* trilogy and Clint Eastwood's *Unforgiven* illustrate the same law. We see the law at work in IRA terrorists who blow up shoppers in downtown London in part because of atrocities committed back in 1649—which in turn were ordered by Oliver Cromwell to avenge a massacre in 1641. We see it in Sri Lanka and in Algeria and the Sudan and in the feuding republics of the former Soviet Union.

Simply acknowledge your crimes against us, say the Armenians to the Turks, and we'll stop blowing up airplanes and assassinating your diplomats. Turkey adamantly refuses. At one point during the Iran hostage crisis, the Iranian government announced they would release all hostages unharmed if the U.S. President apologized for past support of the Shah's oppressive regime. Jimmy Carter, a born-again Christian who understands forgiveness and has gained a deserved reputation as a peacemaker, declined. No apologies, he said. Our national honor was at stake.

I've found that a kind word with a gun gets more than a kind word," said John Dillinger. His observation helps explain why poor countries today spend up to half their annual income on weapons. In a fallen world, force works.

Helmut Thielicke recalls his first Bible study after becoming a pastor in the German state church. Determined to trust Jesus' saying "All power is given unto me in heaven and in earth," he tried to assure himself that even Adolf Hitler, then in power, was a mere puppet hanging by strings in the hands of a sovereign God. The group assembled for Bible study consisted of two elderly ladies and an even older, slightly palsied organist. Meanwhile, outside in the streets marched the spit-shine battalions of Hitler's Youth Corps. "The kingdom of heaven is like a grain of mustard seed ...," Thielicke had to remind himself.

That image—a handful of saints praying indoors while outside goose-step the legions of power—captures how I often feel. The weapons of faith seem virtually powerless deployed against the forces of ungrace. Can one fight nuclear warheads with a slingshot?

Yet history shows that grace has its own power. Great leaders—Lincoln, Gandhi, King, Rabin, and Sadat come to mind, all of whom paid the ultimate price for defying the law of ungrace—can help create a national climate that leads to reconciliation. How different would modern history be if Sadat and not Saddam ruled Iraq. Or if a Lincoln emerged from the ruins of Yugoslavia.

Politics deals with externals: borders, wealth, crimes. Authentic forgiveness deals with the evil in a person's heart, something for which politics has no cure. Virulent evil (racism, ethnic hatred) spreads through society like an airborne disease; one cough infects a whole busload. The cure, like a vaccine, must be applied one person at a time. When moments of grace do occur, the world must pause, fall silent, and acknowledge that indeed forgiveness offers a kind of cure.

In 1987 an IRA bomb went off in a small town west of Belfast, amid a group of Protestants who had gathered to honor the war dead on Veteran's Day. Eleven people died and sixty-three others were wounded. What made this act of terrorism stand out from so many others was the response of one of the wounded, Gordon Wilson, a devout Methodist who had emigrated north from the Irish Republic to work as a draper.

The bomb buried Wilson and his twenty-year-old daughter under five feet of concrete and brick. "Daddy, I love you very much," were the last words Marie spoke, grasping her father's hand as they waited for the rescuers. She suffered severe spinal and brain injuries, and died a few hours later in the hospital.

A newspaper later proclaimed, "No one remembers what the politicians had to say at that time. No one who heard Gordon Wilson will ever forget what he confessed.... His grace towered over the miserable justifications of the bombers." Speaking from his hospital bed, Wilson said, "I have lost my daughter, but I bear no grudge. Bitter talk is not going to bring Marie Wilson back to life. I shall pray, tonight and every night, that God will forgive them."

His daughter's last words were words of love, and Gordon Wilson determined to live out his life on that plane of love. "The world wept," said one report, as Wilson gave a similar interview over the BBC radio that week.

After his release from the hospital, Gordon Wilson led a crusade for Protestant-Catholic reconciliation. Protestant extremists who had planned to avenge the bombing decided, because of the publicity surrounding Wilson, that such behavior would be politically foolish. Wilson wrote a book about his daughter, spoke out against violence, and constantly repeated the refrain, "Love is the bottom line." He met with the IRA, personally forgave them for what they had done, and asked them to lay down their arms. "I know that you've lost loved ones, just like me," he told them. "Surely, enough is enough. Enough blood has been spilled."

The Irish Republic ultimately made Wilson a member of its Senate. When he died in 1995, the Irish Republic, Northern Ireland, and all of Great Britain honored this ordinary Christian citizen who had gained fame for his uncommon spirit of grace and forgiveness. His spirit exposed by contrast the violent deeds of retaliation, and his life of peacemaking came to symbolize the craving for peace within many others who would never make the headlines.

"To bless the people who have oppressed our spirits, emotionally deprived us, or in other ways handicapped us, is the most extraordinary work any of us will ever do," writes Elizabeth O'Connor.

Ten years ago another drama of personal forgiveness captured the world's fleeting attention. Pope John Paul II went into the bowels of Rome's Rebibbia prison to visit Mehmet Ali Agca, a hired assassin who had tried to kill him and nearly succeeded. "I forgive you," said the Pope.

Time magazine, impressed by the event, devoted a cover story to it in which Lance Morrow wrote, "John Paul meant, among other things, to demonstrate how the private and public dimensions of human activity may fuse in moral action.... John Paul wanted to proclaim that great issues are determined, or at least informed, by the elemental impulses of the human breast—hatred or love." Morrow went on to quote a Milan newspaper: "There will be no escape from wars, from hunger, from misery, from racial discrimination, from denial of human rights, and not even from missiles, if our hearts are not changed."

Morrow added,

> The scene in Rebibbia had a symbolic splendor. It shone in lovely contrast to what the world has witnessed lately in the news. For some time, a suspicion has taken hold that the trajectory of history is descendant, that the world moves from disorder to greater disorder, toward darkness—or else toward the terminal global flash. The symbolism of the pictures from Rebibbia is precisely the Christian message, that people can be redeemed, that they are ascendant toward the light.

John Paul's deed shone all the more brightly because of its dim setting: a bare concrete cell, the perfect backdrop for the dreary law of unforgiveness. Assassins are to be imprisoned or executed, not forgiven. Yet, for a moment, the message of forgiveness radiated through prison walls, showing the world a path of transformation, not retribution.

The Pope, of course, was following the example of One who did not survive an attempt against his life. Kangaroo courts of Judea found a way to inflict a sentence of capital punishment on the only perfect man who ever lived. From the cross, Jesus pronounced his own countersentence, striking an eternal blow against the law of unforgiveness. Notably, he forgave those who had not repented: "for they do not know what they are doing."

The Roman soldiers, Pilate, Herod, and members of the Sanhedrin were "just doing their jobs"—the limp excuse later used to explain Auschwitz, My Lai, and the Gulag—but Jesus stripped away that institutional veneer and spoke to the human heart. It was forgiveness they needed, more than anything else. We know, those of us who believe in the atonement, that Jesus had more than his executioners in mind when he spoke those final words. He had us in mind. In the cross, and only in the cross, he put an end to the law of eternal consequences.

Does forgiveness matter in a place like Yugoslavia, where so much evil has been wrought? It must, or the people there will have no hope of living together. As so many abused children learn, without forgiveness we cannot free ourselves from the grip of the past. The same principle applies to nations.

I have a friend whose marriage has gone through tumultuous times. One night George passed a breaking point. He pounded the table and the floor. "I hate you!" he screamed at his wife. "I won't take it anymore! I've had enough! I won't go on! I won't let it happen! No! No! No!"

Several months later my friend woke up in the middle of the night and heard strange sounds coming from the room where his two-year-old son slept. He padded down the hall, stood for a moment outside his son's door, and shivers ran through his flesh. He could not draw a breath. In a soft voice, the two-year-old was repeating word for word with precise inflection the argument between his mother and father. "I hate you.... I won't take it anymore.... No! No! No!"

George realized that in some awful way he had just bequeathed his pain and anger and unforgiveness to the next generation. Is not that what is happening all over Yugoslavia right now?

Apart from forgiveness, the monstrous past may awake at any time from hibernation to devour the present. And also the future.

Only a small crack . . . but cracks make caves collapse.

Alexander Solzhenitsyn

TEN

The Arsenal of Grace

Walter Wink tells of two peacemakers who visited a group of Polish Christians ten years after the end of World War II. "Would you be willing to meet with other Christians from West Germany?" the peacemakers asked. "They want to ask forgiveness for what Germany did to Poland during the war and to begin to build a new relationship."

At first there was silence. Then one Pole spoke up. "What you are asking is impossible. Each stone of Warsaw is soaked in Polish blood! We cannot forgive!"

Before the group parted, however, they said the Lord's Prayer together. When they reached the words "forgive us our sins as we forgive . . . ," everyone stopped praying. Tension swelled in the room. The Pole who had spoken so vehemently said, "I must say yes to you. I could no more pray the Our Father, I could no longer call myself a Christian, if I refuse to forgive. Humanly speaking, I cannot do it, but God will give us his strength!" Eighteen months later the Polish and West German Christians met together in Vienna, establishing friendships that continue to this day.

A recent book, *The Wages of Guilt*, explores the differences in approach to war guilt by Germany and Japan. German survivors, like those who apologized to the Poles, tend to accept responsibility for the crimes committed during the war. For example, when Berlin's mayor Willy Brandt visited Warsaw in 1970, he fell to his knees before the memorial to the victims of the Warsaw ghetto. "This gesture . . . was not planned," he wrote. "Oppressed by the memories of Germany's recent history, I simply did what people do when words fail them."

In contrast, Japan has been reluctant to acknowledge any guilt over their role in the war. Emperor Hirohito announced Japan's surrender with the classic understatement, "The war situation has developed not necessarily to Japan's advantage," and postwar statements have been just as calculated. The Japanese government declined to attend the fiftieth-anniversary commemoration of Pearl Harbor because the United States made the invitation conditional on an apology. "The entire world is responsible for the war," a cabinet secretary insisted. Not until 1995, in fact, did Japan use the word "apology" about their actions.

Today, German schoolchildren learn details of the Holocaust and other Nazi crimes. Their counterparts in Japan learn about the atomic bombs dropped on them, but not about the Massacre of Nanking, the brutal treatment of POWs and vivisection of U.S. prisoners, or the foreign "sex slaves" conscripted to serve Japanese soldiers. As a result, resentment still smolders in countries such as China, Korea, and the Philippines.

The contrast must not be pressed too far because both Japan and Germany have gained acceptance in the world of nations, a token of international "forgiveness" for their aggression. Yet Germany has been welcomed as a full partner in the new Europe, side by side with its former victims, whereas Japan is still negotiating arrangements with its cautious former enemies. Its slowness to apologize has delayed the process of full acceptance.

In 1990 the world watched a drama of forgiveness enacted on the stage of world politics. After East Germany chose a parliament in its first free elections, the representatives convened to take up the reins of government. The Communist bloc was changing daily, West Germany was proposing the radical step of reunification, and the new parliament had many weighty matters of state to consider. For their first official act, however, they decided to vote on this extraordinary statement, drafted in the language of theology, not politics:

> We, the first freely elected parliamentarians of the GDR ... on behalf of the citizens of this land, admit responsibility for the humiliation, expulsion and murder of Jewish men, women and children. We feel sorrow and shame, and acknowledge this bur-

> den of German history. . . . Immeasurable suffering was inflicted on the peoples of the world during the era of national socialism. . . . We ask all the Jews of the world to forgive us. We ask the people of Israel to forgive us for the hypocrisy and hostility of official East German policies toward Israel and for the persecution and humiliation of Jewish citizens in our country after 1945 as well.

East Germany's parliament passed the statement unanimously. Members rose to their feet for a long ovation and then paused for a moment of silence in memory of the Jews who had died in the Holocaust.

What did such an act of parliament accomplish? Certainly it did not bring the murdered Jews back to life or undo the monstrous deeds of Nazism. No, but it helped loosen the stranglehold of guilt that had been choking East Germans for nearly half a century—five decades in which their government had steadfastly denied any need for forgiveness.

For its part, West Germany had already repented officially for the abominations. In addition, West Germany has paid out sixty billion dollars in reparations to Jews. The fact that a relationship exists at all between Germany and Israel is a stunning demonstration of transnational forgiveness. Grace has its own power, even in international politics.

Recent times have seen other public dramas of forgiveness play out in nations formerly controlled by Communists.

In 1983, before the Iron Curtain lifted and during the period of martial law, Pope John Paul II visited Poland, where he conducted a huge open-air mass. Throngs of people, organized in orderly groups by their parishes, marched over the Poniatowski Bridge and streamed toward the stadium. Just before the bridge, the route crossed directly in front of the Communist Party's Central Committee Building, and hour after hour the platoons of marchers chanted in unison, "We forgive you, we forgive you!" as they passed the building. Some said the slogan with heartfelt sincerity. Others shouted it almost with contempt, as if to say, "You're nothing—we don't even hate you."

A few years later Jerzy Popieluszko, a thirty-five-year-old priest whose sermons had electrified Poland, was found floating in the Vistula River with his eyes gouged out and his fingernails torn off. Once again the Catholics took to the streets, marching with banners that read "We forgive. We forgive." Popieluszko had preached the same message Sunday after Sunday to the multitude who filled the square in front of his church: "Defend the truth. Overcome evil with good." After his death they continued to obey him, and in the end it was exactly this spirit of prevailing grace that caused the regime to collapse.

All over Eastern Europe the struggle of forgiveness is still being waged. Should a pastor in Russia forgive the KGB officers who imprisoned him and razed his church? Should Romanians forgive the doctors and nurses who chained sick orphans to their beds? Should citizens of Eastern Germany forgive the stool pigeons—including seminary professors, pastors, and treacherous spouses—who spied on them? When human rights activist Vera Wollenberger learned that it was her husband who had betrayed her to the secret police, resulting in her arrest and exile, she ran to the bathroom and vomited. "I would not want anyone to experience the hell I have been through," she says.

Paul Tillich once defined forgiveness as remembering the past in order that it might be forgotten—a principle that applies to nations as well as individuals. Though forgiveness is never easy, and may take generations, what else can break the chains that enslave people to their historical past?

I will never forget a scene that I witnessed in the Soviet Union in October 1991. I told the story in a small book published just after our visit, but it bears retelling. At the time, the Soviet empire was unraveling, Mikhail Gorbachev was hanging on to office by a string, and Boris Yeltsin was consolidating power by the day. I accompanied a delegation of Christians who met with Russia's leaders in response to their plea for help in "restoring morality" to their country.

Although Gorbachev and all the government officials we visited had received us warmly, old-timers in our group warned us to expect different treatment the evening we visited KGB headquarters. A statue of its founder Feliks Dzerzhinsky may have been toppled by crowds from a pedestal outside the building, but his memory lived on inside. A large photo of the notorious man still hung on one wall of our meeting room. Agents, their faces as blank and impassive as their movie stereotypes, stood at attention by the doorway of the wood-paneled auditorium as General Nikolai Stolyarov, Vice-Chairman of the KGB, introduced himself to our delegation. We braced ourselves.

"Meeting with you here tonight," General Stolyarov began, "is a plot twist that could not have been conceived by the wildest fiction writer." He had that right. Then he startled us by saying, "We here in the USSR realize that too often we've been negligent in accepting those of the Christian faith. But political questions cannot be decided until there is sincere repentance, a return to faith by the people. That is the cross I must bear. In the study of scientific atheism, there was the idea that religion divides people. Now we see the opposite: love for God can only unite."

Our heads spun. Where did he learn the phrase "bear a cross"? And the other word—*repentance?* Did the translator get that right? I glanced at Peter and Anita Deyneka, banned from Russia for thirteen years because of their Christian work, now munching cookies in the KGB headquarters.

Joel Nederhood, a refined, gentle man who made radio and television broadcasts for the Christian Reformed Church, stood with a question for Stolyarov. "General, many of us have read Solzhenitsyn's report of the Gulag. A few of us have even lost family members there." His boldness caught some of his colleagues off guard, and the tension in the room noticeably thickened. "Your agency, of course, is responsible for overseeing the prisons, including the one located in the basement of this building. How do you respond to that past?"

Stolyarov replied in measured tones: "I have spoken of repentance. This is an essential step. You probably know of Abuladze's film by that title. There can be no *perestroika* apart from repentance. The time has come to repent of that past. We have broken the Ten Commandments, and for this we pay today."

I had seen *Repentance* by Tengiz Abuladze, and Stolyarov's allusion to it was stunning. The movie details false denunciations, forced imprisonment, the burning of churches—the very acts that had earned the KGB its reputation for cruelty, especially against religion. In Stalin's era an estimated 42,000 priests lost their lives, and the total number of priests declined from 380,000 to 172. A thousand monasteries, sixty seminaries, and ninety-eight of every hundred Orthodox churches were shuttered.

Repentance portrays atrocities from the vantage point of one provincial town. In the film's most poignant scene, women of the village rummage through the mud of a lumberyard inspecting a shipment of logs that has just floated down the river. They are searching for messages from their husbands who have cut these logs in a prison camp. One woman finds initials carved into the bark and, weeping, caresses the log tenderly, her only thread of connection to a husband she cannot caress. The movie ends with a peasant woman asking directions to a church. Told that she is on the wrong street, she replies, "What good is a street that doesn't lead to a church?"

Now, sitting in the state headquarters of tyranny, in a room built just above the detention rooms where Solzhenitsyn was interrogated, we were being told something very similar by the Vice-Chairman of the KGB. What good is a path that doesn't lead to repentance, to the Ten Commandments, to a church?

Abruptly, the meeting took a more personal turn as Alex Leonovich rose to speak. Alex had been sitting at the head table translating for Stolyarov. A native of Byelorussia, he had escaped during Stalin's reign of terror and had emigrated to the United States. For forty-six years he had been broadcasting Christian programs, often jammed, back to the land of his birth. He knew personally many Christians who had been tortured and persecuted for their faith. For him, to be translating such a message of reconciliation from a high official of the KGB was bewildering and nearly incomprehensible.

Alex, a stout, grandfatherly man, epitomizes the old guard of warriors who have prayed for more than half a century that change might come to the Soviet Union—the very change we were apparently now witnessing. He spoke slowly and softly to General Stolyarov.

"General, many members of my family suffered because of this organization," Alex said. "I myself had to leave the land that I loved. My uncle, who was very dear to me, went to a labor camp in Siberia and never returned. General, you say that you repent. Christ taught us how to respond. On behalf of my family, on behalf of my uncle who died in the Gulag, I forgive you."

And then Alex Leonovich, Christian evangelist, reached over to General Nikolai Stolyarov, the Vice-Chairman of the KGB, and gave him a Russian bear hug. While they embraced, Stolyarov whispered something to Alex, and not until later did we learn what he said. "Only two times in my life have I cried. Once was when my mother died. The other is tonight."

"I feel like Moses," Alex said on the bus home that evening. "I have seen the promised land. I am ready for glory."

The Russian photographer accompanying us had a less sanguine view. "It was all an act," he said. "They were putting on a mask for you. I can't believe it." Yet he too wavered, apologizing a short time later: "Maybe I was wrong. I don't know what to believe anymore."

For the next decades—and perhaps centuries—the former Soviet Union will be confronting issues of forgiveness. Afghanistan, Chechnya, Armenia, the Ukraine, Latvia, Lithuania, Estonia—each of these states bears a grudge against the empire that dominated them. Each of them will question motives, much like the photographer who accompanied us to KGB headquarters. With good reason, Russians do not trust each other or their government. The past must be remembered before it can be overcome.

Even so, overcoming history is possible, however slowly and imperfectly. The chains of ungrace can indeed snap. We in the United States have had experience with reconciliation on a national scale: archenemies in World War II, Germany and Japan are now two of our staunchest allies. Even more significantly—and of more direct relevance to places like the former Soviet Union and Yugoslavia—we fought a bloody Civil War that set family against family and the nation against itself.

I grew up in Atlanta, Georgia, where attitudes toward General Sherman, who burned Atlanta to the ground, suggest how Bosnian Muslims must feel about their Serbian neighbors. It was Sherman, after all, who introduced the "scorched earth" tactics of modern warfare, a policy that would be perfected in the Balkans. Somehow our nation did survive, as one. Southerners still debate the merits of the Confederate flag and the song "Dixie," but I haven't heard much talk of secession lately or of dividing the nation into ethnic enclaves. Two of our recent Presidents have hailed from Arkansas and Georgia.

After the Civil War, politicians and advisers urged Abraham Lincoln to punish the South severely for all the bloodshed it had caused. "Do I not destroy my enemies when I make them my friends?" replied the President, who instead set forth a magnanimous plan of Reconstruction. Lincoln's spirit guided a nation even after his death, perhaps the central reason the "United" States endured.

Even more impressive are the steps toward reconciliation between white and black races, one of which used to *own* the other. The lingering effects of racism prove that it takes many years and much hard work to undo injustice. Still, every step African-Americans take toward participation as citizens implies a move toward forgiveness. Not all blacks forgive and not all whites repent; racism deeply divides this country. Yet compare our situation with what has happened in, say, ex-Yugoslavia. I haven't seen any machine-gunners blocking the routes to Atlanta or artillery shells raining down on Birmingham.

I grew up a racist. Although I am not yet fifty years old, I remember well when the South practiced a perfectly legal form of apartheid. Stores in downtown Atlanta had three rest rooms: White Men, White Women, and Colored. Gas stations had two drinking fountains, one for Whites and one for Colored. Motels and restaurants served white patrons only, and when the Civil Rights Act made such discrimination illegal, many owners shuttered their establishments.*

Lester Maddox, later elected Governor of Georgia, was one of the protesting restaurateurs. After closing his fried chicken outlets, he opened a memorial to the death of freedom, featuring a copy of the Bill of Rights

---

*I visited the Holocaust Museum in Washington, D.C., and was deeply moved by its depiction of Nazi atrocities against the Jews. What struck me most personally, however, was a section early in the exhibit that demonstrated how the early discrimination laws against the Jews—the "Jews Only" shops, park benches, rest rooms, and drinking fountains—were explicitly modeled on segregation laws in the United States.

resting in a black-draped coffin. To support himself he sold clubs and ax handles in three different sizes—Daddy, Mama, and Junior—replicas of the clubs used to beat black civil rights demonstrators. I bought one of those ax handles with money earned from my paper route. Lester Maddox sometimes attended my church (his sister was a member), and it was there I learned a twisted theological basis for my racism.

In the 1960s the church deacon board mobilized lookout squads, and on Sundays these took turns patrolling the entrances lest any black "troublemakers" try to integrate us. I still have one of the cards the deacons printed up to give to any civil rights demonstrators who might appear:

> Believing the motives of your group to be ulterior and foreign to the teaching of God's word, *we cannot extend a welcome to you* and respectfully request you to leave the premises quietly. Scripture does NOT teach "the brotherhood of man and the fatherhood of God." He is the Creator of all, but only the Father of those who have been regenerated.
>
> If any one of you is here with a sincere desire to know Jesus Christ as Saviour and Lord, we shall be glad to deal individually with you from the Word of God.
>
> (Unanimous Statement of Pastor and Deacons, August 1960)

When Congress passed the Civil Rights Act, our church founded a private school as a haven for whites, expressly barring all black students. A few "liberal" members left the church in protest when the kindergarten turned down the daughter of a black Bible professor, but most of us approved of the decision. A year later the church board rejected a Carver Bible Institute student for membership (his name was Tony Evans and he went on to become a prominent pastor and speaker).

We used to call Martin Luther King Jr. "Martin Lucifer Coon." We said that King was a card-carrying Communist, a Marxist agent who merely posed as a minister. Not until much later was I able to appreciate the moral strength of the man who, perhaps more than any other person, kept the South from outright racial war.

My white colleagues in school and in church cheered King's televised encounters with southern sheriffs, police dogs, and fire hoses. Little did we know that by doing so we were playing directly into King's strategy. He deliberately sought out individuals like Sheriff Bull Connor and stage-managed scenes of confrontation, accepting beatings, jailings, and other brutalities, because he believed a complacent nation would rally around his cause only when they saw the evil of racism manifest in its ugliest extreme. "Christianity," he used to say, "has always insisted that the cross we bear precedes the crown we wear."

King recorded his struggle with forgiveness in "Letter from Birmingham City Jail." Outside the jail Southern pastors were denouncing him as a Communist, mobs were yelling "Hang the nigger!" and policemen were swinging nightsticks at his unarmed supporters. King writes that he had to fast for several days in order to achieve the spiritual discipline necessary for him to forgive his enemies.

By forcing evil out into the open, King was attempting to tap into a national reservoir of moral outrage, a concept my friends and I were not equipped to understand. Many historians point to one event as the single moment in which the movement attained at last a critical mass of support for the cause of civil rights. It occurred on the bridge outside Selma, Alabama, when Sheriff Jim Clark turned his policemen loose on unarmed black demonstrators.

The mounted troopers spurred their horses at a run into the crowd of marchers, flailing away with their nightsticks, cracking heads and driving bodies to the ground. As whites on the sidelines whooped and cheered, the troopers shot tear gas into the hysterical marchers. Most Americans got their first glimpse of the scene when ABC interrupted its Sunday movie, *Judgment at Nuremberg*, to show footage. What the viewers saw broadcast live from Alabama bore a horrifying resemblance to what they were watching on film from Nazi Germany. Eight days later President Lyndon Johnson submitted the Voting Rights Act of 1965 to the U.S. Congress.

King had developed a sophisticated strategy of war fought with grace, not gunpowder. He never refused to meet with his adversaries. He opposed policies but not personalities. Most importantly, he countered violence with nonviolence, and hatred with love. "Let us not seek to satisfy our thirst for freedom by drinking from the cup of bitterness and hatred," he exhorted his followers. "We must not allow our creative protest to degenerate into physical violence. Again and again, we must rise to the majestic heights of meeting physical force with soul force."

King's associate Andrew Young remembers those turbulent days as a time when they sought to save "black men's bodies and white men's souls." Their real goal, King said, was not to defeat the white man but "to awaken a sense of shame within the oppressor and challenge his false sense of superiority. . . . The end is reconciliation; the end is redemption; the end is the creation of the beloved community." And that is what Martin Luther King Jr. finally set into motion, even in die-hard racists like me. The power of grace disarmed my own stubborn evil.

Today as I look back on my childhood I feel shame, remorse, and also repentance. It took years for God to break through my armor of blatant racism—I wonder if any of us sheds its more subtle forms—and I now see that sin as one of the most malevolent, with perhaps the greatest societal impact. I hear much talk these days about the underclass and the crisis in urban America. Experts blame in turn drugs, a decline in values, poverty, and the breakdown of the nuclear family. I wonder if all those problems are consequences of a deeper, underlying cause: our centuries-old sin of racism.

Despite the moral and social fallout from racism, somehow the nation did stay together, and people of all colors eventually joined the democratic process, even in the South. For some years now, Atlanta has elected African-American mayors. And in 1976 Americans saw the extraordinary scene of George Wallace appearing before the black leadership of Alabama to apologize for his past behavior to blacks, an apology he repeated on statewide television.

Wallace's appearance—he needed black votes in a tight race for Governor—was easier to understand than the response to it. Black leaders accepted his apology, and black citizens forgave him, voting for him in droves. When Wallace went on to apologize to the Baptist Church in

Montgomery where King had launched the civil rights movement, the leaders who came to offer him forgiveness included Coretta Scott King, Jesse Jackson, and the brother of the murdered Medgar Evers.

Even my childhood church learned to repent. As the neighborhood changed, attendance at that church began to decline. When I attended a service several years ago, I was shocked to find only a few hundred worshipers scattered in the large sanctuary that, in my childhood, used to be packed with fifteen hundred. The church seemed cursed, blighted. It had tried new pastors and new programs, but nothing worked. Though the leaders sought African-American participation, few in the neighborhood responded.

Finally the pastor, a classmate of mine from childhood, took the unusual step of scheduling a service of repentance. In advance of the service he wrote to Tony Evans and to the Bible professor, asking their forgiveness. Then publicly, painfully, with African-American leaders present, he recounted the sin of racism as it had been practiced by the church in the past. He confessed—and received their forgiveness.

Although a burden seemed to lift from the congregation after that service, it was not sufficient to save the church. A few years later the white congregation moved out to the suburbs, and today a rousing African-American congregation, The Wings of Faith, fills the building and rattles its windows once more.

Elton Trueblood notes that the image Jesus used to describe the church's destiny—"the gates of hell will not prevail against it"—is a metaphor of offense, not defense. Christians are storming the gates, and they will prevail. No matter how it looks at any given point in history, the gates guarding the powers of evil will not withstand an assault by grace.

Newspapers prefer to fixate on violent warfare: bombings in Israel and London, assassination squads in Latin America, terrorism in India, Sri Lanka, and Algeria. These produce the grisly images of bleeding faces and amputated limbs that we have come to expect in this most violent of all centuries. And yet no one can deny the power of grace.

Who can forget the images from the Philippines, when common people knelt before fifty-ton tanks, which lurched to a halt as if colliding with an invisible shield of prayer. The Philippines is the only Christian-majority country in Asia, and it was here that the weapons of grace overcame the weapons of tyranny. When Benigno Aquino stepped off the plane in Manila, just before his assassination, he had a speech in his hand with this quote from Gandhi: "The willing sacrifice of the innocent is the most powerful answer to insolent tyranny that has yet been conceived by God or man." Aquino never got the chance to deliver that speech, but his life—and his wife's—proved those words prophetic. The Marcos regime suffered a fatal blow.

The Cold War, says former Senator Sam Nunn, ended "not in a nuclear inferno, but in a blaze of candles in the churches of Eastern Europe." Candlelight processions in East Germany did not show up well on the evening news, but they helped change the face of the globe. First a few hundred, then a thousand, then thirty thousand, fifty thousand, and finally five hundred thousand—nearly the entire population of the city—turned out in Leipzig for candlelight vigils. After a prayer meeting at St. Nikolai Church, the peaceful protestors would march through the dark streets, singing hymns. Police and soldiers with all their weapons seemed powerless against such a force. Ultimately, on the night a similar march in East Berlin attracted one million protestors, the hated Berlin Wall came tumbling down without a shot being fired. A huge banner appeared across a Leipzig street: *Wir danken Dir, Kirche* (We thank you, church).

Like a gale of pure air driving out stagnant clouds of pollution, peaceful revolution spread across the globe. In 1989 alone ten nations—Poland, East Germany, Hungary, Czechoslovakia, Bulgaria, Romania, Albania, Yugoslavia, Mongolia, the Soviet Union—comprising half a billion people experienced nonviolent revolutions. In many of these, the Christian minority played a crucial role. Stalin's mocking question, "How many divisions has the Pope?" got its answer.

Then in 1994 came the most surprising revolution of all, surprising because nearly everyone expected bloodshed. South Africa, though, was also the mother lode of peaceful protest, for it was there that Mohandas Gandhi, studying Tolstoy and the Sermon on the Mount, developed his strategy of nonviolence (which Martin Luther King Jr. later adopted). With much opportunity to practice, South Africans had perfected the use of the weapons of grace. Walter Wink tells of a black woman who was walking on the street with her children when a white man spat in her face. She stopped, and said, "Thank you, and now for the children." Nonplussed, the man was unable to respond.

In one squatter's village, black South African women suddenly found themselves surrounded by soldiers with bulldozers. The soldiers announced through a bullhorn that the residents had two minutes to clear out before their village would be razed. The women had no weapons, and the men of the village were away at work. Knowing the puritanical tendencies of rural Dutch Reformed Afrikaners, the black women stood in front of the bulldozers and stripped off all their clothes. The police fled, and the village remains standing to this day.

News reports barely mentioned the key role that Christian faith played in South Africa's peaceful revolution. After a mediation team led by Henry Kissinger had abandoned all hope of convincing the Inkatha Freedom Party to participate in elections, a Christian diplomat from Kenya met privately with all the principals, prayed with them, and helped change their minds. (A mysteriously malfunctioning compass on an airplane delayed one flight, making this crucial meeting possible.)

Nelson Mandela broke the chain of ungrace when he emerged from twenty-six years of imprisonment with a message of forgiveness and reconciliation, not revenge. F. W. De Klerk himself, elected from the smallest and most strictly Calvinistic of the South African churches, felt what he later described as "a strong sense of calling." He told his congregation that God was calling him to save all the people of South Africa, even though he knew that would mean rejection by his own people.

Black leaders insisted that De Klerk apologize for racial apartheid. He balked, because the people who had started the policy included his own father. But Bishop Desmond Tutu believed it essential that the process of reconciliation in South Africa begin with forgiveness, and he would not relent. According to Tutu, "One lesson we should be able to teach the world, and that we should be able to teach the people of Bosnia, Rwanda, and Burundi, is that we are ready to forgive." Eventually, De Klerk did apologize.

Now that the black majority has political power, they are formally considering issues of forgiveness. The minister of justice sounds downright theological as he formulates a policy. No one can forgive on behalf of victims, he says; victims have to forgive for themselves. And no one can forgive without full disclosure: what happened and who did what must first be revealed. Also, those who committed the atrocities must agree to ask for forgiveness before it can be granted. Step by step, South Africans are remembering their past in order to forget it.

Forgiveness is neither easy nor clear-cut, as South Africans are finding out. The pope may forgive his assassin but not ask for his release from prison. One may forgive the Germans but put restrictions on the armies, forgive a child abuser but keep him away from his victims, forgive Southern racism but enforce laws to keep it from happening again.

Yet nations that pursue forgiveness, in all its complexity, may at least avoid the awful consequences of the alternative—unforgiveness. Instead of scenes of massacre and civil war, the world was treated to the sight of black South Africans in long, snaking lines that stretched in some cases for more than a mile, *dancing* in jubilation over their first-ever opportunity to vote.

Because it goes against human nature, forgiveness must be taught and practiced, as one would practice any difficult craft. "Forgiveness is not just an occasional act: it is a permanent attitude," said Martin Luther King Jr. What greater gift could Christians give to the world than the forming of a culture that upholds grace and forgiveness?

The Benedictines, for example, have a moving service of forgiveness and reconciliation. After giving instruction from the Bible, the leaders ask each one attending to identify issues that require forgiveness. Worshipers then submerge their hands in a large crystal bowl of water, "holding" the grievance in their cupped hands. As they pray for the grace to forgive, gradually their hands open to symbolically "release" the grievance. "Enacting a ceremony like this with one's body," says Bruce Demarest, a participant, "possesses more transforming power than merely uttering the words, 'I forgive.'" What impact might it have if blacks and whites in South Africa—or in the United States of America—plunged their hands repeatedly into a common bowl of forgiveness?

In his book *The Prisoner and the Bomb*, Laurens van der Post recounts the misery of his wartime experiences in a Japanese prison camp in Java. In that unlikely place he concluded,

> The only hope for the future lay in an all-embracing attitude of forgiveness of the peoples who had been our enemies. Forgiveness, my prison experience had taught me, was not mere religious sentimentality; it was as fundamental a law of the human spirit as the law of gravity. If one broke the law of gravity one broke one's neck; if one broke this law of forgiveness one inflicted a mortal wound on one's spirit and became once again a member of the chain-gang of mere cause and effect from which life has laboured so long and painfully to escape.

PART III

Scent of Scandal

ELEVEN

A Home for Bastards: A Story

Will Campbell grew up on a hardscrabble farm in Mississippi. Bookish, never really fitting in with his rural surroundings, he worked hard at his studies and eventually made his way to Yale Divinity School. After graduation he returned south to preach and was named director of religious life at the University of Mississippi. This was the early 1960s, when proper Mississippians circled the wagons against assaults from civil rights activists, and when students and administrators learned of Campbell's liberal views on integration, his stint at the school abruptly ended.

Campbell soon found himself in the thick of battle, leading voter registration drives and supervising the idealistic young Northerners who migrated south to join the civil rights crusade. Among them was a Harvard Divinity School student named Jonathan Daniels, who had responded to Dr. King's call for supporters to descend on Selma. Most of the volunteers went home after the big march, but Jonathan Daniels stayed, and Will Campbell befriended him.

Campbell's theology was undergoing some testing in those days. Much of the opposition to his work came from "good

Christians" who refused to let people of other races into their churches and who resented anyone tampering with laws favoring white people. Campbell found allies more easily among agnostics, socialists, and a few devout Northerners.

"In ten words or less, what's the Christian message?" one agnostic had challenged him. The interlocutor was P. D. East, a renegade newspaper editor who viewed Christians as the enemy and could not understand Will's stubborn commitment to religious faith.

> We were going someplace, or coming back from someplace when he said, "Let me have it. Ten words." I said, "We're all bastards but God loves us anyway." He didn't comment on what he thought about the summary except to say, after he had counted the number of words on his fingers, "I gave you a ten-word limit. If you want to try again you have two words left." I didn't try again but he often reminded me of what I had said that day.

The definition stung P. D. East who, unbeknown to Campbell, was indeed illegitimate and had been called "bastard" all his life. Campbell had chosen the word not merely for shock effect but also for theological accuracy: spiritually we are illegitimate children, invited despite our paternity to join God's family. The more Campbell thought about his impromptu definition of the gospel, the more he liked it.

P. D. East put that definition to a ruthless test, however, on the darkest day of Campbell's life, a day when an Alabama deputy sheriff named Thomas Coleman gunned down Campbell's twenty-six-year-old friend. Jonathan Daniels had been arrested for picketing white stores. On his release from jail he approached a grocery store to make a phone call to arrange a ride when Coleman appeared with a shotgun and emptied it in his stomach. The pellets hit one other person, a black teenager, in the back, critically injuring him.

Campbell's book *Brother to a Dragonfly* records the conversation with P. D. East on that night, which led to what Campbell looks back on as "the most enlightening theological lesson I ever had in my life." P. D. East stayed on the offensive, even at this moment of grief:

> "Yea, Brother. Let's see if your definition of the Faith can stand the test." My calls had been to the Department of Justice, to the American Civil Liberties Union, and to a lawyer friend in Nashville. I had talked of the death of my friend as being a travesty of justice, as a complete breakdown of law and order, as a violation of Federal and State law. I had used words like redneck, backwoods, woolhat, cracker, Kluxer, ignoramus and many others. I had studied sociology, psychology, and social ethics and was speaking and thinking in those concepts. I had also studied New Testament theology.
>
> P. D. stalked me like a tiger. "Come on, Brother. Let's talk about your definition." At one point Joe [Will's brother] turned on him, "Lay off, P. D. Can't you see when somebody is upset?" But P. D. waved him off, loving me too much to leave me alone.

"Was Jonathan a bastard?" P. D. asked first. Campbell replied that though he was one of the most gentle guys he'd ever known, it's true that everyone is a sinner. In those terms, yes, he was a "bastard."

"All right. Is Thomas Coleman a bastard?" That question, Campbell found much easier to answer. You bet the murderer was a bastard.

Then P. D. pulled his chair close, placed his bony hand on Campbell's knee, and looked directly into his red-streaked eyes. "Which one of these two bastards do you think God loves the most?" The question hit home, like an arrow to the heart.

> Suddenly everything became clear. Everything. It was a revelation. The glow of the malt which we were well into by then seemed to illuminate and intensify it. I walked across the room and opened the blind, staring directly into the glare of the street light. And I began to whimper. But the crying was interspersed with laughter. It was a strange experience. I remember trying to sort out the sadness and the joy. Just what I was crying for and what I was laughing for. Then this too became clear.
>
> I was laughing at myself, at twenty years of a ministry which had become, without my realizing it, a ministry of liberal sophistication. . . .
>
> I agreed that the notion that a man could go to a store where a group of unarmed human beings are drinking soda pop and eating moon pies, fire a shotgun blast at one of them, tearing his lungs and heart and bowels from his body, turn on another and send lead pellets ripping through his flesh and bones, and that God would set him free is almost more than I could stand. But unless that is precisely the case then there is no Gospel, there is no Good News. Unless that is the truth we have only bad news, we are back with law alone.

What Will Campbell learned that night was a new insight into grace. The free offer of grace extends not just to the undeserving but to those who in fact deserve the *opposite*: to Ku Klux Klanners as well as civil rights marchers, to P. D. East as well as

Will Campbell, to Thomas Coleman as well as Jonathan Daniels.

This message lodged so deep inside Will Campbell that he underwent a kind of earthquake of grace. He resigned his position with the National Council of Churches and became what he wryly calls "an apostle to the rednecks." He bought a farm in Tennessee, and today is as likely to spend his time among Klansmen and racists as among racial minorities and white liberals. A lot of people, he decided, were volunteering to help minorities; he knew of no one ministering to the Thomas Colemans of the world.

I love the story of Will Campbell because of my upbringing in Atlanta among folks who wore our racism as a badge of honor. In short, I love Will Campbell's story because for a time I more resembled Thomas Coleman than Jonathan Daniels. I never killed anyone, but I surely hated. I laughed when the KKK burned a cross on the front lawn of the first black family to venture into our neighborhood. And when Northerners like Jonathan Daniels got killed, my friends and I shrugged and said, "Serves 'em right, coming down here to stir up trouble."

When time came to see myself for what I really was, a pitiful racist, a hypocrite who cloaked myself in gospel while living anti-gospel, when that time came, I clung like a drowning man to the promise of grace for people who deserve the opposite. People like me.

Ungrace sometimes fights back, enticing me to believe that my now-enlightened self is morally superior to the rednecks and racists who have not yet seen the light. But I know the truth, that "*while we were yet sinners* Christ died for us." I know that I came face-to-face with God's love at my worst, not my best, and that amazing grace saved a wretch like me.

And here in dust and dirt, O here
The lilies of His love appear.

GEORGE HERBERT

TWELVE

No Oddballs Allowed

Only once have I dared to preach a children's sermon. That Sunday morning I brought along a suspiciously squirming and smelly shopping bag, and during the morning service I invited all the children of the church to join me on the platform, where I gradually revealed the bag's contents.

First, I pulled out several packages of barbecued pork rinds (then-President George Bush's favorite snack food) for us to munch on. Next, I brought out a fake snake and a large rubber fly, provoking squeals from my young audience. Then we sampled scallops. Finally, to the children's great delight, I reached cautiously into the bag and extracted a live lobster. Larry the Lobster we called him, and Larry responded by waving his claws in a most menacing fashion.

The church janitor worked overtime that day, and so did I, for after the children had marched downstairs I took on the task of explaining to their parents why God once disapproved of all these foods. Levitical laws of the Old Testament specifically forbade each morsel we had eaten, and no Orthodox Jew would touch any of the contents of my shopping bag. "What did God have against lobster?" I titled my sermon.

Together we turned to a fascinating passage in the New Testament, the account of the apostle Peter's vision on a rooftop. Having climbed to the roof to pray in privacy, Peter began feeling hunger pangs. His mind wandered, he fell into a trance, and then an appalling scene played out before him. A large sheet descended from heaven, overflowing with "unclean" mammals, reptiles, and birds. Acts 10 does not get more specific, but a good clue to the species can be found in Leviticus 11: pigs, camels, rabbits, vultures, ravens, horned owls, screech owls, storks, bats, ants, beetles, bears, lizards, skinks, weasels, rats, snakes.

Simon, that's nasty! Don't even touch it. Go wash your hands this instant! he had doubtless heard his mother shout. Why? *Because we're different, that's why. We don't eat pigs. They're nasty, unclean. God told us not to touch them.* To Peter, as to every Jew in Palestine, such foods were more than distasteful—they were taboo, even abominable. "You are to detest them," God had said.

If during the course of a day Peter happened to touch the carcass of an insect, he would wash himself and his clothes and remain impure till evening, unable to visit the temple in such a state. And if, say, a gecko or a spider happened to fall from the ceiling onto a clay cooking pot, he would have to discard the pot's contents and smash it.

Now these contraband items were descending in a sheet, with a celestial voice commanding, "Get up, Peter. Kill and eat."

Peter reminded God of his own rules. "Surely not, Lord!" he protested. "I have never eaten anything impure or unclean."

The voice replied, "Do not call anything impure that God has made clean." Twice more this scene repeated itself until Peter, shaken to the core, descended the stairs to encounter the next jolt of the day: a group of "unclean" Gentiles who wanted to join the band of Jesus-followers.

Christians today who enjoy pork chops, scallops, oysters on the half shell, and lobster may easily miss the force of this scene that transpired on a rooftop so many years ago. For shock value, the closest parallel I can think of would be if, in the midst of a Southern Baptist convention in Texas Stadium, a fully stocked bar supernaturally lowered onto the playing field, with a booming voice from heaven urging the teetotalers to "Drink up!"

I can imagine the reaction: "Surely not, Lord! We're Baptists. We've never touched the stuff." That was the kind of conviction Peter had against unclean foods.

The incident in Acts 10 may have expanded the diet of the fledgling church, but it does not provide an answer to my original question, "What did God have against lobster?" For that I must turn to the book of Leviticus, where God explains the ban: "I am the LORD your God; consecrate yourselves and be holy, because I am holy." God's brief explanation allows much room for interpretation, and scholars have long debated the reasons behind the reason.

Some have pointed out the health benefits of the Levitical laws. The ban against pork removed the threat of trichinosis, and a ban against shellfish kept the Israelites safe from the viruses sometimes found in oysters and mussels. Others note that many of the forbidden animals are scavengers, feeding on carrion. Still others observe that specific laws seem directed against the customs of the Israelites' pagan neighbors. For example, the ban against cooking a young goat in its mother's milk was likely given to keep the Israelites from mimicking a magic-spell ritual of the Canaanites.

All these explanations make sense and may indeed shed light on the logic behind God's curious list. Some animals, though, cannot be explained away. Why lobster? Or what about rabbits, which carry no health risk and eat grass, not carrion? And why did camels and donkeys, the ubiquitous work animals of the Middle East, make the list? Clearly the laws have an arbitrariness about them.*

What did God have against lobster? The Jewish writer Herman Wouk says that "fit" is the best English equivalent for the Hebraic word "kosher" that guides Jewish customs to this day. Leviticus judges some animals "fit," or proper, and others unfit. Anthropologist Mary Douglas goes further, noting that in each case God forbids animals that show an anomaly. Since fish are supposed to have fins and scales, shellfish and eel do not qualify. Birds are meant to fly, and thus emus and ostriches do not qualify. Land animals should walk on all fours, not crawl along the ground like a snake. Domesticated cattle, sheep, and goats chew the cud and have cloven hooves; therefore so should all such edible mammals.

---

*Of course, all societies' eating habits are arbitrary, and every culture makes a distinction between "clean" and "unclean" animals. The French eat horses, Chinese eat dogs and monkeys, Italians eat songbirds, New Zealanders eat kangaroo, Africans eat insects, and cannibals eat other people. Americans find most of these customs offensive because our society has its own ingrained list of acceptable foods. For vegetarians, the list is much shorter.

Rabbi Jacob Neusner echoes her argument: "If I had to say in a few words what makes something unclean, it is something that, for one reason or another, is abnormal."

After studying the various theories, I have come up with an all-encompassing principle that, I believe, expresses the essence of the Old Testament laws on uncleanness: No Oddballs Allowed. The Israelites' diet scrupulously excluded any abnormal or "oddball" animals, and the same principle applied also to "clean" animals used in worship. No worshiper could bring a maimed or defective lamb to the temple, for God wanted the unblemished of the flock. From Cain onward, people had to follow God's precise instructions or risk having their offerings rejected. God demanded perfection; God deserved the best. No Oddballs Allowed.

The Old Testament applies a similar, far more troubling, ranking to people. I remember attending a church service in Chicago in which the pastor, Bill Leslie, divided our sanctuary so it would resemble the temple in Jerusalem. Gentiles could assemble in the balcony, designated the Court of the Gentiles, but were excluded from the main sanctuary. Jewish women could enter the main floor, but only the women's zone. Jewish laymen had a spacious area near the front, yet even they could not approach the platform, reserved for priests alone.

The rear of the platform, where the altar stood, Bill designated as the Most Holy Place. "Imagine a foot-thick curtain walling off this area," he said. "Only one priest went inside on one day a year—the holy day of Yom Kippur—and even he had to wear a rope around his ankle. If he did something wrong and died inside, the other priests would have to pull him out with the rope. They dared not enter the Most Holy Place, where God lived."

No one, not even the most pious person, would think of barging into the Most Holy Place, for the penalty was certain death. The very architecture reminded Israelites that God was set apart, other, *holy*.

Consider the modern parallel of a person who wishes to send a message to the President of the United States. Any citizen may write the President, or send a telegram or e-mail message. But even if she traveled to Washington, D.C., and stood in line with the tourists at the White House, she would not expect to gain a personal appointment with the President. Though she may speak to a secretary or with her Senator's help perhaps arrange a meeting with a cabinet official, no ordinary citizen expects to be able to barge into the Oval Office and present a petition. Government runs by hierarchy, setting apart its highest officials according to strict protocol. Similarly, in the Old Testament a ladder of hierarchy separated people from their God, this one based not on prestige but on "cleanness" or "holiness."

It is one thing to label animals unclean and quite another to label people unclean, but Old Testament laws did not shrink from that step.

> For the generations to come none of your descendants who has a defect may come near to offer the food of his God. No man who has any defect may come near: no man who is blind or lame, disfigured or deformed; no man with a crippled foot or hand, or who is hunchbacked or dwarfed, or who has any eye defect, or who has festering or running sores or damaged testicles.

In sum, those with damaged bodies or damaged family lines (bastards) failed to qualify: No Oddballs Allowed. Menstruating women, men who had recently had a nocturnal emission, women who had undergone childbirth, people with skin diseases or running sores, anyone who had touched a corpse—all these were declared ceremonially unclean.

In this age of political correctness, such blatant ranking of individuals based on gender, race, and even bodily health seems almost inconceivable, and yet this was the environment that defined Judaism. Each day Jewish men began their morning prayers by giving thanks to God "who hast not made me a Gentile . . . who has not made me a slave . . . who hast not made me a woman."

Acts 10 shows clearly the results of such an attitude, "the deadly logic of the politics of purity," as Croatian theologian Miroslav Volf describes it. When Peter, under duress, finally agreed to visit the house of a Roman centurion, he introduced himself by saying, "You are well aware that it is against our law for a Jew to associate with a Gentile or visit him." He made such a concession only after losing the argument with God on the rooftop.

Peter continued, "But God has shown me that I should not call any man impure or unclean." A revolution of grace was under way, one that Peter could hardly comprehend.

Before writing *The Jesus I Never Knew*, I spent several months researching the background to Jesus' life. I learned to appreciate the ordered world of first-century Judaism. I admit that the ranking of people rankled my American sensibilities—it seemed a formal pattern of ungrace, a religious caste system—but at least the Jews had found a place for such groups as women, aliens, slaves, and the poor. Other societies treated them far worse.

Jesus appeared on earth just as Palestine was experiencing a religious revival. The Pharisees, for example, spelled out precise rules for staying clean: never enter the home of a Gentile, never dine with sinners, perform no work on the Sabbath, wash your hands seven times before eating. Thus when rumors spread that Jesus could be the long-awaited Messiah, pious Jews were more scandalized than galvanized. Had he not touched unclean persons, such as those suffering from leprosy? Had he not let a woman of ill repute wash his feet with her hair? He dined with tax collectors—one even joined his inner circle of the Twelve—and was notoriously lax about the rules of ritual cleanness and Sabbath observance.

Moreover, Jesus deliberately crossed into Gentile territory and got involved with Gentiles. He praised a Roman centurion as having more faith than anyone in Israel and volunteered to enter the centurion's house to heal his servant. He healed a half-breed Samaritan with leprosy and had a lengthy conversation with a Samaritan woman—to the consternation of his disciples, who knew that "Jews do not associate with Samaritans." This woman, rejected by Jews on account of her race, rejected by neighbors on account of her serial marriages, became the first "missionary" appointed by Jesus and the first person to whom he openly revealed his identity as

Messiah. Then Jesus culminated his time on earth by giving his disciples the "Great Commission," a command to take the gospel to unclean Gentiles "in all Judea and Samaria, and to the ends of the earth."

Jesus' approach to "unclean" people dismayed his countrymen and, in the end, helped to get him crucified. In essence, Jesus canceled the cherished principle of the Old Testament, No Oddballs Allowed, replacing it with a new rule of grace: "We're all oddballs, but God loves us anyhow."

The Gospels record only one occasion when Jesus resorted to violence: the cleansing of the temple. Brandishing a whip, he overturned tables and benches and drove out the merchants who had set up shop there. As I have said, the very architecture of the temple expressed the Jewish hierarchy: Gentiles could enter only the outer court. Jesus resented that merchants had turned the Gentiles' area into an oriental bazaar filled with the sounds of animals bleating and merchants haggling over prices, an atmosphere hardly conducive to worship. Mark records that after the cleansing of the temple, the chief priests and teachers of the law "began looking for a way to kill him." In a real sense, Jesus sealed his fate with his angry insistence on the Gentiles' right to approach God.

Rung by rung, Jesus dismantled the ladder of hierarchy that had marked the approach to God. He invited defectives, sinners, aliens, and Gentiles—the unclean!—to God's banquet table.

Had not Isaiah prophesied of a great banquet to which all nations would be invited? Over the centuries, Isaiah's exalted vision had clouded over so that some groups restricted the invitation list to Jews who were not physically defective. In direct contrast, Jesus' version of the great banquet has the host sending messengers into the streets and alleys to invite "the poor, the crippled, the lame, the blind."*

---

*The Old Testament contains many indications that God planned all along to expand his "family" beyond the Jewish race to encompass those from every tribe and nation. In a delicious irony, Peter received the vision of the unclean animals in Joppa, the very seaport from which Jonah tried to escape God's command to carry God's message to the pagan Ninevites.

Jesus' most memorable story, the Prodigal Son, likewise ends with a banquet scene, featuring as its hero a good-for-nothing who has soiled the family reputation. Jesus' point: those judged undesirable by everyone else are infinitely desirable to God, and when one of them turns to God, a party breaks out. We're all oddballs but God loves us anyhow.

Another famous parable, the Good Samaritan, teased its original audience by introducing two religious professionals who gave the robbery victim a wide berth, unwilling to risk contamination from an apparent corpse. Jesus made the hero of this story a despised Samaritan—a choice as startling to that audience as it would be if a modern-day rabbi told a story glorifying a PLO fighter.

In his social contacts as well, Jesus overturned Jewish categories of "clean" and "unclean." Luke 8, for example, records three incidents in quick succession that, taken together, must have confirmed the Pharisees' misgivings about Jesus. First Jesus sails into a region populated by Gentiles, healing a naked madman and commissioning him as a missionary to his hometown. Next we see Jesus touched by a woman with a twelve-year hemorrhage, a "female problem" that has disqualified her from worship and no doubt caused her much shame. (The Pharisees taught that such illnesses came about because of a person's sin; Jesus directly contradicted them.) From there Jesus proceeds to the home of a synagogue ruler whose daughter has just died. Already "unclean" from the Gentile madman and the hemorrhaging woman, Jesus enters the inner room and touches the corpse.

Levitical laws guarded against contagion: contact with a sick person, a Gentile, a corpse, certain kinds of animals, or even mildew and mold would contaminate a person. Jesus reversed the process: rather than becoming contaminated, he made the other person whole. The naked madman did not pollute Jesus; he got healed. The pitiful woman with the flow of blood did not shame Jesus and make him unclean; she went away whole. The twelve-year-old dead girl did not contaminate Jesus; she was resurrected.

I sense in Jesus' approach a fulfillment, not an abolition, of the Old Testament laws. God had "hallowed" creation by separating the sacred from the profane, the clean from the unclean. Jesus did not cancel out the hallowing principle, rather he changed its source. We ourselves can be agents of God's holiness, for God now dwells within us. In the midst of an unclean world we can stride, as Jesus did, seeking ways to be a source of holiness. The sick and the maimed are for us not hot spots of contamination but potential reservoirs of God's mercy. We are called upon to extend that mercy, to be conveyers of grace, not avoiders of contagion. Like Jesus, we can help make the "unclean" clean.

It took the church some time to adjust to this dramatic change—otherwise Peter would not have needed the rooftop vision. Similarly, the church needed a supernatural prod before carrying the gospel to Gentiles. The Holy Spirit was happy to oblige, sending Philip first to Samaria and then directing him to a desert road where he met a foreigner, a black man, and one judged unclean under Old Testament rules (as a eunuch, he had damaged testicles). A short time later, Philip baptized the first missionary to Africa.

The apostle Paul—initially one of the most resistant to change, a "Pharisee of the Pharisees" who had daily thanked God he was not a Gentile, slave, or woman—ended up writing these revolutionary words: "There is neither Jew nor Greek, slave nor free, male nor female, for you are all one in Christ Jesus." Jesus' death, he said, broke down the temple barriers, dismantling the dividing walls of hostility that had separated categories of people. Grace found a way.

In this day, when tribalism sparks massacres in Africa, when nations redraw boundaries based on ethnic background, when racism in the United States mocks our nation's great ideals, when minorities and splinter groups lobby for their rights, I know of no more powerful message of the gospel than this, the message that got Jesus killed. The walls separating us from each other, and from God, have been demolished. We're all oddballs, but God loves us anyhow.

Almost twenty centuries have passed since God enlightened the apostle Peter on a rooftop. In that time, many circumstances have changed (no one is worrying about de-Judaizing the church anymore). Yet the shift that Jesus introduced has important consequences for every Christian. Jesus' revolution of grace affects me deeply in at least two ways.

First, it affects my access to God. In the same church service in which Bill Leslie divided our sanctuary into the approximate proportions of the Jewish temple, members of the congregation acted out a skit. Several petitioners approached the platform to deliver a message to the priest — with the women, of course, relying on their male representatives. Some brought sacrifices for the priest to present to God. Others made specific requests: "Could you talk to God about my problem?" they asked. Each time the "priest" would mount the platform, go through a prescribed ritual, and submit the request to God inside the Most Holy Place.

Suddenly, in the midst of this ceremony, a young woman came running down the aisle, disregarding the boundary set for her gender, with a Bible open to the book of Hebrews. "Hey, any of us can talk to God directly!" she proclaimed. "Listen to this."

> Therefore, since we have a great high priest who has gone through the heavens, Jesus the Son of God, let us hold firmly to the faith we profess. . . . Let us then approach the *throne of grace* with confidence.

"And here it is again,"

> . . . since we have confidence to enter the Most Holy Place by the blood of Jesus, by a new and living way opened for us through the curtain, that is, his body, and since we have a great priest over the house of God, let us draw near to God. . . .

"Any of us can enter the Most Holy Place!" she said before running offstage. "Any of us can come to God directly!"

In his sermon, the pastor spoke of the remarkable change of "God drawing near." You need only read the book of Leviticus and then turn to Acts to sense the seismic change. Whereas Old Testament worshipers purified themselves before entering the temple and presented their offerings to God through a priest, in Acts God's followers (good Jews, most of them) were meeting in private homes and addressing God with the informal *Abba.* It was a familiar term of family affection, like "Daddy," and before Jesus no one would have thought of applying such a word to Yahweh, the Sovereign Lord of the Universe. After him, it became the standard word used by early Christians to address God in prayer.

Earlier, I drew a parallel of a visitor in the White House. No such visitor, I said, could expect to barge into the Oval Office to see the President without an appointment. There are exceptions. During John F. Kennedy's administration, photographers sometimes captured a winsome scene. Seated around the President's desk in gray suits, cabinet members are debating matters of world consequence, such as the Cuban missile crisis. Meanwhile, a toddler, the two-year-old John-John, crawls atop the huge Presidential desk, oblivious to White House protocol and the weighty matters of state. John-John was simply visiting his daddy, and sometimes to his father's delight he would wander into the Oval Office with nary a knock.

That is the kind of shocking accessibility conveyed in Jesus' word *Abba.* God may be the Sovereign Lord of the Universe, but through his Son, God has made himself as approachable as any doting human father. In Romans 8, Paul brings the image of intimacy even closer. God's Spirit lives inside us, he says, and when we do not know what we ought to pray "the Spirit himself intercedes for us with groans that words cannot express."

We need not approach God by a ladder of hierarchy, anxious about cleanliness issues. If God's kingdom had a "No Oddballs Allowed" sign posted, none of us could get in. Jesus came to demonstrate that a perfect and holy God welcomes pleas for help from a widow with two mites and from a Roman centurion and a miserable publican and a thief on a cross. We need only call out "Abba" or, failing that, simply groan. God has come that close.

The second way in which Jesus' revolution affects me centers on how we are to view "different" people. Jesus' example convicts me today, because I sense a subtle shift in the reverse direction. As society unravels and immorality increases, I hear calls from some Christians that we show less mercy and more morality, calls that hark back to the style of the Old Testament.

A phrase used by both Peter and Paul has become one of my favorite images from the New Testament. We are to administer, or "dispense," God's grace, say the two apostles. The image brings to mind one of the old-fashioned "atomizers" women used before the perfection of spray technology. Squeeze a rubber bulb, and droplets of perfume come shooting out of the fine holes at the other end. A few drops suffice for a whole body; a few pumps change the atmosphere in a room. That is how grace should work, I think. It does not convert the entire world or an entire society, but it does enrich the atmosphere.

Now I worry that the prevailing image of Christians has changed from that of a perfume atomizer to a different spray apparatus: the kind used by insect exterminators. *There's a roach!* Pump, spray, pump, spray. *There's a spot of evil!* Pump, spray, pump, spray. Some Christians I know have taken on the task of "moral exterminator" for the evil-infested society around them.

I share a deep concern for our society. I am struck, though, by the alternative power of mercy as demonstrated by Jesus, who came for the sick and not the well, for the sinners and not the righteous. Jesus never countenanced evil, but he did stand ready to forgive it. Somehow, he gained the reputation as a lover of sinners, a reputation that his followers are in danger of losing today. As Dorothy Day put it, "I really only love God as much as I love the person I love the least."

These are difficult issues, I realize, and for this reason they deserve a chapter of their own.

"Don't the Bible say we must love everybody?"

"O, the Bible! To be sure, it says a great many things; but, then, nobody ever thinks of doing them."

HARRIET BEECHER STOWE, *UNCLE TOM'S CABIN*

THIRTEEN

Grace-Healed Eyes

Whenever I felt bored I would call my friend Mel White. I knew no one who lived with more verve and abandon. He had traveled all over the world, and he regaled me with his tales: scuba diving among barracudas in the Caribbean, stepping through a millennium's accumulation of pigeon droppings in order to film at sunrise from atop a Moroccan minaret, crossing the Atlantic in the *Queen Elizabeth II* as guest of a famous television producer, interviewing survivors of the Jim Jones cult after the massacre in Guyana.

Generous to a fault, Mel made a perfect target for any huckster. If we were sitting in an outdoor cafe and a flower-seller walked by, he would buy a bouquet just to see my wife's eyes light up. If a photographer offered to take our photo for some outlandish fee, Mel would instantly agree. "It's a memory," he would say over our objections. "You can't put a price tag on a memory." His jokes and witticisms kept the waiter, the *maître d'*, and the cashier in stitches.

When we lived in downtown Chicago, Mel used to visit us on his way to Michigan, where he worked as a consultant for Christian films. We would eat out, visit an art gallery, stroll the streets, catch a movie, and walk along the lakefront until midnight or so. Then at four o'clock in the morning Mel would awake, get dressed, and type furiously for four hours, producing a thirty-page document he would deliver that afternoon to his client in Michigan. When we put Mel in a cab to the airport, my wife and I would feel exhausted but happy. More than anyone we knew, Mel made us feel fully alive.

Many homosexuals populated the neighborhood we lived in, especially along Diversey Avenue (known as "Perversey" to the locals). I remember joking about them to Mel. "Know the difference between a gay and a Nazi?" I once said as we walked down Diversey. "Sixty degrees," and I dropped my hand from the stiff Nazi salute to a limp-wrist imitation.

"You can always tell the homosexuals around here," my wife added. "There's something about them. I always know."

We had been friends for about five years when I got a call from Mel asking if we could meet at the Marriott Hotel near O'Hare Airport. I arrived at the appointed time, then sat alone in the restaurant for an hour and a half reading the newspaper, the menu, the backs of sugar packets, and anything else I could find. No Mel. Just as I got up to leave, peeved at the inconvenience, Mel dashed in. He was apologetic, even trembling. He had gone to the wrong Marriott and then got stuck in a massive Chicago traffic jam. He had only an hour before his plane. Could I sit with him a little longer to help him calm down? "Of course."

Rattled by the morning's events, Mel seemed harried and distracted, on the verge of tears. He shut his eyes, breathed deeply a few times, and began our conversation with a sentence I will never forget. "Philip, you've probably already figured out that I'm gay."

The thought had never once crossed my mind. Mel had a loving and devoted wife and two children. He taught at Fuller Seminary, served as pastor of an Evangelical Covenant church, and made films and wrote best-selling books for Christians. Mel, gay? Is the Pope Muslim?

At that time, despite the neighborhood I lived in, I did not know one gay person. I knew nothing about the subculture. I joked about it and told stories about the Gay Pride Parade (which marched down my street) to my suburban friends, but I had no homosexual acquaintances, much less friends. The idea repulsed me.

Now I was hearing that one of my best friends had a secret side I knew nothing about. I sat back in my chair, took a few deep breaths of my own, and asked Mel to tell me his story.

I am not breaking Mel's confidence by relating this story, because he has already gone public in his book *Stranger at the Gate: To be Gay and*

Christian in America. The book mentions his friendship with me and also tells of some of the conservative Christians he previously worked with as a ghostwriter: Francis Schaeffer, Pat Robertson, Oliver North, Billy Graham, W. A. Criswell, Jim and Tammy Faye Bakker, Jerry Falwell. None of these people knew about Mel's secret life at the time he worked with them, and understandably some of them feel upset with him now.

I should make clear that I have no desire to delve into the theological and moral issues surrounding homosexuality, important as they may be. I write about Mel for one reason only: my friendship with him has strongly challenged my notion of how grace should affect my attitude toward "different" people, even when those differences are serious and perhaps unresolvable.

I learned from Mel that homosexuality is not the casual lifestyle choice I had blithely assumed it to be. As Mel spells out in his book, he felt homosexual longings from adolescence, tried hard to repress those longings, and as an adult fervently sought a "cure." He fasted, prayed, and was anointed with oil for healing. He went through exorcism rites led by Protestants and also by Catholics. He signed up for aversion therapy, which jolted his body with electricity every time he felt stimulated by photos of men. For a time, chemical treatments left him drugged and barely coherent. Above all else, Mel wanted desperately *not* to be gay.

I remember a phone call that woke me up late one night. Without bothering to introduce himself, Mel said in a flat voice, "I am standing on a fifth-floor balcony overlooking the Pacific Ocean. You have ten minutes to tell me why I should not jump." This was no prank to get attention; Mel had nearly succeeded in a bloody suicide attempt not long before. I pled with him, using every personal, existential, and theological argument I could think of in my groggy state. Thankfully, Mel did not jump.

I also remember a tearful scene a few years later in which Mel brought me mementos from his gay lover. Handing me a blue wool sweater, he asked me to throw it in the fireplace. He had sinned and now repented, he said, and he was leaving that life behind him and returning to his wife and family. We rejoiced and prayed together.

I remember another tearful scene when Mel destroyed his California Bath Club membership card. A mysterious disease had begun showing up among the gay population of California, and hundreds of gay men were dropping out of the bath club scene. "I'm not doing this because of fear of disease, but because I know it's the right thing to do," Mel told me. He took a pair of scissors and cut apart the hard plastic card.

Mel had wild swings between promiscuity and fidelity. Sometimes he would act like a hormone-flooded teenager, and sometimes like a sage. "I have learned the distinction between virtuous grief and guilty grief," he once told me. "Both are real, both are excruciating, but the latter is far worse. Virtuous grief, such as celibate people feel, knows what it lacks but does not know what it has lost. Guilty grief never stops knowing." For Mel, guilty grief meant the haunting awareness that if he chose to come out of the closet he would lose his marriage as well as his career and ministry and quite possibly his faith.

Despite these guilt feelings, Mel finally concluded that his options narrowed down to two: insanity or wholeness. Attempts to repress homosexual desires and live either in heterosexual marriage or in gay celibacy, he believed, would lead to certain insanity. (At the time he was seeing a psychiatrist five days a week, at a hundred dollars a session.) Wholeness, he decided, meant finding a gay partner and embracing his homosexual identity.

Mel's odyssey confused and disturbed me. My wife and I stayed up many long nights with Mel discussing his future. Together we went over all the relevant biblical passages and what they might mean. Mel kept asking why Christians highlighted any reference to same-sex unions while disregarding other behavior mentioned in the same passages.

At Mel's request I attended the first gay march on Washington, in 1987. I went not as a marcher, or even as a journalist, but as Mel's friend.

He wanted me nearby as he sorted through some of the decisions bearing down on him.

About 300,000 gay rights marchers had gathered, and a minority clearly intended to shock the public, wearing outfits that no evening newscast could televise. The October day was chilly, and gray clouds spit raindrops on the columns parading through the capital.

As I stood on the sidelines, directly in front of the White House, I watched an angry confrontation. Mounted policemen had formed a protective circle around a small group of counterdemonstrators who, thanks to their orange posters featuring vivid illustrations of hellfire, had managed to attract most of the press photographers. Despite being outnumbered fifteen thousand to one, these Christian protesters were yelling inflammatory slogans at the gay marchers.

"Faggots go home!" their leader screamed into a microphone, and the others took up the chant: "Faggots go home, faggots go home. . . ." When that got wearisome, they switched to "Shame-on-you-for-what-you-do." Between chants the leader delivered brimstone sermonettes about God reserving the hottest fires in hell for sodomites and other perverts.

"AIDS, AIDS, it's comin' your way" was the last taunt in the protesters' repertoire, and the one shouted with the most ardor. We had just seen a sad procession of several hundred persons with AIDS: many in wheelchairs, with the gaunt bodies of concentration camp survivors. Listening to the chant, I could not fathom how anyone could wish that fate on another human being.

For their part, the gay marchers had a mixed response to the Christians. Rowdy ones blew kisses or retorted, "Bigots! Bigots! Shame on you!" One group of lesbians got a few laughs from the press by yelling in unison to the protesters, "We want your wives!"

Among the marchers were at least three thousand who identified themselves with various religious groups: the Catholic "Dignity" movement, the Episcopalian group "Integrity," and even a sprinkling of Mormons and Seventh-Day Adventists. More than a thousand marched under the banner of the Metropolitan Community Church (MCC), a denomination that professes a mostly evangelical theology except for its stance on homosexuality. This last group had a poignant reply to the beleaguered Christian protesters: they drew even, turned to face them, and sang, "Jesus loves us, this we know, for the Bible tells us so."

The abrupt ironies in that scene of confrontation struck me. On the one side were Christians defending pure doctrine (not even the National Council of Churches has accepted the MCC denomination for membership). On the other side were "sinners," many of whom openly admit to homosexual practice. Yet the more orthodox group spewed out hate and the other group sang of Jesus' love.

During the weekend in Washington, Mel introduced me to many of the leaders of the religious groups. I can't remember attending so many church services in one weekend. To my surprise, most of the services used the hymns and order of worship of mainstream evangelicals, and I heard nothing suspect in the theology preached from the pulpit. "Most gay Christians are quite conservative theologically," one of the leaders explained to me. "We get such hatred and rejection from the church that there's no reason to bother with church at all unless you really do believe the gospel is true." I heard numerous personal stories to back up his claim.

Every gay person I interviewed could tell hair-raising tales of rejection, hatred, and persecution. Most had been called names and beaten up too many times to count. Half of the people I interviewed had been disowned by their families. Some of the AIDS patients had tried to contact their estranged families to inform them of the disease but had received no response. One man, after ten years of separation, was invited home for Thanksgiving dinner in Wisconsin. His mother seated him apart from the family, at a separate table set with Chinette plates and plastic utensils.

Some Christians say, "Yes, we should treat gays with compassion but at the same time we must give them a message of judgment." After all these interviews, I began to understand that every gay person has heard the message of judgment from the church—again and again, nothing but judgment. The more theologically inclined gay people I interviewed interpret the biblical passages on homosexuality differently. Some of them told me they had offered to sit down and discuss these differences with conservative scholars, but no one had agreed.

I left Washington with my head reeling. I had attended packed-out worship services marked by fervent singing, praying, and testifying—all oriented around what the Christian church has always taught to be a sin. Also, I could sense my friend Mel edging closer and closer to a choice that I knew would be morally wrong—to divorce his wife and lose his ministry in order to begin a scary new life fraught with temptation.

It occurred to me that my own life would be much simpler if I had never met Mel White. But he was my friend—how should I treat him? What would grace have me do? What would Jesus do?

After Mel came out of the closet and his story became publicized, his former colleagues and employers treated him frostily. Famous Christians who had hosted him, traveled with him, and made hundreds of thousands of dollars off his work suddenly turned away. In an airport Mel walked up to a leading Christian statesman he knew well and held out his hand. The man scowled, turned his back, and would not even speak. When Mel's book came out, some of the Christians he had worked for called press conferences to denounce it, denying any past close association.

For a time, Mel was in hot demand on radio talk shows and on television programs such as *60 Minutes.* The secular media loved the angle of a stealth homosexual working for leaders of the religious right, and in search of gossip they probed his stories about evangelical celebrities. Appearing on these shows, Mel heard from many Christians. "Virtually every talk show I have been on," Mel tells me, "someone has called to say that I am an abomination and should be treated according to the laws of Leviticus—meaning, I should be stoned to death."

Simply because I was mentioned in Mel's book, I heard from some of these Christians as well. One man enclosed a copy of a letter he had written Mel, which concluded,

> I truly pray that one day, you will truly repent, truly desire freedom from the sin that enslaves you, and renounce the false teaching of the so-called "gay church." If you don't, thankfully

you will receive what you deserve, an eternity in Hell, reserved for all who are enslaved to Sin and refuse to Repent.

When I replied, I asked the writer if he really meant the word "thankfully," and he sent back a long letter, full of Scripture references, affirming that indeed he did.

I started making it a point to meet other gay people in our neighborhood, including some who came from a Christian background. "I still believe," one told me. "I would love to go to church, but whenever I've tried someone spreads a rumor about me and suddenly everyone withdraws." He added a chilling remark, "As a gay man, I've found it's easier for me to get sex on the streets than to get a hug in church."

I met other Christians who have sought to treat homosexuals in a loving way. Barbara Johnson, for example, is a best-selling Christian writer who first learned her son was gay and then learned that the church did not know how to handle that fact. She began an association called "Spatula Ministries" (as in, "You had to scrape me off the ceiling with a spatula") to minister to other parents in her predicament. Convinced that the Bible forbids it, Barbara opposes homosexual practice and always makes that clear. She is simply trying to form a refuge for other families who find no such refuge in the church. Barbara's newsletters are filled with stories of families that are riven apart, then painfully stitched back together. "These are our sons, these are our daughters," Barbara says. "We cannot simply shut the door on them."

I also talked with Tony Campolo, a high-profile Christian speaker who opposes homosexual practice, while at the same time admitting that homosexual orientation is ingrained and almost impossible to change. He holds up an ideal of sexual celibacy. Partly because of his wife's ministry to the gay community, Tony has been slandered by other Christians, resulting in many canceled speaking engagements. At one convention, protesters distributed purported correspondence between Tony and gay leaders at Queer Nation, a letter that was proved spurious, part of a smear campaign.

Much to my surprise, I learned a great deal about the treatment of "different" people from Edward Dobson, a graduate of Bob Jones University, formerly Jerry Falwell's right-hand man, and founder of the *Fundamentalist Journal.* Dobson left Falwell's organization to take a pastorate in Grand Rapids, Michigan, and while there he became concerned about the AIDS problem in his city. He asked to meet with some of the gay leaders in town and volunteered the services of members of his church.

Although Dobson's belief in the wrongness of homosexual practice had not changed, he felt constrained to reach out to the gay community in Christian love. The gay activists were leery, to say the least. They knew Dobson's reputation as a fundamentalist, and to them, as to many gays, "fundamentalist" brings to mind people like the demonstrators I saw in Washington, D.C.

In time Ed Dobson won the trust of the gay community. He began encouraging his congregation to provide Christmas gifts for people with HIV and to offer other practical means of assistance to the sick and dying. Many of them had never met a homosexual before. A few refused to cooperate. Gradually, though, both groups began seeing each other in a new light. As one gay person said to Dobson, "We understand where you stand, and know that you do not agree with us. But you still show the love of Jesus, and we're drawn to that."

To many AIDS patients in Grand Rapids, the word *Christian* now carries a very different connotation than it did a few years ago. Dobson's experience has proved that Christians can have firm views about ethical behavior and yet still demonstrate love. Ed Dobson once said to me, "If I die and someone stands up at my funeral and says nothing but, 'Ed Dobson loved homosexuals,' I would feel proud."

I also interviewed Dr. C. Everett Koop, who was then serving as Surgeon General of the United States. Koop's credentials as an evangelical Christian were impeccable. It was he, teamed with Francis Schaeffer, who helped mobilize the conservative Christian community to enter the political fray over pro-life issues.

In his role as "the nation's doctor," Koop visited AIDS patients. Their bodies skeletal, emaciated, and covered with purplish sores, he began to feel for them a deep compassion, both as a doctor and as a Christian. He had vowed to look out for the weak and disenfranchised, and there was no more weak or disenfranchised group in the nation.

For seven weeks Koop addressed only religious groups, including Jerry Falwell's church, the National Religious Broadcasters' convention, conservative groups within Judaism, and Roman Catholics. In those addresses, delivered in full Public Health Service uniform, Koop affirmed the need for abstinence and monogamous marriage. But he added, "I am the Surgeon General of the heterosexuals and the homosexuals, of the young and the old, of the moral and the immoral." He admonished fellow Christians, "You may hate the sin, but you are to love the sinner."

Koop always expressed his personal abhorrence of sexual promiscuity—consistently he used the word "sodomy" when referring to homosexual acts—but as Surgeon General he lobbied on homosexuals' behalf and cared for them. Koop could hardly believe it when he spoke to twelve thousand gay people in Boston and they chanted, *Koop! Koop! Koop! Koop!* "They give unbelievable support—in spite of what I say about their practices. I guess it's because I'm the person who came out and said, I'm the Surgeon General of all the people and I'll meet them where they are. In addition, I've asked for compassion for them, and for volunteers to go and care for them." Koop never compromised his beliefs—even now he persists in using the emotionally charged word "sodomy"—but no evangelical Christian gets a warmer reception among homosexuals.

Finally, I learned an important insight into "different" people from Mel White's parents. A network television crew did a segment in which they interviewed Mel, his wife, his friends, and his parents. Remarkably, Mel's wife continued to support him and speak highly of him after the divorce; she even wrote the foreword to his book. Mel's parents, conservative Christians and respected pillars of the community (Mel's father had been his city's mayor), had a tougher time accepting the situation. After Mel broke the news to them, they went through various stages of shock and denial.

At one point, a TV interviewer asked Mel's parents on-camera, "You know what other Christians are saying about your son. They say he's an abomination. What do you think about that?"

"Well," the mother answered in a sweet, quavery voice, "he may be an abomination, but he's still our pride and joy."

That line has stayed with me because I came to see it as a heartrending definition of grace. I came to see that Mel White's mother expressed how God views every one of us. In some ways we are all abominations to God—*All have sinned and fall short of the glory of God*—and yet somehow, against all reason, God loves us anyhow. Grace declares that we are still God's pride and joy.

Paul Tournier wrote about a friend who was obtaining a divorce:

> I cannot approve of his course of action, because divorce is always disobedience of God. I should be betraying my belief if I were to hide it from him. I know that there is always a solution other than divorce to a marital conflict, if we are really prepared to seek it under God's guidance. But I know that this disobedience is no worse than the slander, the lie, the gesture of pride of which I am guilty every day. The circumstances of our life are different, but the reality of our hearts is the same. If I were in his place, would I act any differently from him? I have no idea. At least I know that I should need friends who loved me unreservedly just as I am, with all my weaknesses, and who would trust me without judging me. If he gets his divorce, he will no doubt meet even greater difficulties than those he is in today. He will need my affection all the more, and this is the assurance I must give him.

I got a call from Mel White in the midst of one of his activist campaigns. He was fasting in a camper in Colorado Springs, Colorado, a pocket of conservatism dubbed "ground zero" by gay rights activists. Inside the camper Mel was displaying "gay-bashing" mailings sent out by Colorado Springs' Christian organizations. Mel was asking the Christian leaders there to desist from inflammatory rhetoric, for in many parts of the country hate crimes against gays were epidemic.

Mel was having a rough week. A local radio commentator had made some veiled threats against him, and at night joyriders would circle his camper, honking their horns to keep him from sleeping.

"A reporter is trying to get us all together for once," Mel told me over the phone. "He's invited hard-liners from ACT UP, and some lesbian ministers in the MCC church as well as executives from places like Focus on the Family and the Navigators. I don't know what's going to happen. I'm hungry and exhausted and afraid. I need you to be there."

So I went. Mel is the only person I know who could convene such a gathering. Folks from the political right and the political left sat in the same living room, with a palpable tension hanging in the air. I remember many things about that evening, but one thing above all. When Mel asked me to speak to some of the issues, he introduced me as his friend and told a little about our history together. He ended by saying, "I don't know how Philip feels about every aspect of the issue of homosexuality, and to tell you the truth I'm afraid to ask. But I do know how he feels about me—he loves me."

My friendship with Mel has taught me much about grace. On the surface the word may seem a shorthand expression for the fuzzy tolerance of liberalism: can't we all just get along? Grace is different, though. Traced back to its theological roots, it includes an element of self-sacrifice, a cost.

I have seen Mel demonstrate a graceful spirit time and again to Christians who revile him. Once I asked to see a batch of the hate-mail he gets from Christians, and I could barely make it through the letters. The pages were septic with hatred. In the name of God, writers rained down curses and profanity and threats. I kept wanting to protest, "Wait, Mel is my friend. You don't know him." To the letter writers, though, Mel was a label—*pervert!*—not a person. Knowing Mel, I understand better the dangers Jesus discussed so incisively in the Sermon on the Mount: how quickly we accuse others of murder and neglect our own anger, or of adultery and neglect our own lust. Grace dies when it becomes us versus them.

I have also read some of the letters Mel received in response to his book *Stranger at the Gate*. Most came from gay people and simply told a story. Like Mel, many of the letter writers had attempted suicide. Like Mel, many had experienced nothing but rejection from the church. Eighty thousand books sold, forty-one thousand reader responses—could that ratio say something about the hunger for grace in the homosexual community?

I have watched Mel try to forge a new career. He lost all his former clients, his income dropped by seventy-five percent, and he had to move from a luxury house to an apartment. As Minister of Justice for the MCC denomination, he now spends much of his time speaking to small church groups of gay men and women, groups which, to put it kindly, do nothing to feed a speaker's ego.

The whole notion of a "gay church" seems bizarre to me. I have met celibate, nonpracticing homosexuals who wish desperately that another church would welcome them, but have found none. I feel sad that the churches I attend are missing out on the spiritual gifts of these Christians, and sad too that the MCC denomination seems to me so fixated on sexual issues.

Mel and I have deep differences. I cannot condone many of the decisions he has made. "One day we may face each other on the other side of the picket lines," he predicted several years ago. "What will happen to our friendship then?"

I remember one difficult confrontation in a Red Lion Inn coffee shop just after I returned from Russia. I was bursting with news of the fall of communism, of the new openness to Christ in nearly a third of the world, of incredible words I had heard straight from the lips of Gorbachev and from the KGB. It seemed a rare moment of grace in a century that has known so little.

Mel, though, had an entirely different agenda. "Can you support my ordination?" he asked. At the time homosexuality, not to say sexuality, was far from my mind. I was thinking about the fall of Marxism, the end of the Cold War, the emancipation of the Gulag.

"No," I told Mel after a moment's thought. "Based on your history and what I read in the Epistles, I don't think you qualify. If I were voting on your ordination, I would vote no."

It took months for our friendship to recover from that one conversation. I had responded honestly, off the cuff, but to Mel it sounded like a direct and personal rejection. I try to put myself in his place, to understand what it must be like for him to remain friends with a person who writes for *Christianity Today* magazine and who represents the evangelical establishment that has caused him such pain. How easy it would be for him to surround himself with like-minded supporters.

Frankly, I think our friendship takes far more grace on Mel's part than on mine.

I can predict what kind of letters I will receive in reaction to this story. Homosexuality is such a flash-point issue that it attracts passionate responses from both sides. Conservatives will lambaste me for coddling a sinner, and liberals will attack me for not endorsing their position. Again, I am not discussing my views of homosexual behavior, only my attitudes toward homosexuals. I have used the example of my relationship with Mel White—deliberately evading some of the issues—because for me it has been an intense and ongoing test on how grace calls me to treat "different" people.

Such profound differences, in whatever arena, form a kind of crucible of grace. Some must grapple with how to treat fundamentalists who wounded them in the past. Will Campbell took on the task of reconciling with rednecks and Kluxers. Still others contend with the arrogance and close-mindedness of "politically correct" liberals. Whites must deal with how they differ from African-Americans, and vice versa. Inner-city blacks must also sort out complicated relationships with Jews and Koreans.

An issue like homosexuality presents a special case because the difference centers on a moral, not a cross-cultural, issue. For most of history the church has overwhelmingly viewed homosexual behavior as a serious sin. Then the question becomes, "How do we treat sinners?"

I think of the changes that have occurred within the evangelical church in my lifetime over the issue of divorce, an issue on which Jesus is absolutely clear. Yet today a divorced person is not shunned, banned from churches, spit upon, screamed at. Even those who consider divorce a sin have come to accept the sinners and treat them with civility and even love. Other sins on which the Bible is also clear—greed, for example—seem to pose no barrier at all. We have learned to accept the person without approving of the behavior.

My study of Jesus' life convinces me that whatever barriers we must overcome in treating "different" people cannot compare to what a holy God—who dwelled in the Most Holy Place, and whose presence caused fire and smoke to belch from mountaintops, bringing death to any unclean person who wandered near—overcame when he descended to join us on planet Earth.

A prostitute, a wealthy exploiter, a demon-possessed woman, a Roman soldier, a Samaritan with running sores and another Samaritan with serial husbands—I marvel that Jesus gained the reputation as being a "friend of sinners" like these. As Helmut Thielicke wrote:

> Jesus gained the power to love harlots, bullies, and ruffians . . . he was able to do this only because he saw through the filth and crust of degeneration, because his eye caught the divine original which is hidden in every way—in *every* man! . . . First and foremost he gives us new eyes. . . .
>
> When Jesus loved a guilt-laden person and helped him, he saw in him an erring child of God. He saw in him a human being whom his Father loved and grieved over because he was going wrong. He saw him as God originally designed and meant him to be, and therefore he saw through the surface layer of grime and dirt to the real man underneath. Jesus did not *identify* the person with his sin, but rather saw in this sin something alien, something that really did not belong to him, something that merely chained and mastered him and from which he would free him and bring him back to his real self. Jesus was able to love men because he loved them right through the layer of mud.

We may be abominations, but we are still God's pride and joy. All of us in the church need "grace-healed eyes" to see the potential in others for the same grace that God has so lavishly bestowed on us. "To love a person," said Dostoevsky, "means to see him as God intended him to be."

The Catholic novelist believes that you destroy your freedom by sin; the modern reader believes, I think, that you gain it in that way. There is not much possibility of understanding between the two.

FLANNERY O'CONNOR

FOURTEEN

Loopholes

Historian and art critic Robert Hughes tells of a convict sentenced to life imprisonment on a maximum-security island off the coast of Australia. One day, with no provocation he turned on a fellow prisoner and beat him senseless and killed him. Authorities shipped the murderer back to the mainland to stand trial, whereupon he gave a straightforward, passionless account of the crime. He showed no sign of remorse and denied having held any grudge against the victim. "Why, then?" asked the bewildered judge. "What was your motive?"

The prisoner replied that he was sick of life on the island, a notoriously brutal place, and saw no reason to keep on living. "Yes, yes, I understand all that," said the judge. "I can see why you might drown yourself in the ocean. But murder? Why murder?"

"Well, I figure it's like this," said the prisoner. "I'm a Catholic. If I commit suicide I'll go straight to hell. But if I murder I can come back here to Sydney and confess to a priest before my execution. That way, God will forgive me."

The Australian prisoner's logic was the mirror image of Prince Hamlet's, who would not kill the king at prayer in the chapel lest he be forgiven his foul deeds and go straight to heaven.

Anyone who writes about grace must confront its apparent loopholes. In W. H. Auden's poem "For the Time Being," King Herod shrewdly grasps the logical consequences of grace: "Every crook will argue: 'I like committing crimes. God likes forgiving them. Really the world is admirably arranged.'"

To this point, I freely admit, I have presented a one-sided picture of grace. I have portrayed God as a lovesick father eager to forgive, and grace as a force potent enough to break the chains that bind us, and merciful enough to overcome deep differences between us. Depicting grace in such sweeping terms makes people nervous, and I concede that I have skated to the very edge of danger. I have done so because I believe the New Testament does too. Consider this pointed reminder from the grand old preacher Martyn Lloyd-Jones:

> There is thus clearly a sense in which the message of "justification by faith only" can be dangerous, and likewise with the message that salvation is entirely of grace. . . .
>
> I would say to all preachers: If your preaching of salvation has not been misunderstood in that way, then you had better examine your sermons again, and you had better make sure that you really are preaching the salvation that is offered in the New Testament to the ungodly, to the sinner, to those who are enemies of God. There is this kind of dangerous element about the true presentation of the doctrine of salvation.

Grace has about it the scent of scandal. When someone asked theologian Karl Barth what he would say to Adolf Hitler, he replied, "Jesus Christ died for your sins." Hitler's sins? Judas's? Has grace no limit?

Two giants of the Old Testament, Moses and David, committed murder and still God loved them. As I have mentioned, another man who led a campaign of torture went on to set a missionary standard that has never been matched. Paul never tired of describing that miracle of forgiveness: "Even though I was once a blasphemer and a persecutor and a violent man, I was shown mercy because I acted in ignorance and unbelief. The *grace* of our Lord was poured out on me abundantly, along with the faith and love that are in Christ Jesus. Here is a trustworthy saying that deserves full acceptance: Christ Jesus came into the world to save sinners—of whom I am the worst."

Ron Nikkel, who heads up Prison Fellowship International, has a standard talk that he delivers to prisoners around the world. "We don't know who will make it into heaven," he says. "Jesus indicated a lot of people will face surprises: 'Not everyone who says to me, "Lord, Lord," will enter the kingdom of heaven.' But we do know that some thieves and murderers will be there. Jesus promised heaven to the thief on the cross, and the apostle Paul was an accomplice to murder." I have watched the expressions on the faces of prisoners in places like Chile, Peru, and Russia as Ron's point sinks in. For them, the scandal of grace sounds too good to be true.

When Bill Moyers filmed a television special on the hymn "Amazing Grace," his camera followed Johnny Cash into the bowels of a maximum-security prison. "What does this song mean to you?" Cash asked the prisoners after singing the hymn. One man serving time for attempted murder replied, "I'd been a deacon, a churchman, but I never knew what grace was until I ended up in a place like this."

The potential for "grace abuse" was brought home to me forcefully in a conversation with a friend I'll call Daniel. Late one night I sat in a restaurant and listened as Daniel confided to me that he had decided to leave his wife after fifteen years of marriage. He had found someone younger and prettier, someone who "makes me feel alive, like I haven't felt in years." He and his wife had no strong incompatibilities. He simply wanted a change, like a man who gets an itch for a newer model car.

A Christian, Daniel knew well the personal and moral consequences of what he was about to do. His decision to leave would inflict permanent damage on his wife and three children. Even so, he said, the force pulling him toward the younger woman, like a powerful magnet, was too strong to resist.

I listened to Daniel's story with sadness and grief, saying little as I tried to absorb the news. Then, during the dessert course, he dropped the bombshell: "Actually, Philip, I have an agenda. The reason I wanted to see you tonight was to ask you a question that's been bothering me. You study the Bible. Do you think God can forgive something as awful as I am about to do?"

Daniel's question lay on the table like a live snake, and I went through three cups of coffee before I dared attempt an answer. In that interval I thought long and hard about the repercussions of grace. How can I dissuade my friend from committing a terrible mistake if he knows forgiveness lies just around the corner? Or, as in Robert Hughes's grim story from Australia, what's to keep a convict from murdering if he knows in advance he'll be forgiven?

There is one "catch" to grace that I must now mention. In the words of C. S. Lewis, "St. Augustine says 'God gives where He finds empty hands.' A man whose hands are full of parcels can't receive a gift." Grace, in other words, must be received. Lewis explains that what I have termed "grace abuse" stems from a confusion of condoning and forgiving: "To condone an evil is simply to ignore it, to treat it as if it were good. But forgiveness needs to be accepted as well as offered if it is to be complete: and a man who admits no guilt can accept no forgiveness."

Here is what I told my friend Daniel, in a nutshell. "Can God forgive you? Of course. You know the Bible. God uses murderers and adulterers. For goodness' sake, a couple of scoundrels named Peter and Paul led the New Testament church. Forgiveness is *our* problem, not God's. What we have to go through to commit sin distances us from God—we change in the very act of rebellion—and there is no guarantee we will ever come back. You ask me about forgiveness now, but will you even want it later, especially if it involves repentance?"

Several months after our conversation, Daniel made his choice and left his family. I have yet to see evidence of repentance. Now he tends to rationalize his decision as a way of escaping an unhappy marriage. He has branded most of his former friends "too narrow-minded and judgmental," and looks instead for people who celebrate his newfound liberation. To me, though, Daniel does not seem very liberated. The price of "freedom" has meant turning his back on those who cared about him most. He also tells me God is not a part of his life right now. "Maybe later," he says.

God took a great risk by announcing forgiveness in advance, and the scandal of grace involves a transfer of that risk to us.

"Truly it is an evil to be full of faults," said Pascal, "but it is a still greater evil to be full of them, and to be unwilling to recognize them."

People divide into two types: not the guilty and the "righteous," as many people think, but rather two different types of guilty people. There are guilty people who acknowledge their wrongs, and guilty ones who do not, two groups who converge in a scene recorded in John 8.

The incident takes place in the temple courts, where Jesus is teaching. A group of Pharisees and teachers of the law interrupt this "church service" by dragging in a woman caught in adultery. Following the custom, she is stripped to the waist as a token of her shame. Terrified, defenseless, publicly humiliated, the woman cowers before Jesus, her arms covering her bare breasts.

Adultery takes two, of course, but the woman stands alone before Jesus. (Perhaps she was caught in bed with a Pharisee?) John makes clear that the accusers have less interest in punishing a crime than in setting a trap for Jesus, and quite a clever trap it is. Moses' law specifies death by stoning for adultery, yet Roman law forbids the Jews from carrying out executions. Will Jesus obey Moses or Rome? Or will he, notorious for his mercy, find some way to let this adulteress off the hook? If so, he must defy Moses' law before a crowd assembled in the very courts of the temple. All eyes fix on Jesus.

At that moment crackling with tension, Jesus does something unique: he bends down and writes on the ground with his finger. This is, in fact, the only scene from the Gospels that shows Jesus writing. For his only written words he chose as his medium a palette of sand, knowing that footsteps, wind, or rain would soon erase them.

John does not tell us what Jesus wrote in the sand. In his movie of Jesus' life, Cecil B. DeMille depicts him spelling out the names of various sins: Adultery, Murder, Pride, Greed, Lust. Each time Jesus writes a word, a few more Pharisees file away. DeMille's guess, like all others, is conjecture. We know only that in this moment freighted with danger Jesus pauses, keeps silent, and fingers words on the ground. Irish poet Seamus Heaney comments that Jesus "marks time in every possible sense of that phrase," concentrating everyone's attention and creating a rift of meaning between what is going to happen and whatever the audience wishes to happen.

Those in the audience no doubt see two categories of actors in the drama: the guilty woman, caught red-handed, and the "righteous" accusers who are, after all, religious professionals. When Jesus finally speaks, he demolishes one of those categories. "If any one of you is without sin," he says, "let him be the first to throw a stone at her."

Again he stoops to write, marking more time, and one by one all the accusers slink away.

Next, Jesus straightens up to address the woman, left alone before him. "Woman, where are they? Has no one condemned you?"

"No one, sir," she says.

And to this woman, dragged in terror to her expected execution, Jesus grants absolution: "Then neither do I condemn you.... Go now and leave your life of sin."

Thus in a brilliant stroke Jesus replaces the two assumed categories, righteous and guilty, with two different categories: sinners who admit and sinners who deny. The woman caught in adultery helplessly admitted her guilt. Far more problematic were people like the Pharisees who denied or repressed guilt. They too needed hands empty for grace. Dr. Paul Tournier expresses this pattern in the language of psychiatry: "God blots out conscious guilt, but He brings to consciousness repressed guilt."

The scene from John 8 rattles me because by nature I identify more with the accusers than the accused. I deny far more than I confess. Cloaking my sins under a robe of respectability, I seldom if ever let myself get caught in a blatant, public indiscretion. Yet if I understand this story correctly, the sinful woman is the one nearest the kingdom of God. Indeed, I can only advance in the kingdom if I become like that woman: trembling, humbled, without excuse, my palms open to receive God's grace.

That stance of openness to receive is what I call the "catch" to grace. It must be received, and the Christian term for that act is *repentance*, the doorway to grace. C. S. Lewis said repentance is not something God arbitrarily demands of us; "It is simply a description of what going back is like." In terms of the parable of the Prodigal Son, repentance is the flight home that leads to joyful celebration. It opens the way to a future, to a relationship restored.

The Bible's many fierce passages on sin appear in a new light once I understand God's desire to press me toward repentance, the doorway to grace. Jesus told Nicodemus, "For God did not send his Son into the world to condemn the world, but to save the world through him." In other words, he awakes guilt for my own benefit. God seeks not to crush me but to liberate me, and liberation requires a defenseless spirit like that of the woman caught red-handed, not the haughty spirit of the Pharisees.

Unless a flaw comes into the light, it cannot be healed. Alcoholics know that unless a person acknowledges the problem—"I am an alcoholic"—there is no hope of cure. For skilled deniers, such a confession may require excruciating interventions by family and friends, who "write on the ground" the shameful truth until the alcoholic admits it.*

In Tournier's words,

> . . . believers who are most desperate about themselves are the ones who express most forcefully their confidence in grace. There is a St. Paul . . . and a St. Francis of Assisi, who affirmed that he was the greatest sinner of all men; and a Calvin, who asserted that man was incapable of doing good and of knowing God by his own power. . . .
>
> "It is the saints who have a sense of sin," as Father Daniélou says; "the sense of sin is the measure of a soul's awareness of God."

---

*Alcoholics use the term "dry drunk" to describe an alcoholic who stops drinking but remains in denial, refusing to admit he has a problem. Dry but miserable, he makes everyone around him miserable also. He still manipulates others and pulls the strings of codependency. Yet because he no longer drinks, he no longer has intervals of happiness. Family members may even try to get such an alcoholic to drink again, for relief; they want their "happy drunk" back. Author Keith Miller likens this person to a hypocrite in church, who changes the outside but not the inside. Real change, for the alcoholic as well as for the Christian, must begin with admitting the need for grace. Denial blocks grace.

It is possible, warns the biblical writer Jude, to "change the grace of our God into a license for immorality." Not even an emphasis on repentance erases this danger completely. Both my friend Daniel and the Australian convict would agree in theory to the need for repentance, and both were scheming to exploit a loophole of grace by getting what they wanted now and then repenting of it later. At first a devious idea forms in the back of the mind. *It's something I want. Yeah, I know, it's wrong. But why don't I just go ahead anyway? I can always get forgiveness later.* The idea grows into an obsession, and ultimately grace becomes "a license for immorality."

Christians have responded to this danger in various ways. Martin Luther, intoxicated with God's grace, sometimes scoffed at the potential for abuse. "If you are a preacher of grace, do not preach a fictitious, but a true, grace; and if the grace is true, carry a true, and not a fictitious sin," he wrote his friend Melanchthon. "Be a sinner and sin vigorously.... It is sufficient that we recognize through the wealth of God's glory, the lamb who bears the sin of the world; from this, sin does not sever us, even if thousands, thousands of times in one day we should fornicate or murder."

Others, alarmed at the prospect of Christians fornicating or murdering thousands of times in one day, have called Luther to task for his hyperbole. The Bible, after all, presents grace as a healing counterforce to sin. How can the two coexist in the same person? Shouldn't we "grow in grace," as Peter commands? Shouldn't our family likeness to God increase? "Christ accepts us as we are," wrote Walter Trobisch, "but when he accepts us, we cannot remain as we are."

Twentieth-century theologian Dietrich Bonhoeffer coined the phrase "cheap grace" as a way of summarizing grace abuse. Living in Nazi Germany, he was appalled by the cowardly way in which Christians were responding to Hitler's threat. Lutheran pastors preached grace from the pulpit on Sundays, then kept quiet the rest of the week as the Nazis pursued their policies of racism, euthanasia, and finally genocide. Bonhoeffer's book *The Cost of Discipleship* highlights the many New Testament passages commanding Christians to attain holiness. Every call to conversion, he insisted, includes a call to discipleship, to Christ-likeness.

In the book of Romans, Paul bores in on these very issues. No other biblical passage gives such a focused look at grace in all its mystery, and for perspective on the scandal of grace we must turn to Romans 6–7.

The first few chapters of Romans have tolled a bell on the miserable state of humanity, with the damning conclusion: "All have sinned and fall short of the glory of God." Like a fanfare introducing a new symphonic movement, the next two chapters tell of a grace that wipes out any penalty: "But where sin increased, grace increased all the more." Grand theology to be sure, but such a sweeping declaration introduces the very practical problem I have been circling around: Why be good if you know in advance you will be forgiven? Why strive to be Just As God Wants when he accepts me Just As I Am?

Paul knows he has opened a theological floodgate. Romans 6 asks bluntly, "What shall we say, then? Shall we go on sinning so that grace may increase?" and again "What then? Shall we sin because we are not under law but under grace?" Paul gives a short, explosive answer to both questions: "By no means!" Other translations are more colorful: the King James Version, for example, has it, "God forbid!"

What absorbs the apostle in these dense, passionate chapters is, quite simply, the scandal of grace. The question "Why be good?" lies at the heart of Paul's argument. If you know in advance you'll be forgiven, why not join the bacchanalian pagans? Eat, drink, and be merry, for tomorrow God will forgive. Paul cannot ignore this apparent loophole.

Paul's first illustration (Romans 6:1–14) speaks directly to the point. He poses the question, If grace increases as sin increases, then why not sin as much as possible in order to give God more opportunity to extend grace? Although such reasoning may sound perverse, at various times Christians have followed exactly that loopy logic. A third-century bishop was shocked to see devout martyrs of the Christian faith devote their last nights in prison to drunkenness, revelry, and promiscuity. Since martyrs' death would make them perfect, they reasoned, what would it matter if they spent their last hours sinning? And in Cromwell's England, an extremist sect known as the Ranters developed a doctrine of the "holiness of sin." One leader cursed for an entire hour in the pulpit of a London church; others got drunk and blasphemed in public.

Paul has no time for such ethical convolutions. To refute them, he begins with a basic analogy that starkly contrasts death and life. "We died to sin; how can we live in it any longer?" he asks, incredulous. No Christian resurrected to new life should be pining for the grave. Sin has the stench of death about it. Why would anyone choose it?

Paul's vivid imagery of death versus life does not fully settle the question at hand, however, for wickedness does not always have the stench of death about it—at least, not to fallen human beings. Grace abuse is a real temptation. Flip through the ads in any current magazine and you'll see temptations toward lust, greed, envy, and pride that make sin downright appealing. Like farm pigs, we enjoy a good wallow in the mud.

Moreover, although Christians may have "died to sin" in some theoretical way, it keeps popping back to life. A friend of mine who led a Bible study on this passage had one college coed come to him afterwards with a puzzled expression. "I know it says we've died to sin," she said. "But in my life sin seems very much alive." Paul, a realist, recognized this fact, or else he would not have advised us in the same passage, "*Count* yourselves dead to sin" and "Do not let sin reign in your mortal body."

Harvard biologist Edward O. Wilson performed a rather bizarre experiment on ants that may supplement Paul's illustration. After noticing that it took ants a few days to recognize one of their crumpled nestmates as having died, he determined that ants identified death by clues of smell, not visually. As the ant's body began to decompose, other ants would infallibly carry it out of the nest to a refuse pile. After many tries, Wilson narrowed down the precise chemical clue to oleic acid. If the ants smelled oleic acid, they would carry out the corpse; any other smell, they ignored. Their instinct was so strong that if Wilson daubed oleic acid on bits of paper, other ants would dutifully carry the paper to the ant cemetery.

In a final twist, Wilson painted oleic acid on the bodies of living ants. Sure enough, their nestmates seized them and marched them, their legs and antennae wriggling in protest, out to the ant cemetery. Thus deposited, the indignant "living dead" cleaned themselves off before returning to the nest. If they did not remove every trace of the oleic acid, the nestmates would promptly seize them again and return them to the cemetery. They had to be certifiably alive, judged solely by smell, before being accepted back into the nest.

I think of that image, "dead" ants acting very much alive, when I read Paul's first illustration in Romans 6. Sin may be dead, but it stubbornly wriggles back to life.

Immediately, Paul restates the dilemma in a subtly different way: "Shall we sin because we are not under law but under grace?" (6:15). Does grace offer a license, a sort of free pass through the ethical maze of life? I have already described an Australian murderer and an American adulterer who came to this very conclusion.

"I suppose there's some reason for keeping rules while you're young . . . so you'll have enough energy left to break them all when you get old," said Mark Twain, who valiantly tried to follow his own advice. Why not, if you know in advance you'll be forgiven? Again Paul lets out an incredulous "God forbid!" How do you answer someone whose main goal in life is to push the outer edges of the envelope of grace? Has such a person ever truly experienced grace?

Paul's second analogy (6:15–23), human slavery, adds a new dimension to the discussion. "You used to be slaves to sin," he begins, drawing a very apt comparison. Sin is a slave master that controls us whether we like it or not. Paradoxically, a headlong pursuit of freedom often turns into bondage: insist on the freedom to lose your temper whenever you feel anger, and you will soon find yourself a slave to rage. In modern life, those things that teenagers do to express their freedom—tobacco, alcohol, drugs, pornography—become their relentless masters.

For many, sin feels like a kind of slavery—or in modern terms, an addiction. Any member of a twelve-step group can describe the process. Set a firm resolution against yielding to your addiction, and for a time you bask in freedom. How many, though, experience the sad return to bondage.

Here is a precise description of the paradox from the novelist François Mauriac:

> One by one the passions awake, prowl around and sniff at the object of their covetousness; they are attacking the poor undecided soul from the back and he is done for. How often has he got to be hurled into the ditch, to be stifled by the mud, to grasp at the edges and arise to the light again, to feel his hands give way and return again to the darkness, before he finally submits to the law of the spiritual life—the least understood law in the world and the one that repels him most though without it he cannot attain the grace of perseverance. What is required is the renunciation of the ego, and this is expressed perfectly in the phrase of Pascal: "Entire and sweet renunciation. Absolute submission to Jesus Christ and to my spiritual director."
>
> People may laugh and scoff at you for being unworthy of the title of free man and for having to submit yourself to a master.... But this enslavement is really a miraculous liberation, for even when you were free you spent the whole time forging chains for yourself and putting them on, riveting them tighter and tighter each moment. During the years when you thought you were free you submitted like an ox to the yoke of your countless hereditary ills. From the hour of your birth not one of your crimes has failed to go on living, has failed to imprison you more and more every day, has failed to beget other crimes. The Man you submit yourself to *does not want you to be free to be a slave:* he breaks the circle of your fetters, and, against your half-extinguished and still-smouldering desires, He kindles and re-kindles the fire of Grace.

In yet a third illustration (7:1–6), Paul likens the spiritual life to marriage. The basic analogy is not new, for the Bible often presents God as a lover pursuing a fickle bride. The intensity of feeling we have for the one person we choose to spend life with mirrors the passion God feels toward us, and God wants his passion returned in kind.

Far more than death, far more than slavery, the analogy of marriage provides an answer to the question Paul started with: Why be good? Really, that is the wrong question. It should be: Why love?

One summer I had to learn basic German in order to finish a graduate degree. What a wretched summer! On delightful evenings while my friends sailed on Lake Michigan, rode bikes, and sipped cappuccinos in patio cafés, I was holed up with a Kapomeister tutor, parsing German verbs. Five nights a week, three hours a night I spent memorizing vocabulary and word endings that I would never again use. I endured such torture for one purpose only: to pass the test and get my degree.

What if the school registrar had promised me, "Philip, we want you to study hard, learn German, and take the test, but we promise you in advance that you'll get a passing grade. Your diploma has already been filled out." Do you think I would have spent every delectable summer evening inside a hot, stuffy apartment? Not a chance. In a nutshell, that was the theological dilemma Paul confronts in Romans.

Why learn German? There are noble reasons, to be sure—languages broaden the mind and expand the range of communication—but these had never motivated me to study German before. I studied for selfish reasons, to finish a degree, and only the threat of consequences hanging over me caused me to reorder my summer priorities. Today, I remember very little of the German I crammed into my brain. "The old way of the written code" (Paul's description of the Old Testament law) produces short-term results at best.

What would inspire me to learn German? I can think of one powerful incentive. If my wife, the woman I fell in love with, spoke only German, I would have learned the language in record time. Why? I would have a desperate desire to communicate *mit einer schönen Frau.* I would have stayed up late at night parsing verbs and placing them properly at the ends of my love-letter sentences, treasuring each addition to my vocabulary as a new way of expressing myself to the one I loved. I would have learned German unbegrudgingly, with the relationship itself as my reward.

That reality helps me understand Paul's gruff "God forbid!" response to the question "Shall we go on sinning that grace may increase?" Would a groom on his wedding night hold the following conversation with his bride? "Honey, I love you so much, and I'm eager to spend my life with you. But I need to work out a few details. Now that we're married, how far can I go with other women? Can I sleep with them? Kiss them? You don't mind a few affairs now and then, do you? I know it might hurt you, but just think of all the opportunities you'll have to forgive me after I betray you!" To such a Don Juan the only reasonable response is a slap in the face and a "God forbid!" Obviously, he does not understand the first thing about love.

Similarly, if we approach God with a "What can I get away with?" attitude, it proves we do not grasp what God has in mind for us. God wants something far beyond the relationship I might have with a slave master, who will enforce my obedience with a whip. God is not a boss or a business manager or a magic genie to serve at our command.

Indeed, God wants something more intimate than the closest relationship on earth, the lifetime bond between a man and a woman. What God wants is not a good performance, but my heart. I do "good works" for my wife not in order to earn credit but to express my love for her. Likewise, God wants me to serve "in the new way of the Spirit": not out of compulsion but out of desire. "Discipleship," says Clifford Williams, "simply means the life which springs from grace."

If I had to summarize the primary New Testament motivation for "being good" in one word, I would choose *gratitude*. Paul begins most of his letters with a summary of the riches we possess in Christ. If we comprehend what Christ has done for us, then surely out of gratitude we will strive to live "worthy" of such great love. We will strive for holiness not to make God love us but because he already does. As Paul told Titus, it is the grace of God that "teaches us to say 'No' to ungodliness and worldly passions, and to live self-controlled, upright and godly lives."

In her memoir *Ordinary Time*, the Catholic writer Nancy Mairs tells of her years of mutiny against childhood images of a "Daddy God," who could only be pleased if she followed a list of onerous prescriptions and prohibitions:

> The fact that these took their most basic form as commandments suggested that human nature had to be forced into goodness; left to its own devices, it would prefer idols, profanity, leisurely Sunday mornings with bagels and the *New York Times*, disrespect for authority, murder, adultery, theft, lies, and everything belonging to the guy next door.... I was forever on the perilous verge of doing a don't, to atone for which I had to beg forgiveness from the very being who had set me up for trespass, by forbidding behaviors he clearly expected me to commit, in the first place: the God of the Gotcha, you might say.

Mairs broke a lot of those rules, felt constantly guilty, and then, in her words, "learned to thrive in the care of" a God who "asks for the single act that will make transgression impossible: love."

The best reason to be good is to want to be good. Internal change requires relationship. It requires love. "Who can be good, if not made so by loving?" asked Augustine. When Augustine made the famous statement, "If you but love God you may do as you incline," he was perfectly serious. A person who truly loves God will be inclined to please God, which is why Jesus and Paul both summed up the entire law in the simple command, "Love God."

If we truly grasped the wonder of God's love for us, the devious question that prompted Romans 6 and 7—What can I get away with?—would never even occur to us. We would spend our days trying to fathom, not exploit, God's grace.

But can he want the grape, who hath the wine?

George Herbert

FIFTEEN

Grace Avoidance

I have had many close-up encounters with legalism. I came out of a Southern fundamentalist culture that frowned on coed swimming, wearing shorts, jewelry or makeup, dancing, bowling, and reading the Sunday newspaper. Alcohol was a sin of a different order, with the sulfurous stench of hellfire about it.

Later I attended a Bible college where, in an era of miniskirts, deans legislated a skirt length below the knee. If a student wore a skirt of dubious length, the Dean of Women would require her to kneel to see if it touched the floor. Slacks on women were forbidden except during hayrides, when they must be worn *under skirts* for modesty's sake. A rival Christian college went so far as to ban polka-dot dresses, since the dots might draw attention to a "suggestive" part of the body. Male students at our school had their own rules, including a restriction against hair covering the ears and a ban on facial hair. Dating was strictly regulated: although I got engaged before my senior year, I could see my fiancée only during the dinner hour and could not kiss her or even hold hands.

The college also attempted to monitor a student's relationship with God. Early each morning a bell rang, summoning us to rise and have personal devotions. If caught sleeping in, we would have to read and write a report on a book such as *The Christian's Secret of a Happy Life*. (I wonder whether the authorities considered the long-term impact of assigning such books as punishment.)

Some students dropped out of school, some gladly kept the rules, and some learned to fake it, leading a double life. I survived in part because of the insights I gained in reading Erving Goffman's classic work *Asylums.* The great sociologist examined a series of what he termed "total institutions," including monasteries, private boarding schools, insane asylums, prisons, and military academies. Each of these had a long list of arbitrary, depersonalizing rules which they used as a means to break down individuality and enforce conformity. Each was a finely tuned system of ungrace.

Goffman's book helped me to see the Bible college, and fundamentalism in general, as a controlled environment, a subculture. I had been resenting that environment, but now I began to realize that everyone grows up in a subculture. Some (Hasidic Jews, fundamentalist Moslems) are more legalistic even than Southern fundamentalists; some (inner-city gangs, right-wing militia groups) are far more dangerous; some (the video game/MTV subculture) seem benign on the surface but may prove insidious. My resistance to fundamentalism subsided as I considered the alternatives.

I began to see the Bible college as a kind of spiritual West Point Academy: both required neater beds, shorter hair, and more rigid posture than other schools. If I did not like that, I could go elsewhere.

What bothers me most, in retrospect, was the Bible college's attempt to relate all their rules to God's law. In the sixty-six-page rule book—we joked that it included one page for each book of the Bible—and in chapel services, the deans and professors would painstakingly try to ground each rule in biblical principles. I seethed at their contorted attempts to condemn long hair on men, aware that Jesus and most of the biblical characters we studied probably had longer hair than ours and facial hair to boot. The rule about hair length had more to do with the likelihood of offending supporters than with anything in Scripture, but no one dared admit it.

I could not find one word in the Bible about rock music, skirt lengths, or cigarette smoking, and the ban against alcohol put us on the side of John the Baptist, not Jesus. Yet authorities in that school made a determined effort to present all these rules as part of the gospel. The subculture got muddled with the message.

I should clarify that in many ways I am now grateful for the severity of fundamentalism, which may have kept me out of trouble. Strict legalism pulls in the bounds of deviance: we might sneak off to a bowling alley, but would never think of touching liquor or—horrors!—drugs. Though I can find nothing in the Bible against cigarettes, I am glad that fundamentalism scared me away from them even before the Surgeon General mounted a bully pulpit.

In short, I have little resentment against these particular rules but much resentment against the way they were presented. I had the constant, pounding sense that following an external code of behavior was the way to please God—more, to make God love me. It has taken me years to distill the gospel out of the subculture in which I first encountered it. Sadly, many of my friends gave up on the effort, never getting to Jesus because the pettiness of the church blocked the way.

I hesitate to write about the dangers of legalism at a time when both church and society seem to be careening in the opposite direction. At the same time, I know nothing that represents a greater threat to grace. Legalism may "work" in an institution such as a Bible college or the Marine Corps. In a world of ungrace, structured shame has considerable power. But there is a cost, an incalculable cost: ungrace does not work in a relationship with God. I have come to see legalism in its pursuit of false purity as an elaborate scheme of grace avoidance. You can know the law by heart without knowing the heart of it.

I have a friend who tried to help a middle-aged man overcome his allergic reaction to the church, in his case due to an overly strict upbringing in Catholic schools. "Are you really going to let some little old nuns dressed in black and white keep you from entering the kingdom of God?" my friend asked. Tragically, for many the answer is yes.

As I study the life of Jesus, one fact consistently surprises me: the group that made Jesus angriest was the group that, externally at least, he most resembled. Scholars agree that Jesus closely matched the profile of a Pharisee. He obeyed the Torah, or Mosaic law, quoted leading Pharisees, and often took their side in public arguments. Yet Jesus singled out the Pharisees for his strongest attacks. "Snakes!" he called them. "Brood of vipers! Fools! Hypocrites! Blind guides! Whitewashed tombs!"

What provoked such outbursts? The Pharisees had much in common with those whom the press might call Bible-belt fundamentalists today. They devoted their lives to following God, gave away an exact tithe, obeyed every minute law in the Torah, and sent out missionaries to gain new converts. Against the relativists and secularists of the first century, they held firm to traditional values. Rarely involved in sexual sin or violent crime, the Pharisees made model citizens.

Jesus' fierce denunciations of the Pharisees show how seriously he viewed the toxic threat of legalism. Its dangers are elusive, slippery, hard to pin down, and I have scoured the New Testament in search of them—especially Luke 11 and Matthew 23, where Jesus morally dissects the Pharisees. I mention them here because I believe these dangers represent as great a threat in the twentieth century as they did in the first. Legalism takes different forms now than it did in my childhood, but by no means has it gone away.

Overall, Jesus condemned the legalists' emphasis on *externals.* "You Pharisees clean the outside of the cup and dish, but inside you are full of greed and wickedness," he said. Expressions of love for God had, over time, evolved into ways of impressing others. In Jesus' day, religious people wore gaunt and hungry looks during a brief fast, prayed grandiosely in public, and wore portions of the Bible strapped to their bodies.

In his Sermon on the Mount, Jesus denounced the motives behind such seemingly harmless practices:

> So when you give to the needy, do not announce it with trumpets, as the hypocrites do in the synagogues and on the streets, to be honored by men. I tell you the truth, they have received their reward in full. But when you give to the needy, do not let your left hand know what your right hand is doing, so that your giving may be in secret. Then your Father, who sees what is done in secret, will reward you.
>
> And when you pray, do not be like the hypocrites, for they love to pray standing in the synagogues and on the street corners to be seen by men. I tell you the truth, they have received their reward in full. But when you pray, go into your room, close the door and pray to your Father, who is unseen.

I have seen what happens when Christians ignore Jesus' commands. For instance, the church of my childhood conducted an annual funding drive for foreign missions.* From the pulpit, the pastor would call out the names and amounts of each pledge that came in: "Mr. Jones, five hundred dollars . . . and listen to this—the Sanderson family, two thousand dollars! Praise the Lord!" We all applauded and said "Amen!" and the Sandersons beamed. As a child I craved that kind of public recognition, not to further the cause of foreign missions but to get approval and acclaim. Once, I hauled a large bag of pennies down front, and never did I feel more righteous than when the pastor stopped the proceedings, commended me, and prayed over my pennies. I had my reward.

Today, the temptation still exists. When I gave a substantial contribution to a nonprofit organization, the recipients put me in a President's Club, with my name highlighted in the organizational newsletter. I got special mailings from the president, which, I was assured, only went to an elite group of donors. I admit that I relished the flattering letters and thank-you gifts. They made me feel generous and righteous—until I went back and read the Sermon on the Mount.

Leo Tolstoy, who battled legalism all his life, understood the weaknesses of a religion based on externals. The title of one of his books says it well: *The Kingdom of God Is Within You.* According to Tolstoy, all religious systems tend to promote external rules, or moralism. In contrast, Jesus refused to define a set of rules that his followers could then fulfill with a sense of satisfaction. One can never "arrive" in light of such sweeping commands as "Love the Lord your God with all your heart and with all your soul and with all your mind. . . . Be perfect, therefore, as your heavenly Father is perfect."

Tolstoy drew a contrast between Jesus' approach and that of all other religions:

> The test of observance of external religious teachings is whether or not our conduct conforms with their decrees [Observe

*Yes, this is the same church that excluded black members. We would raise over a hundred thousand dollars—big money in the 1950s and 1960s—to send missionaries to people of other color, but not allow any inside our doors.

> the Sabbath. Get circumcised. Tithe.] Such conformity is indeed possible.
>
> The test of observance of Christ's teachings is our consciousness of our failure to attain an ideal perfection. The degree to which we draw near this perfection cannot be seen; all we can see is the extent of our deviation.
>
> A man who professes an external law is like someone standing in the light of a lantern fixed to a post. It is light all round him, but there is nowhere further for him to walk. A man who professes the teaching of Christ is like a man carrying a lantern before him on a long, or not so long, pole: the light is in front of him, always lighting up fresh ground and always encouraging him to walk further.

In other words, the proof of spiritual maturity is not how "pure" you are but awareness of your impurity. That very awareness opens the door to grace.

Woe to you, because you load people down with burdens they can hardly carry." Over time, the spirit of law-keeping stiffens into *extremism.* I know of no legalism that does not seek to enlarge its domain of intolerance.

The scribes and Pharisees who studied Moses' law, for example, tacked on many additions to its 613 regulations. The rabbi Eliezer the Great specified how often a common laborer, ass driver, camel driver, or sailor should have sex with his wife. Pharisees added scores of emendations on Sabbath behavior alone. A man could ride a donkey without breaking the Sabbath rules, but if he carried a switch to speed up the animal he would be guilty of laying a burden on it. A woman could not look in the mirror on the Sabbath lest she see a gray hair and be tempted to pluck it out. You could swallow vinegar but not gargle it.

Whatever Moses had said, the Pharisees could improve on. The third commandment, "You shall not misuse the name of the Lord," became a ban against using the Lord's name at all, and thus to this day devout Jews write "G–d" instead of "God," and never speak the word. Just to be on the safe side scholars interpreted the law "Do not cook a young goat in its mother's milk" as forbidding the mixture of meat and dairy products, and for this reason kosher apartments, hospitals, and nursing homes still come equipped with two kitchens, one for meat and one for dairy. "You shall not commit adultery" led to Pharisees' rules against talking to or even looking at women who were not their wives. "Bleeding Pharisees," who had lowered their heads and bumped into walls, wore their bruises as badges of holiness.

(A disregard for these additions to Moses' law got Jesus into constant trouble. On the Sabbath he healed people and let his disciples pick corn if they got hungry. He conversed with women in broad daylight. He ate with the "unclean" and claimed that nothing people ate could make them unclean. Most shockingly, he addressed God as "Abba.")

Church history reveals that Christians sometimes outdid the Pharisees in their extremism. By the fourth century monks were living on a diet of bread, salt, and water. One devised a cell so small he had to double up his body to enter it; another spent ten years in a circular cage. Grazier-monks lived in the forests and grubbed for wild herbs and roots; some wore only a loincloth of thorns. Simeon Stylites set the standard for extremism: he lived on top of a column for thirty-seven years and prostrated himself 1,244 times a day.

Christians in the United States, a bastion of freedom and pragmatism, have had their own flings with extremism. Sects like the Shakers forbade marriage and sex (guaranteeing their eventual extinction). The great revivalist Charles Finney refrained from coffee and tea, and insisted that the school he founded, Oberlin College, bar such stimulants as pepper, mustard, oil, and vinegar. More recently, a friend of mine actually preached a funeral sermon for a young Seventh-Day Adventist who had starved himself to death out of concern over which foods were permissible to eat.

We laugh, or cry as the case may be, at such symptoms of extremism, yet Christians must acknowledge that these tendencies are a relentless part of our heritage. Worldwide, the pattern has shifted, with the "Christian

West" now known for its decadence, not its extreme legalism. Meanwhile, some Muslim countries deploy morals police to club women who dare to drive or who venture into public without veils. And hotels in Israel install "Shabbat" elevators, which on the Sabbath stop at every floor so that Orthodox Jews can avoid work by not having to push the buttons.

The pendulum swings, though, and in some Christian groups extremism is on the rise. Where legalism takes root, the prickly thorns of extremism eventually branch out.

Legalism is a subtle danger because no one thinks of himself as a legalist. My own rules seem necessary; other people's rules seem excessively strict.

You give a tenth of your spices—mint, dill and cummin. But you have neglected the more important matters of the law—justice, mercy and faithfulness.... You blind guides! You strain out a gnat but swallow a camel."

Jesus did not fault the Pharisees for extremism in itself—I doubt he really cared what they ate or how many times they washed their hands. But he did care that they imposed extremism on others and that they focused on *trivialities,* neglecting more weighty matters. The same teachers who tithed their kitchen spices had little to say about the injustice and oppression in Palestine. And when Jesus healed a person on the Sabbath, his critics seemed far more concerned about protocol than about the sick person.

The low point of legalism played itself out at Jesus' execution: the Pharisees took pains to avoid entering Pilate's palace before the Passover feast and arranged the crucifixion so as not to interfere with Sabbath rules. Thus the greatest crime in history was carried out with strict attention to legalistic detail.

I have seen many modern-day illustrations of legalism's trend toward trivialities. The church I grew up in had much to say about hairstyle, jewelry, and rock music but not a word about racial injustice and the plight of blacks in the South. In Bible college, not once did I hear a reference to the Holocaust in Germany, perhaps the most heinous sin in all history. We were too busy measuring skirts to worry about such contemporary political issues as nuclear war, racism, or world hunger. I met South African students who came from churches where young Christians did not chew gum or pray with their hands in their pockets, and where blue jeans made a person spiritually suspect. Yet those same churches vigorously defended the racist doctrine of apartheid.

A U.S. delegate to the Baptist World Alliance Congress in Berlin in 1934 sent back this report of what he found under Hitler's regime:

> It was a great relief to be in a country where salacious sex literature cannot be sold; where putrid motion pictures and gangster films cannot be shown. The new Germany has burned great masses of corrupting books and magazines along with its bonfires of Jewish and communistic libraries.

The same delegate defended Hitler as a leader who did not smoke or drink, who wanted women to dress modestly, and who opposed pornography.

It is all too easy to point fingers at German Christians of the 1930s, southern fundamentalists in the 1960s, or South African Calvinists of the 1970s. What sobers me is that contemporary Christians may someday be judged just as harshly. What trivialities do we obsess over, and what weighty matters of the law—justice, mercy, faithfulness—might we be missing? Does God care more about nose rings or about urban decay? Grunge music or world hunger? Worship styles or a culture of violence?

Author Tony Campolo, who makes a regular circuit as a chapel speaker on Christian college campuses, for a time used this provocation to make a point. "The United Nations reports that over ten thousand people starve to death each day, and most of you don't give a sh––. However, what is even more tragic is that most of you are more concerned about the fact that I just said a bad word than you are about the fact that ten thousand people are going to die today." The responses proved his point: in nearly every case Tony got a letter from the chaplain or president of the college protesting his foul language. The letters never mentioned world hunger.

Much of the behavior considered sinful in my upbringing is now common practice in many evangelical churches. Although the manifestations have changed, the spirit of legalism has not. Now I am more likely to encounter a legalism of thought. Author friends of mine who dare to question the received doctrine on abortion or homosexuality, for example, face the same judgment today that a "social drinking" Christian faced in the fundamentalist subculture.

I have already mentioned the abuse Tony Campolo has received for his pleas that we show more compassion to homosexuals. Another friend, Karen Mains, lost her career as a broadcaster after a campaign critical of her writings. Eugene Peterson's "tampering with God's Word" in his New Testament paraphrase, *The Message*, made him the target of a self-proclaimed cult-watcher. Richard Foster dared to use words like "meditation" in his writings on spiritual discipline, which put him under suspicion as a New Ager. Chuck Colson told me the ugliest mail he has ever received came from Christians in response to his accepting the Templeton Prize for Progress in Religion, which sometimes goes to non-Christians. "Our brethren were far less charitable than the secular media during the days of Watergate," he said, in a terrible indictment. The mail heated up even more when he signed a statement of mutual cooperation with Catholics.

Be on your guard against the yeast of the Pharisees, which is hypocrisy.... Do not do what they do, for they do not practice what they preach." The word *hypocrisy* means, simply, "putting on a mask." Evidently Jesus himself coined the word, borrowing it from the Greek actors, or *hypocritēs,* who entertained crowds at an outdoor theater near his home. It describes a person who puts on a face to make a good impression.

As part of his Fulbright fellowship, my friend Terry Muck studied legalism among Buddhist monks in Sri Lanka. The monks had all agreed to follow the 212 rules of the Buddha, many of which were now outdated and impractical. Terry wondered how the monks could reconcile their need to live in the modern world with their adherence to an ancient legalistic code. For example, the Buddha had specified that no monk should carry money, and yet Terry regularly observed monks paying fares on city buses. "Do you follow the 212 rules?" he asked them. "Yes." "Do you handle money?" "Yes." "Are you aware of the rule against money?" "Yes." "Do you follow all the rules?" "Yes."

The rules also forbade eating after noon, for the monks lived on handouts and the Buddha did not want his followers to burden housewives. Modern monks got around that rule by stopping the clock at noon each day; after the evening meal, they reset the clock to the correct time.

I have used examples from Buddhism, but in my experience hypocrisy is one of the most common reasons why people reject Christianity. Christians profess "family values," but some studies show that they rent X-rated videos, divorce their spouses, and abuse their children at about the same rate as everybody else.

By its very nature legalism encourages hypocrisy because it defines a set of behavior that may cloak what is going on inside. At a Bible college or Christian camp, and even in church, everyone learns how to look "spiritual." The emphasis on externals makes it easy for a person to fake it, to conform even while suppressing, or hiding, inner problems. Years after I left Bible college I learned that some of my fellow students suffered from deep inner turmoil—depression, homosexuality, addictions—that had gone unaddressed during their time there. They concentrated instead on conforming to the behavior around them.

One of the most sobering passages in the New Testament, and one of few that shows direct punishment, appears in Acts 5: the story of Ananias and Sapphira. This couple had done a very good deed, selling a piece of property and donating much of the proceeds to the church. They did only one thing wrong: in an effort to appear more spiritual, they acted as if they were donating *all* the proceeds. In other words, they misrepresented themselves spiritually. The harsh response to Ananias and Sapphira shows how seriously God views hypocrisy.

I know of only two alternatives to hypocrisy: perfection or honesty. Since I have never met a person who loves the Lord our God with all her heart, mind, and soul, and loves her neighbor as herself, I do not view perfection as a realistic alternative. Our only option, then, is honesty that leads to repentance. As the Bible shows, God's grace can cover any sin, including murder, infidelity, or betrayal. Yet by definition grace must be received, and hypocrisy disguises our need to receive grace. When the masks fall, hypocrisy is exposed as an elaborate ruse to avoid grace.

Everything they do is done for men to see . . . they love the place of honor at banquets and the most important seats in the synagogues; they love to be greeted in the marketplaces and to have men call them 'Rabbi.'"

Jesus' critique centered on what legalism does to the law-keeper: it fosters feelings of *pride* and *competition.* Instead of getting on with the task of creating a just society that would shine as a light to the Gentiles, the Pharisees narrowed their vision and began competing with each other. Caught up in trying to impress each other with spiritual calisthenics, they lost contact with the real enemy, as well as with the rest of the world. "From silly devotions and sour-faced saints, spare us, O Lord," prayed Teresa of Ávila.

As a recovering legalist, I have to remind myself that for all their strictness the Pharisees did not seem to resent the obligations of the law. They kept inventing new rules, after all. The Pharisees saw strictness as a means of achieving, of gaining status. Jesus condemned that pride, and also condemned the tiered spirituality that ranked some sins as acceptable (hatred, materialism, lust, divorce) and others as unacceptable (murder, adultery, breaking Sabbath rules).

We Christians have our own grouping of "acceptable" and "unacceptable" sins. As long as we avoid the most egregious sins, we feel pretty good about our spiritual status. The problem is, our understanding of egregious sins keeps changing. In the Middle Ages, charging interest was considered immoral, so much so that Jews were conscripted to do the dirty work. Nowadays Christians enjoy credit cards, home mortgage loans, and mutual fund accounts without a pang of guilt. The list of seven deadly sins included gluttony, envy, and spiritual sloth or "melancholy"—behavior that rarely attracts a sermon today.

During the Victorian era sexual sins ranked at the very top—or bottom, depending on how you look at it—so much so that the word "immorality" came to denote sexual sins. When I grew up divorce and drinking headed the list. Now, in the modern evangelical church, abortion and homosexuality probably rank highest.

Jesus took an altogether different approach to sin. Rather than ranking sins as significant or less significant, he raised his listeners' sights to a perfect God, before whom all of us are sinners. We all fall back on the grace of God. Isaiah put it in earthy language: all our righteous acts, he said, are as "filthy rags," literally, "soiled undergarments."

In an ironic way, blatant sinners have a kind of advantage when it comes to grace. The author Graham Greene used to say his religious faith intensified when he slipped into some immorality, for then he would go to church and confession out of desperation. He had no excuse, no grounds on which to defend his behavior.

Jesus' story of the Prodigal Son makes a similar point. The prodigal son had no leg to stand on, no possible basis for spiritual pride. By any measure of spiritual competition he had failed, and now he had nothing to lean against but grace. God's love and forgiveness extended equally to the virtuous elder brother, of course, but that son, too busy comparing himself to his irresponsible sibling, was blinded to the truth about himself. In the words of Henri Nouwen, "The lostness of the resentful 'saint' is so hard to reach precisely because it is so closely wedded to the desire to be good and virtuous." Nouwen confesses:

> I know, from my own life, how diligently I have tried to be good, acceptable, likable, and a worthy example for others. There was always the conscious effort to avoid the pitfalls of sin and the constant fear of giving in to temptation. But with all of that there came a seriousness, a moralistic intensity—and even a touch of fanaticism—that made it increasingly difficult to feel at home in my Father's house. I became less free, less spontaneous, less playful. . . .

> The more I reflect on the elder son in me, the more I realize how deeply rooted this form of lostness really is and how hard it is to return home from there. Returning home from a lustful escapade seems so much easier than returning home from a cold anger that has rooted itself in the deepest corners of my being.

The spiritual games we play, many of which begin with the best of motives, can perversely lead us away from God, because they lead us away from grace. Repentance, not proper behavior or even holiness, is the doorway to grace. And the opposite of sin is grace, not virtue.

If Jesus' critique of legalism was not devastating enough, the apostle Paul added another, fundamental complaint. Legalism fails miserably at the one thing it is supposed to do: encourage obedience. In a strange twist, a system of strict laws actually puts new ideas of lawbreaking in a person's mind. Paul explains, "For I would not have known what coveting really was if the law had not said, 'Do not covet.' But sin, seizing the opportunity afforded by the commandment, produced in me every kind of covetous desire." In a demonstration of this principle, some surveys show that people raised in teetotaling denominations are three times as likely to become alcoholics.

I remember reading Augustine's account of stealing pears. He and his friends had plenty of pears of higher quality, but they felt obliged to raid a neighbor's tree just to disobey the man's warning against stealing pears. Having spent four years on a campus governed by a sixty-six-page rule book, I can understand this odd pattern. I learned to rebel by hearing all the stern admonitions against rebellion. Partly out of immaturity, I am sure, I felt a constant temptation to resist the demands of authority simply because they were imposed demands. I had never felt a desire to grow a beard until I read a rule book forbidding beards.

"The finer the net is woven, the more numerous are the holes," wrote the Catholic theologian Hans Küng. Having sworn allegiance to the 2,414 canons in the Roman Code of Canon Law, one day he realized his energy was going toward either keeping or getting around those canons, rather than accomplishing the work of the gospel.

For those who do not rebel, but rather strive sincerely to keep the rules, legalism sets another trap. The feelings of failure may cause long-lasting scars of shame. As a young monk, Martin Luther would spend as long as six hours racking his brain to confess the sins he might have committed the previous day! Luther wrote:

> Although I lived a blameless life as a monk, I felt that I was a sinner with an uneasy conscience before God. I also could not believe that I had pleased him with my works. Far from loving that righteous God who punished sinners, I actually loathed him. I was a good monk, and kept my order so strictly that if ever a monk could get to heaven by monastic discipline, I was that monk. All my companions in the monastery would confirm this.... And yet my conscience would not give me certainty, but I always doubted and said, "You didn't do that right. You weren't contrite enough. You left that out of your confession."

The failure of relationship works both ways. As I read the history of the Israelites and their binding contract with God, I see sparse references to God's delight or pleasure. With a few shining exceptions, the history books—and especially the prophets—portray a God who seems irritated, disappointed, or downright furious. The law did not encourage obedience, rather it magnified disobedience. Law merely indicated the sickness; grace brought about the cure.

Neither Jesus nor Paul mentioned one final complaint against legalism that burdens me in a deeply personal way. I have referred to friends who rejected the Christian faith in large part because of the church's petty legalism. My own brother broke up with the first girl he truly loved because she wasn't "spiritual" enough by his legalistic standards. For thirty years he has tried to escape that ironclad moralism—and so far has succeeded in escaping God as well.

Legalism creates a subculture, and we in the United States, a nation of immigrants, surely know that subcultures can be repudiated. How many immigrant parents have watched their children abandon the language, heritage, and customs of the family in order to adopt the teenage subculture of modern America? Likewise, how many strict Christian families have watched as a child abandons faith, casting aside rules and beliefs as easily as one casts aside a too-small jacket? Legalism makes apostasy easy.

Samuel Tewk, an English reformer in the nineteenth century, introduced a radical new approach to treatment of the mentally ill. At the time, asylum workers were chaining lunatics to the walls and beating them, in the belief that punishment would defeat the evil forces within. Tewk taught the mentally afflicted how to behave at tea parties and at church. He dressed them the way everyone else was dressed, so that no one would recognize them as mentally ill. On the outside, they looked fine. He did nothing to address their suffering, however, and no matter how they behaved, they remained mentally ill.

One day I realized that I was like one of Tewk's patients: although the church of my childhood had taught me the proper way to behave, and a Bible college had given me more advanced knowledge, neither had cured the deep illness within. Though I had mastered the external behavior, inside the sickness and pain remained. For a time I cast aside the beliefs of my childhood, until God wonderfully revealed himself to me as a God of love and not hate, of freedom and not rules, of grace and not judgment.

To this day some of my friends who rebelled along with me remain alienated from God because of their deep distrust of the church. Amid all the distractions of the subculture, somehow they missed the ultimate goal: knowing God. The church, says Robert Farrar Capon, "has spent so much time inculcating in us the fear of making mistakes that she has made us like ill-taught piano students: we play our songs, but we never really hear them because our main concern is not to make music but to avoid some flub that will get us in dutch." I have now heard the strains of grace, and I grieve for my friends who have not.

Now that several decades have passed, I look back on my own legalistic upbringing with some bemusement. Frankly, I don't think God cares whether I wear a mustache or not, any more than God cares whether I use a zipper to close my pants or whether, like the Amish, I use buttons. When I attended a Bible college, I observed people who followed the rules and missed God, and people who broke the rules and missed God. What burdens me, though, is that group of people who still believe that they missed God *because* they broke the rules. They never heard the melody of the gospel of grace.

I have written about legalism partly because of my own bruising encounters with it and partly because I believe it represents such a powerful temptation to the church. Legalism stands like a stripper on the sidelines of faith, seducing us toward an easier way. It teases, promising some of the benefits of faith but unable to deliver what matters most. As Paul wrote to the legalists of his day, "For the kingdom of God is not a matter of eating and drinking, but of righteousness, peace and joy in the Holy Spirit."

Jay Kesler, president of Taylor University, told me about his own brush with legalism. Shortly after deciding to follow Christ as a teenager, he felt overwhelmed by all the new rules imposed on him. Confused, Jay walked around his backyard in Indiana and noticed his faithful collie Laddy, merrily gnawing on a bone while stretched out in the glistening wet grass. It struck Jay that Laddy was possibly the best Christian he knew. Laddy did not smoke, drink, go to movies, dance, or carry protest signs. He was harmless, docile, and inactive. At once Jay saw how far he had strayed from the life of freedom and passion to which Jesus had called him.

At first glance legalism seems hard, but actually freedom in Christ is the harder way. It is relatively easy not to murder, hard to reach out in love; easy to avoid a neighbor's bed, hard to keep a marriage alive; easy to pay taxes, hard to serve the poor. When living in freedom, I must remain open to the Spirit for guidance. I am more aware of what I have neglected than what I have achieved. I cannot hide behind a mask of behavior, like the hypocrites, nor can I hide behind facile comparisons with other Christians.

The Reformed theologian J. Gresham Machen wrote, "A low view of law leads to legalism in religion; a high view makes one a seeker after grace." The ultimate effect of legalism is to lower one's view of God. We tend to think of the stricter denominations and Christian institutions as more "spiritual." In truth, the differences between Bob Jones and Wheaton College, or between Mennonites and Southern Baptists, are minuscule when compared to a holy God.

I once read that proportionally the surface of the earth is smoother than a billiard ball. The heights of Mount Everest and the troughs of the Pacific Ocean are very impressive to those of us who live on this planet. But from the view of Andromeda, or even Mars, those differences matter not at all. That is how I now see the petty behavioral differences between one Christian group and another. Compared to a holy and perfect God, the loftiest Everest of rules amounts to a molehill. You cannot earn God's acceptance by climbing; you must receive it as a gift.

Jesus proclaimed unmistakably that God's law is so perfect and absolute that no one can achieve righteousness. Yet God's grace is so great that we do not have to. By striving to prove how much they deserve God's love, legalists miss the whole point of the gospel, that it is a gift from God to people who don't deserve it. The solution to sin is not to impose an ever-stricter code of behavior. It is to know God.

PART IV

Grace Notes for a Deaf World

SIXTEEN

Big Harold: A Story

My father died of polio a month after my first birthday, and so I grew up fatherless. Out of kindness, one man in our church took my brother and me under his wing. Big Harold, we called him. He sat patiently in playgrounds as we spun ourselves silly on the merry-go-round. When we grew older, he taught us how to play chess and helped us build a soap-box racer. In the ignorance of childhood, we had no idea that a lot of people in the church seemed to think him strange.

Eventually Big Harold left our church. It was too liberal, he decided. Some of the women there wore lipstick and makeup. Also, he had found some biblical passages that led him to disapprove of musical instruments in a church, and he sought a church that agreed with his views. I attended Big Harold's wedding: the rule against music evidently pertaining only to the sanctuary, a long yellow extension cord snaked down the main aisle to the outdoors, where a record player coughed out a scratchy rendition of Mendelssohn's "Wedding March."

Big Harold was obsessed about morality and politics. The United States, he believed, would soon fall under the judgment of God because of its permissiveness. He quoted Communist leaders who talked about the West rotting from the inside out, like an overripe fruit. He believed, in fact, that Communists working through the Trilateral Commission and the Federal Reserve Bank would soon take over our government. He gave me literature from the John Birch Society, printed on cheap paper, bound with red-white-and-blue covers, and he insisted I read the book *None Dare Call It Treason.*

Big Harold hated black people. He often talked about how dumb and lazy they were, and told stories about the good-for-nothing blacks who worked around him. About that time, Congress started passing civil rights bills and Atlanta began to integrate. Before, white people always had certain motels and restaurants to themselves, and shopping centers catered either to blacks or whites, never both. Now the government was forcing changes, and Big Harold saw these changes as one more sign of a Communist conspiracy. The final straw came when courts ordered forced busing of Atlanta schoolchildren. Big Harold had two children of his own by then, and he could not bear the thought of sending them in a bus full of black children to a school run by secular humanists.

When Big Harold started looking into emigration, I thought he was joking. He sent off for literature from places like Rhodesia, South Africa, Australia, New Zealand, the Falkland Islands—places where white people still seemed firmly in control. He pored over atlases and studied the racial makeup of these societies. Not only did he want a white-dominated country, he also wanted a moral one. That ruled out Australia, despite its white majority, because its society seemed more permissive than the United States. It had topless beaches, and everyone drank beer.

One day, Big Harold announced that he was moving to South Africa. Back then, no one could imagine the white minority loosening their grip on power. They had the guns, after all. The United Nations was voting measure after measure condemning apartheid, but South Africa stood its ground, defying the entire world. Big Harold liked that.

He also liked the fact that religion played an important role in the South African government. The leading political party leaned heavily on the Reformed Church, which in return provided a theological basis for apartheid. The government had no qualms about enforcing morality. Abortion was illegal, as was interracial marriage. Customs inspectors censored magazines like *Playboy* and banned questionable movies or books. Big Harold laughed as he told us that for years *Black Beauty*, the children's story about a horse, had been banned because of its title; none of the inspectors had bothered to read it.

At the Atlanta airport we bade a tearful farewell as Big Harold, his wife, Sarah, and his two young children waved goodbye to the only country they had ever known. They had no jobs, no friends, not even a place to live in South Africa. Don't worry, they assured us, white people are welcomed with open arms.

Big Harold proved a faithful correspondent, always in his signature style. He became a lay preacher in a small church and used the back of his sermon notes to write letters to his family and friends in America. Typically, these sermons had twelve or fourteen major points, each supported by a veritable concordance of Bible references. It was sometimes difficult to tell the back of one of these letters from the front, because both sides sounded like sermons. Big Harold railed against communism and false religions, against the immorality of today's young people, against churches and people who did not agree with him in every detail.

He seemed to thrive in South Africa. America had a lot to learn, he wrote me. At his church young people did not chew gum, pass notes, or whisper to each other during the sermon.

In school (all white), students stood and addressed their teachers with respect. Big Harold subscribed to *Time* magazine, and he could hardly believe what was happening in America. South Africa kept minorities in their place, and lobby groups for feminism and gay rights were unheard of. The government should be an agent of God, he told us, and stand up for what is right against the forces of darkness.

Even when writing about his family, Big Harold managed to convey a cranky, judgmental tone. His children never seemed to please him, especially his son, William, who was always making the wrong decision and getting into trouble.

Anyone else picking up one of Big Harold's letters might have judged him a kook. Yet because of fond memories from childhood, I never took the letters quite seriously. Underneath the gruff exterior, I knew, was a man who had devoted himself to help a widow with her two young sons.

I was a teenager when Big Harold moved away. I went on to college and graduate school, got a job as a magazine editor, and eventually became a full-time writer. All this time Big Harold sent a steady stream of letters. His father died, and then his mother, but he never thought seriously about returning to the United States for a visit. As far as I know, no one from Big Harold's family nor any of his friends ever visited him in South Africa either.

The letters darkened in the 1990s, when for the first time it became conceivable that whites and blacks would share power in South Africa. Big Harold sent me copies of letters he had sent to newspapers there. The South African government was betraying him just as the U.S. government had. He said he could prove that Nelson Mandela and Desmond Tutu were card-carrying Communists. He called Americans traitors for their support of economic sanctions. And he pointed to Communist agitation as the main reason behind a decline of morality. Striptease clubs were now opening in border towns, and in downtown Johannesburg you could actually see racially mixed couples holding hands. The tone of his letters grew more and more hysterical.

With some misgivings, I decided to visit Big Harold in 1993. For twenty-five years I had received only judgment and disapproval from him. He had sent lengthy rebuttals of my books until one of them, *Disappointment with God*, made him so mad that he asked me to send no more. He fired off a three-page letter condemning it—not the book itself, but the title. Though he had not opened the book, he had much to say about the title, which he found offensive.

Still, since I was traveling to South Africa on business, how could I resist a five-hundred-mile detour to visit Big Harold? Perhaps he was different in person, more like the man I had once known. Perhaps he needed exposure to the broader world. I wrote him months in advance to ask if I could stop by, and right away his letters took on a softer, more conciliatory tone.

The only flight to Big Harold's city left Johannesburg at 6:30 A.M., and by the time my wife and I reached the airport we were buzzed on coffee. Caffeine jitters merely added to our general nervousness about the visit. We had no idea what to expect. Big Harold's children were now grown adults who, no doubt, would speak with South African accents. Would I even recognize the parents, Harold and Sarah? I made a mental note to drop the Big Harold label, a carryover from childhood.

Thus began one of the most bizarre days of my life. When the plane landed and we disembarked, I recognized Sarah immediately. Her hair had gone gray and her shoulders slumped with age, but that sad, thin face could belong to no one else. She hugged me and introduced us to her son William and his fiancée, Beverly. (The daughter lived far away and could not join us.)

William was in his late twenties, friendly, handsome, and a great fan of America. He let it drop that he had met his fiancée at a methadone clinic for recovering drug addicts. Obviously, some facts had never made it into Big Harold's letters.

William had borrowed a beat-up Volkswagen van, thinking we might have lots of luggage. The van's middle seats having been stripped out, William, Beverly, and Sarah sat up front while my wife and I occupied the lone seat in the rear, directly above the engine. It was hot, well over ninety degrees, and exhaust from the engine leaked through the rusted floor. To make matters worse, Beverly and William, like many recovering drug addicts, were chain-smokers, and clouds of smoke drifted back through the van, mixing with the diesel exhaust.

William took us on a weaving, brake-riding, daredevil drive through town. He kept turning around in his seat to point out sights of interest—"Heard of Dr. Christiaan Barnard? He used to live in that house"—and as he did so the van lurched from side to side, the luggage slid across the floor, and we fought hard to keep down the gallons of coffee and the airplane breakfast.

One question I had not yet asked: Where was Big Harold? I assumed he would be waiting for us at the house. But when we pulled up, no one appeared at the door. "Where's Harold?" I asked William as we unloaded the luggage, remembering my commitment to drop the "Big."

"Oh, we were going to tell you but didn't have a chance. You see, Dad's in jail." He fished in his pocket for a fresh cigarette.

"Jail?" My brain flinched.

"Right. He was hoping to be out by now, but his release got delayed."

I stood staring until he offered more explanation. "It's like—well, Dad sometimes loses his temper. He writes angry letters . . ."

"I know, I've received some of those letters," I interrupted.

"Yeah, well. He sent one too many and got in trouble. We'll tell you more later. Come on in the house."

I stood for a moment longer, trying to absorb the news, but William ducked inside. I grabbed our suitcases and entered the small, gloomy bungalow. Inside, a double layer of venetian blinds and room-darkening shades sealed us from outside light. The furniture was comfortable and well-worn, its style more American than other homes I had visited in South Africa. Sarah put on a teakettle, and we made polite conversation for a few minutes, skirting the one topic everyone knew was on our minds.

Soon I encountered a major distraction. William raised beautiful tropical birds: lorikeets, cockatiels, macaws, parrots. Since his apartment manager did not allow pets, he kept them at his parents' house, where they flew uncaged. Raised from eggs, they were tame enough to land on my shoulder as I sat on the couch. A rainbow lorikeet startled me by lunging at my tongue, nearly causing me to drop my teacup.

"Oh, don't mind Jerry," William laughed. "I've trained him to eat chocolate. I chew on chocolate candy a while, then stick out my tongue and he licks it off." I kept my mouth shut, and chose not to look at the expression on my wife's face.

There, queasy from an overdose of coffee, cigarette smoke, and Volkswagen exhaust, sitting in a dark bungalow with a bird dropping moist deposits on my shoulder and making passes at my tongue, I heard the truth about Big Harold's dark side. Yes, Harold preached fire and brimstone on Sunday, and wrote screeds of venom and judgment to his friends back in America. Yes, he railed against the decline of morals. But at the same time, out of this small, musty house I was now sitting in, he had been running a pornography ring. He brought in illegal foreign publications, clipped out photos, and sent them to famous women in South Africa with notes saying,

"This is what I want to do to you." One of these women, a television newscaster, had grown alarmed enough to call the police. By tracing the typewriter, the police narrowed the search to Harold and moved in.

Sarah could hardly bear to tell the details of the day when a SWAT team surrounded the house, forced their way in, and ransacked every drawer and closet. They impounded her husband's copy machine and typewriter. They found his private stash of porn. And they hauled him off to jail, handcuffed, a baseball cap pulled down over his face. All the while, television news trucks were parked outside, and a helicopter hovered over the scene. The story hit the evening news: "Preacher arrested on morals charge."

Sarah said she did not leave the house for four days, ashamed to face the neighbors' stares. She finally forced herself to go to church, only to endure more humiliation. Harold had been the moral center of the tiny church, and the others now felt confused, even betrayed. If such a thing could happen to him ...

Later that same day, after hearing the story in bits and pieces, I got to see Harold himself. We packed a picnic lunch in plastic containers and took it to the minimum-security prison, where Harold met us in the exercise yard. It was our first face-to-face meeting in twenty-five years, and we embraced. He was in his sixties now, bone-thin, nearly bald, with sunken eyes and an unhealthy complexion the color of weak milk. I could hardly believe I once thought of him as *Big* Harold.

He seemed a ghost compared to the other prisoners, most of whom were using the time for body-building and working on their tans. He had a look of overwhelming sadness about him. He had been exposed, laid raw for all the world to see. He had nowhere to hide.

In our several hours together, I saw glimpses of the Harold I used to know. I told him about changes in the old neighborhood and about the improvements being made to ready Atlanta for the '96 Olympics. He brightened as I mentioned friends and family members. He pointed out the various birds flitting about the grounds, exotic South African birds I had never seen before.

We talked around, but never directly about, the events that had put him in prison. He admitted fear. "I've heard what they do to sex offenders here," he said. "That's why I grew this beard and started wearing a hat. It's a kind of disguise."

Visiting hours ended, and along with all the other visitors we were ushered out through the rows of razor-wire fences. I embraced Harold again, and walked away, knowing I would probably never see him again.

When our plane left South Africa a few days later, my wife and I were still in a state of shock. She, who knew Harold mainly through his letters, had expected to meet a prophet dressed in camel skin, a John the Baptist urging the world to *Repent!* I expected some combination of that and also the gentle man from my childhood. In a million years, neither of us would have guessed we would visit a prisoner serving time.

After our visit, the first few letters from Harold had a humbler tone. When he got out, though, he began to harden again. He bullied his way back into the church (they had "dis-fellowshipped" him), bought a new typewriter, and started sending out more pronouncements on the state of the world. I had hoped that such an experience would draw him up short, make him more compassionate of others, less haughty and morally sure. Yet several years have passed and never again have I detected the slightest sign of humility in his letters.

Saddest of all, I have never detected any sign of grace. Big Harold was well-schooled in morality. For him, the world divided neatly into the pure and the impure, and he kept drawing the circle tighter and tighter until finally he could trust no one but himself. Then he could not trust himself. Perhaps for the first time in his life he found himself in a place where he had nowhere to turn but grace. Yet as far as I could see, he never turned there. Morality, even flawed morality, seemed a far safer place.

The best lack all conviction, while the worst
Are full of passionate intensity.

W. B. YEATS

SEVENTEEN

Mixed Aroma

I had a rude introduction to contemporary culture wars when I visited the White House during Bill Clinton's first term. My invitation came in a roundabout manner. I have little personal involvement in politics, and mostly avoid the subject in my writing. But in late 1993 I grew concerned about the alarm, even hysteria, over the state of society being voiced in evangelical circles. I wrote a column that concluded, "Our real challenge should not be to Christianize the United States (always a losing battle) but rather to strive to be Christ's church in an increasingly hostile world."

The editors of *Christianity Today* magazine titled my column rather sensationally, "Why Clinton Isn't the Antichrist." I got a handful of letters, mostly from people contending that Bill Clinton *is* the Antichrist. Somehow the column found its way to the President's desk, and a few months later when President Clinton invited twelve evangelicals to a private breakfast, my name made the list. Some of the guests represented church or parachurch organizations; some hailed from Christian academia; I got invited thanks mainly to the catchy title on my column. ("Well, Bill, you've got to start somewhere," said Al Gore when he saw the title "Why Clinton Isn't the Antichrist.")

"The President has no agenda," we were assured. "He simply wants to hear your concerns. You'll have five minutes each to say anything you want to the President." It took little political savvy to realize that the President was convening us primarily because of his low standing among evangelical Christians. Mr. Clinton addressed some of those concerns in his opening remarks, confessing, "Sometimes I feel like a spiritual orphan."

As a lifelong Southern Baptist, he was finding it difficult to locate a Christian community in Washington, D.C.—"the most secular city I've ever lived in," he told us. When the First Family went to church, they attracted a media circus, hardly conducive to a worship experience. Few of Clinton's staff members (whom, of course, he had appointed) shared his concern for faith.

Moreover, the conservative Christian community had disassociated itself from him. When the President jogged through the streets of Washington he saw bumper stickers like this one: "A vote for Bill Clinton is a sin against God." Operation Rescue founder Randall Terry had publicly labeled the Clintons "Ahab and Jezebel." And Clinton's own Southern Baptist denomination was under pressure to censure his home church in Arkansas for not kicking the President off its membership rolls.

In short, the President had not experienced much grace from Christians. "I've been in politics long enough to expect criticism and hostility," the President told us. "But I was unprepared for the *hatred* I get from Christians. Why do Christians hate so much?"

Of course, everyone in the Lincoln Dining Room that morning knew why the President stirred up such animosity among Christians. His policies on abortion and homosexual rights, in particular, along with reports of his own moral failings, made it difficult for many Christians to take seriously his profession of faith. A respected Christian leader had told me flatly, "Bill Clinton cannot possibly be sincere about his faith and hold the views that he does."

I wrote an article about that breakfast, and a few months later another invitation came from the White House, this time offering an exclusive magazine interview with the President. The interview took place in February 1994, most of it conducted in the Presidential limousine. After Mr. Clinton gave a speech at an inner-city school, David Neff, the editor of *Christianity Today*, and I accompanied him on the long ride back to the White House, where we would continue the conversation in the Oval Office. The limousine, though spacious, still cramped Clinton's long legs as we sat facing him. Taking occasional sips of water from a paper Dixie cup in order to soothe his perennially strained throat, the President answered our questions.

Much of our conversation revolved around the abortion issue. David Neff and I had planned strategically how to bring up the tough questions, but as it turned out they came up naturally. That morning all of us had attended the National Prayer Breakfast and heard Mother Teresa boldly dress down the President for the plague of abortion in this country. Clinton had met with her privately after the breakfast, and he seemed anxious to continue the discussion with us.

My article that resulted, "The Riddle of Bill Clinton's Faith," reported his views and also explored the question raised by my friend. Can Bill Clinton possibly be sincere about his faith, holding the views that he does? I had done much research, including conversations with his friends and associates from childhood, and the evidence seemed clear: Clinton's faith was not posturing for political expediency but an integral part of who he was. Except during college days he had attended church faithfully, had been a lifelong supporter of Billy Graham, and was an avid student of the Bible. When I asked what Christian books he'd read most recently, he mentioned titles by Richard Mouw (president of Fuller Theological Seminary) and Tony Campolo.

In fact, I found it almost impossible to understand the Clintons apart from their religious faith. Hillary Clinton, a lifelong Methodist, believes we were placed on earth to do good by serving others. Bill Clinton, a Southern Baptist, was raised in the tradition of revivalism and "going forward" to confess sins. Sure, he messes up during the week—doesn't everyone?—but come Sunday he goes to church, confesses his sins, and starts over.

After our interview I wrote what I thought was a balanced account of President Clinton and his faith, giving considerable space to the issue of abortion, in which I contrasted his waffling views with the moral absolutes of Mother Teresa. I was totally unprepared for the firestorm of reaction. I wonder if my mailman will ever recover from the strain of lugging bags of angry letters to my mailbox.

"You say Clinton has biblical knowledge," said one; "well, so does the Devil! You got snowed." Many writers contended that evangelicals should never have met with the President. Six drew parallels with Adolf Hitler, who cynically used pastors for his own purposes. Several more likened us to the church browbeaten by Stalin. Others recalled biblical scenes of confrontation: John the Baptist and Herod, Elijah and Ahab, Nathan and David. Why hadn't I acted more like a prophet, shaking my finger in the President's face?

One person wrote, "If Philip Yancey saw a child about to be run over by a freight train, I believe he would stand comfortably out of the way and lovingly ask the child to move instead of making an effort to scream and push the child out of harm's way."

Less than ten percent of the letters had positive things to say, and the vicious tone of personal attack caught me off guard. One reader wrote, "Perhaps the move from the flatlands of the Midwest to the rarefied and reclusive atmosphere of Colorado has short-circuited Mr. Yancey's oxygen supply and dimmed his discernment." And another, "I hope Phil Yancey enjoyed his cozy eggs Benedict breakfast at the White House because as he was busy wiping the yolk off his fuzzy face (lest it run down his back), the Clinton Administration was forging ahead with its radically anti-theistic and amoral agenda."

In twenty-five years of journalism I have received my share of mixed reviews. Even so, as I read through stacks of vituperative letters I got a strong sense for why the world does not automatically associate the word "grace" with evangelical Christians.

The apostle Paul's writings follow a familiar pattern. The first part of each letter explores lofty theological concepts, such as "the riches of God's grace." At that point, Paul typically pauses to answer potential objections. Only then does he proceed to make a practical application, spelling out how these riches translate into the mess of everyday life. How should a "graced" person act as a husband or wife, as a church member, as a citizen?

Using that same pattern, I have presented grace as a wonderful force that can break the chains of ungrace binding nations, tribes, and families. It conveys the best news possible, that the God of the universe loves us—news so good it bears the scent of scandal. But my task is not over.

The time has come to return to a practical question: If grace is so amazing, why don't Christians show more of it?

How is it that Christians called to dispense the aroma of grace instead emit the noxious fumes of ungrace? In the United States in the 1990s, one answer to that question springs readily to mind. The church has allowed itself to get so swept up in political issues that it plays by the rules of power, which are rules of ungrace. In no other arena is the church at greater risk of losing its calling than in the public square.

My experience in writing about Bill Clinton brought this point home to me. For perhaps the first time I had caught a good whiff of the aroma given off by some Christians, and it was not a pleasant smell. I began paying closer attention to how Christians are perceived by the world at large. An overwrought editorial in the *New York Times*, for example, warned that the activism of religious conservatives "poses a far greater threat to democracy than was presented by communism." Could they seriously believe that?

Because cartoons reveal a lot about the general drift of culture, I began noticing how they portrayed Christians. The *New Yorker* magazine, for instance, pictured a waiter in an expensive restaurant explaining the menu to a patron: "The ones with asterisks are those recommended by the religious right." Yet another political cartoon showed a classic American church building with the sign out front, "First Church of Anti-Clinton."

I fully support the right, and indeed the responsibility, of Christians to get involved politically: in moral crusades such as abolition, civil rights, and anti-abortion, Christians have led the way. And I believe the media grossly exaggerate the "threat" posed by the religious right. The Christians I know who are involved in politics bear little resemblance to their caricatures. Nevertheless I do worry about the recent tendency for the labels "evangelical Christian" and "religious right" to become interchangeable. The cartoons show that Christians increasingly are perceived as rigid moralists who want to control other lives.

I know why some Christians are acting ungraciously: out of fear. We feel under attack in schools, in courts, and sometimes in Congress. Meanwhile we see around us the kind of moral change that marks society's decay. In such categories as crime, divorce, youth suicide, abortion, drug use, children on welfare, and illegitimate births the United States outranks every other industrialized country. Social conservatives feel more and more like an embattled minority, their values under constant attack.

How can Christians uphold moral values in a secular society while at the same time conveying a spirit of grace and love? As the psalmist expressed it, "When the foundations are being destroyed, what can the righteous do?" Behind the gruffness of the people who wrote me letters, I'm sure, lies a deep and proper concern for a world that has little place for God. Yet I also know that, as Jesus pointed out to the Pharisees, a concern for moral values alone is not nearly enough. Moralism apart from grace solves little.

Andy Rooney, commentator on the *60 Minutes* television show, once said, "I've decided I'm against abortion. I think it's murder. But I have a dilemma in that I much prefer the pro-choice to the pro-life people. I'd much rather eat dinner with a group of the former." It matters little who Andy Rooney dines with, but it matters a lot whether Andy Rooney misses encountering the grace of God from Christians in all their pro-life zeal.

When I ask my airplane seatmates, "What comes to mind when I say the words 'evangelical Christian'?" they usually respond in political terms. Yet the gospel of Jesus was not primarily a political platform. In all the talk of voting blocs and culture wars, the message of grace—the main distinctive Christians have to offer—tends to fall aside. It is difficult, if not impossible, to communicate the message of grace from the corridors of power.

The church is becoming more and more politicized, and as society unravels I hear calls that we emphasize mercy less and morality more. Stigmatize homosexuals, shame unwed mothers, persecute immigrants, harass the homeless, punish lawbreakers—I get the sense from some Christians that if we simply pass enough harsh laws in Washington, we can turn our country around. One prominent spiritual leader insists, "The only way to have a genuine spiritual revival is to have legislative reform." Could he have that backwards?

In the 1950s and 1960s, mainline denominations moved away from proclaiming the gospel toward a more political agenda, and the pews began to empty, cutting membership by half. Many of these disaffected churchgoers sought out evangelical churches, where they heard messages more directed to their spiritual needs. It would be ironic indeed if evangelical churches repeated the error and drove away members because of an overemphasis on politics of the conservative stripe.

Another book deserves to be written addressing the intolerance of the secular left, where meanness and inflexibility also thrive. In this book, however, I have a single concern: What about grace? Does the Christians' concern for morality drown out our message of God's love for sinners? Evangelical Christians are my heritage, my family. I work among them, worship with them, write books for them. If my family seems in danger of misrepresenting the gospel of Christ, I must speak out. It is, in fact, a form of self-criticism.

True, the media distort the religious right and misunderstand Christians in general. But we Christians share the blame. On a visit to my city Randall Terry called for Christians to become "intolerant zealots" when it comes to "baby killers, sodomites, condom-pushers, and that pluralism nonsense." Terry described our Congresswoman as "a snake, witch, and evil woman." He said that "Christians need to stop being little scaredy-cats in Christian ghettoes playing spiritual tiddlywinks." We need rather to clean out the "moral cesspool this nation has become" and make this a Christian nation again. More, we need to make a Christian conquest of other nations.

Although Randall Terry may not typify mainstream evangelicals, his comments did make the front page of our local papers, feeding public images of ungrace. So did these comments from Terry: "I want you to let a wave of hatred wash over you. Yes, hate is good. . . . We have a biblical duty, we are called by God to conquer this country."

Ralph Reed, formerly of the Christian Coalition, is usually a circumspect speaker. But these words from him have probably been reprinted more widely than any others: "It's better to move quietly, with stealth, under the cover of night. . . . I want to be invisible. I do guerrilla warfare.

I paint my face and travel at night. You don't know it's over until you're in a body bag. You don't know until election night."

I imagine most people, as I do, take such pronouncements with a grain of salt. We are accustomed to public posturing, to the press reporting the juiciest sound bites. I could easily match their words with intemperate comments from the opposite side. I do wonder, however, what such comments sound like to a young woman who has actually undergone an abortion and may now regret it. I know what such comments sound like to a homosexual who struggles with his or her identity, for I interviewed many of them in Washington, D.C.

I think back to the prostitute's comment that originally prompted me to write this book. "Church! Why would I ever go there? I was already feeling terrible about myself. They'd just make me feel worse!" And I think back to the life of Jesus, who attracted as if by reverse magnetism the most unsavory of characters, the moral outcasts. He came for the sinners, not the righteous. And when he was arrested it was not the notorious sinners of Palestine, but the moralists, who called for his death.

My neighbor, an official in the state Republican Party, told me of the concern among fellow Republicans that "stealth candidates" (Ralph Reed's term) of the religious right are plotting to take over the party. One of his coworkers cautioned that such stealth candidates could often be identified by their frequent use of the word "grace." Although he had no idea what grace meant, he had noticed that stealth candidates came from organizations and churches with that word prominent in their titles or in their literature.

Will grace, "the last best word," the only unsullied theological word remaining in our language, go the way of so many others? In the political arena, has it come to mean its opposite?

In another context, Nietzsche gave this warning, which applies to modern Christians: "Be careful, lest in fighting the dragon you become the dragon."

William Willimon, Chaplain at Duke University and a lifelong Methodist, cautions evangelicals against their current fixation with politics. "Pat Robertson has become Jesse Jackson. Randall Terry of the nineties is Bill Coffin of the sixties. And the average American knows no answer to human longing or moral deviation other than legislation." Willimon speaks from experience: his own denomination built a four-story office building on Capitol Hill in order to lobby Congress more effectively. Yes, they lobbied effectively, but along the way they neglected their primary mission as a church, and members forsook Methodist churches by the thousands. Now, as Willimon calls his denomination to return to biblical preaching, he looks to evangelicals and finds sermons about politics, not God.

I see the confusion of politics and religion as one of the greatest barriers to grace. C. S. Lewis observed that almost all crimes of Christian history have come about when religion is confused with politics. Politics, which always runs by the rules of ungrace, allures us to trade away grace for power, a temptation the church has often been unable to resist.

Those of us who live under the strict separation of church and state may not fully appreciate how historically rare that arrangement is or why it came about. Thomas Jefferson's phrase, "a wall of separation between church and state," first appeared in a letter to Connecticut Baptists who *welcomed* such a wall of separation. Baptists, Puritans, Quakers, and other splinter groups had made the long voyage to America in hopes of finding a place that did separate church and state, for they had all been victims of state-sponsored religious persecution. When the church joined with the state, it tended to wield power rather than dispense grace.

As Mark Galli of *Christian History* magazine has pointed out, Christians at the end of the twentieth century complain about the disunity of the church, the lack of godly leaders in politics, and the dearth of Christian influence in popular culture. None of these complaints applied to the Middle Ages, an era when the church was unified, Christians appointed key political leaders, and the faith permeated all of popular culture. Yet who would look back on the results with nostalgia? Crusaders devastated lands to the East. Priests, marching alongside soldiers, "converted" whole continents at the point of a sword. Inquisitors hounded Jews, hunted down witches, and even subjected loyal Christians to cruel tests of faith. Truly the church had become the "morals police" of society. Grace gave way to power.

When the church has occasion to set the rules for all society, it often veers toward the extremism Jesus warned against. Consider just one example, the Geneva of John Calvin. There, officials could summon anyone for questioning about matters of faith. Church attendance was compulsory. Laws covered such issues as how many dishes could be served at each meal and the appropriate colors of garments.

William Manchester records some of the diversions forbidden by Calvin:

> feasting, dancing, singing, pictures, statues, relics, church bells, organs, altar candles; "indecent or irreligious" songs, staging or attending theatrical plays; wearing rouge, jewelry, lace, or "immodest" dress; speaking disrespectfully of your betters; extravagant entertainment, swearing, gambling, playing cards, hunting, drunkenness; naming children after anyone but figures in the Old Testament; reading "immoral or irreligious" books.

A father who christened his son Claude, a name not found in the Old Testament, spent four days in jail, as did a woman whose hairdo reached an "immoral" height. The Consistory beheaded a child who struck his parents. They drowned any single woman found pregnant. In separate incidents, Calvin's stepson and daughter-in-law were executed when found in bed with their lovers.

After reporting on such moments in church history, Paul Johnson concludes, "Attempts to perfect Christian societies in this world, whether conducted by popes or revolutionaries, have tended to degenerate into red terrors." This fact should give us pause as voices today call on us to break down the walls between church and state and restore morality to our society. In the words of Lesslie Newbigin, "The project of bringing heaven down to earth always results in bringing hell up from below."

We in the modern United States, besieged by secularism and living in a culture of deteriorating morality, can easily lose sight of where we have come from. I grow alarmed when I hear the National Secretary for the Moral Majority praying for the death of his opponents, and saying, "We're tired of turning the other cheek . . . good heavens, that's all that we have done." I grow alarmed when I read of an organization in California working to elect government officials in order that government can become the "police department within the Kingdom of God on earth," ready to "impose God's vengeance upon those who abandon God's laws of justice."

Early on, America teetered on the brink of becoming a strict theocracy along the lines of Calvin's Geneva. The Code of Connecticut, for example, includes these laws: "No one shall run on the Sabbath Day, or walk in his garden, or elsewhere except reverently to and from meeting. No one shall travel, cook victuals, make beds, sweep house, cut hair, or shave on the Sabbath. If any man shall kiss his wife, or wife her husband on the Lord's Day, the party in fault shall be punished at the discretion of the court of magistrates." Anglican forces who took over Maryland passed a rule requiring citizens to convert from Catholicism before sitting in the assembly. Parts of New England restricted eligible voters to godly people who could testify to a personal experience of salvation.

Eventually, however, the colonies agreed that there would be no nationally established church and that freedom of religion could be practiced throughout the nation. It was an unprecedented step in history and a gamble that appears to have paid off: as historian Garry Wills says, the first nation to separate Christianity from government produced perhaps the most religious nation on earth.

Jesus came to found a new kind of kingdom that could coexist in Jerusalem and also spread into Judea, Samaria, and the uttermost parts of the earth. In a parable he warned that those farmers who concentrate on pulling up weeds (his image for "sons of the evil one") may destroy the wheat along with the weeds. Leave matters of judgment to the one true Judge, Jesus advised.

The apostle Paul had much to say about the immorality of individual church members but little to say about the immorality of pagan

Rome. He rarely railed against the abuses in Rome—slavery, idolatry, violent games, political oppression, greed—even though such abuses surely offended Christians of that day as much as our deteriorating society offends Christians today.

When I went to the White House to visit President Clinton, I knew well that his reputation among conservative Christians hinged on two issues: abortion and homosexual rights. I agree fully that these are important moral issues which Christians must address. But when I went through the New Testament I could find very little related to either one. Both practices existed then, in a different and more egregious form. Roman citizens did not rely principally on abortion for birth control. The women bore their babies, then abandoned them by the side of the road for wild animals or vultures. Likewise, Romans and Greeks also practiced a form of same-gender sex: older men commonly used young boys as their sex slaves, in pederasty.

Thus in Jesus' and Paul's day both these moral issues asserted themselves in ways that today would be criminal in any civilized country on earth. No country allows a person to kill a full-term, delivered baby. No country legally permits sex with children. Jesus and Paul doubtless knew of these deplorable practices. And yet Jesus said nothing about either one, and Paul made only a few references to cross-gender sex. Both concentrated not on the pagan kingdom around them but on the alternative kingdom of God.

For this reason, I wonder about the enormous energy being devoted these days to restoring morality to the United States. Are we concentrating more on the kingdom of this world than on the kingdom that is not of this world? The public image of the evangelical church today is practically defined by an emphasis on two issues that Jesus did not even mention. How will we feel if historians of the future look back on the evangelical church of the 1990s and declare, "They fought bravely on the moral fronts of abortion and homosexual rights," while at the same time reporting that we did little to fulfill the Great Commission, and we did little to spread the aroma of grace in the world?

The church . . . is not the master or servant of the state, but rather the conscience of the state. It must be the guide and the critic of the state, and never its tool.

Martin Luther King Jr.

EIGHTEEN

Serpent Wisdom

When I grew up in the 1950s, the school principal began each day with a prayer read over the intercom system. In school we pledged allegiance to a nation "under God," and in Sunday school we pledged allegiance to both the American and the Christian flags. It never occurred to me that America might one day present Christians with a new challenge: how to "grace" a society increasingly hostile to them.

Until recently American history—the official version, at least—presented a waltz between two dancing partners, church and state. Religion runs so deep that the United States has been described as a nation with the soul of a church. *The Mayflower Compact* specified the Pilgrims' goal as "undertaken, for the Glory of God and advancement of the Christian Faith and Honour of our King and Country." Our founders thought religious faith essential for a democracy to work: in John Adams' words, "Our constitution was made only for a moral and religious people. It is wholly inadequate for the government of any other."

For most of our history, even the Supreme Court echoed the Christian consensus. In 1931 the court declared, "We are a Christian people, according to one another the equal right of religious freedom, and acknowledging with reverence the duty of obedience to the will of God." In 1954 Earl Warren, a Chief Justice notorious to many conservatives, said in a speech, "I believe no one can read the history of our country without realizing that the Good Book and the spirit of the Savior have from the beginning been our guiding geniuses." Charters for the original colonies, he added, all pointed to the same objective: "a Christian land governed by Christian principles."

We live amid daily reminders of our Christian heritage. The very names of government agencies—the civil *service*, the *ministry* of justice—give off religious overtones. Americans respond quickly to disasters, protect the rights of the disabled, stop to help stranded motorists, give billions of dollars to charity—these and many other "habits of the heart" reflect a national culture that grew from Christian roots. Only someone who travels overseas can appreciate the fact that not all cultures include such grace notes.

(Under the surface, of course, history tells a different story. Native Americans were nearly exterminated in this "Christian" country. Women were denied basic rights. "Good Christians" in the South beat their slaves without a twinge of conscience. Having grown up in the South, I know that African-Americans as a group do not look back nostalgically on the "godly" days of our early history. "I would have been a slave back then," John Perkins reminds us. To these minorities, the message of grace got lost.)

Nowadays few people confuse church and state in the United States, and the change occurred with such breathtaking speed that anyone born in the last thirty years may wonder what Christian consensus I am talking about. It seems incredible that the words "under God" were added to the Pledge of Allegiance only in 1954, and the phrase "In God we trust" became the nation's official motto in 1956. Since then the Supreme Court has banned prayer in schools and some teachers have tried to prohibit their students from writing about any religious themes. Movies and television shows rarely mention Christians except in derogation, and courts routinely strip religious symbols from public places.

Much of the outrage of the religious right stems from the swiftness of this cultural shift. Harold O. J. Brown, one of the early evangelical activists against abortion, says that he and others experienced the *Roe v. Wade* ruling as a wake-up call in the middle of the night. Christians had viewed the Supreme Court as a mostly trustworthy group of sages who drew their conclusions from the moral consensus of the rest of the country. Suddenly the bombshell dropped, a decision that divided the country along fault lines.

Other court decisions—establishing a "right to die," redefining marriage, protecting pornography—have sent conservative Christians reeling. Now Christians are much more likely to view the state as the church's antagonist, not its friend. James Dobson captures the tone when he says, "Nothing short of a great Civil War of Values rages today throughout North America. Two sides with vastly differing and incompatible worldviews are locked in a bitter conflict that permeates every level of society."

The culture war is under way. Ironically, every year the church in the United States draws closer and closer to the situation faced by the New Testament church: an embattled minority living in a pluralistic, pagan society. Christians in places like Sri Lanka, Tibet, Sudan, and Saudi Arabia have faced open hostility from their governments for years. But in the United States, with a history so congenial to the faith, we don't like it.

How can Christians dispense grace in a society that seems to be veering away from God? The Bible offers many different models of response. Elijah hid out in caves and made lightning raids on Ahab's pagan regime; his contemporary Obadiah worked within the system, running Ahab's palace while sheltering God's true prophets on the side. Esther and Daniel were employed by heathen empires; Jonah called down judgment on another. Jesus submitted to the judgment of a Roman governor; Paul appealed his case all the way to Caesar.

To complicate matters, the Bible gives no direct advice for citizens of a democracy. Paul and Peter urged their readers to submit to authorities and honor the king, but in a democracy we the citizens are the "king." We can hardly ignore the government when, by constitutional right, we comprise the government. And if Christians make up a majority, why not proclaim ourselves a "moral majority" and fashion culture in our own likeness?

When some form of Christian consensus held sway in the United States, these issues were less urgent. Now all of us who love our faith and also our nation must decide how best to express that care. I offer three preliminary conclusions that ought to apply no matter what the future brings.

First, as should be clear by now, I believe that dispensing God's grace is the Christian's main contribution. As Gordon MacDonald said, the world can do anything the church can do except one thing: it cannot show grace. In my opinion, Christians are not doing a very good job of dispensing grace to the world, and we stumble especially in this field of faith and politics.

Jesus did not let any institution interfere with his love for individuals. Jewish racial and religious policies forbade him to speak with a Samaritan woman, let alone one with a checkered moral background; Jesus selected one as a missionary. His disciples included a tax collector, viewed as a traitor by Israel, and also a Zealot, a member of the superpatriot party. He praised the countercultural John the Baptist. He met with Nicodemus, an observant Pharisee, and also with a Roman centurion. He dined in the home of another Pharisee named Simon and also in the home of an "unclean" man, Simon the Leper. For Jesus, the person was more important than any category or label.

I know how easy it is to get swept away by the politics of polarization, to shout across picket lines at the "enemy" on the other side. But Jesus commanded, "Love your enemies." For Will Campbell, that meant the redneck Kluxers who killed his friend. For Martin Luther King Jr., that meant the white sheriffs who sicked their police dogs on him.

Who is *my* enemy? The abortionist? The Hollywood producer polluting our culture? The politician threatening my moral principles? The drug lord ruling my inner city? If my activism, however well-motivated, drives out love, then I have misunderstood Jesus' gospel. I am stuck with law, not the gospel of grace.

The issues facing society are pivotal, and perhaps a culture war is inevitable. But Christians should use different weapons in fighting wars, the "weapons of mercy" in Dorothy Day's wonderful phrase. Jesus declared that we should have one distinguishing mark: not political correctness or moral superiority, but *love*. Paul added that without love nothing we do—no miracle of faith, no theological brilliance, no flaming personal sacrifice—will avail (1 Corinthians 13).

Modern democracy badly needs a new spirit of civility, and Christians could show the way by demonstrating the "fruit" of God's Spirit: love, joy, peace, patience, kindness, goodness, faithfulness, gentleness, and self-control.

The weapons of mercy can be potent. I have told of my visit to the White House, which prompted a passel of angry letters. Two of the Christian leaders present at our meeting felt the need to apologize to the President for the ungrace shown by fellow Christians. Said one, "Christians have tainted the credibility of the Gospel by the viciousness of . . . personal attacks against the President and his family." While there, we also heard a firsthand account from Hillary Clinton, target of many of these attacks.

Susan Baker, a Republican and wife of former Secretary of State James Baker, invited Mrs. Clinton to meet with her bipartisan Bible study. The First Lady admitted she felt skeptical about visiting with a group of women who described themselves as "conservative and liberal, Republican and Democrat, but all committed to Jesus." She went with her guard up, ready to defend her positions and absorb some verbal blows.

The meeting began, however, with one of the women saying, "Mrs. Clinton, all of us in this room have agreed to pray for you faithfully. We want to apologize for the way you've been treated by some people, including some Christians. We have wronged you, defamed you, treated you unchristianly. Will you forgive us?"

Hillary Clinton said that she had come prepared for anything that morning except an apology. All her suspicion melted away. Later, she devoted an entire speech at the National Prayer Breakfast to enumerating the spiritual "gifts" she had received from the group. She asked if they could start a similar group for young people her daughter's age; Chelsea had not met many "grace-full" Christians.

It grieves me that mailings from conservative religious groups read, in tone, much like mailings from the ACLU and People for the American Way. Both sides appeal to hysteria, warn against rabid conspiracies, and engage in character assassination of their enemies. In short, both exude the spirit of ungrace.

To his credit, Ralph Reed has publicly renounced such methods. He now regrets using language lacking the "redemptive grace that should always characterize our words and deeds." "If we succeed," Reed wrote in *Active Faith*, "it will be because we have followed [Martin Luther] King's example always to love those who hate us, doing battle 'with Christian weapons and with Christian love.' If we fail, it will not be a failure of money or methods, but a failure of the heart and soul. . . . Every word we say and every action we take should reflect God's grace."

Ralph Reed rightly looks to Martin Luther King Jr., who has much to teach us about the politics of confrontation. "Attack the false idea, not the person who holds that idea," King insisted. King strove to put into practice Jesus' command to "Love your enemies," even while sitting in a jail cell taunted by those enemies. We can only persuade our adversaries on the basis of truth alone, he said, not by resorting to half-truth, exaggeration, or lie. Every volunteer in King's organization pledged to follow eight principles, including these: meditate daily on the teachings and life of Jesus, walk and talk in the manner of love, and observe with both friend and foe the ordinary rules of courtesy.

I was present for a public scene of confrontation that followed the gracious pattern Dr. King laid down. The morning I interviewed President Clinton, as I have mentioned, we both attended the National Prayer Breakfast where we heard Mother Teresa speak. It was a remarkable event. The Clintons and the Gores sat at elevated head tables on either side of Mother Teresa. Rolled out in a wheelchair, the frail, eighty-three-year-old Nobel Peace Prize laureate needed help to stand up. A special platform had been positioned to allow her to see over the podium. Even so, hunched over, four-feet-six-inches tall, she could barely reach the microphone. She spoke clearly and slowly with a thick accent in a voice that nonetheless managed to fill the auditorium.

Mother Teresa said that America has become a selfish nation, in danger of losing the proper meaning of love: "giving until it hurts." The greatest proof, she said, is abortion, the effects of which can be seen in escalating violence. "If we accept that a mother can kill even her own child, how can we tell other people not to kill each other? . . . Any country that accepts abortion is not teaching its people to love, but to use any violence to get what they want."

We are inconsistent, said Mother Teresa, to care about violence, and to care about hungry children in places like India and Africa, and yet not care about the millions who are killed by the deliberate choice of their own mothers. She proposed a solution for those pregnant women who don't want their children: "Give that child to me. I want it. I will care for it. I am willing to accept any child who would be aborted and to give that child to a married couple who will love the child and be loved by the child." Already she has placed three thousand children in adoptive homes in Calcutta.

Mother Teresa filled her talk with poignant stories of people she had ministered to, and no one who heard it could go away unmoved. After the breakfast, Mother Teresa met with President Clinton, and later that day I could tell the conversation had moved him too. Clinton himself brought up several of her stories during our interview.

Courageously, firmly, but with courtesy and love, Mother Teresa had managed to reduce the controversy of abortion to its simplest moral terms: life or death, love or rejection. A skeptic could say about her offer, *Mother Teresa, you don't understand the complexities involved. There are more than a million abortions in the United States alone each year. I'm sure you're going to take care of all those babies!*

But she is Mother Teresa, after all. She has lived out her distinct calling from God, and if God sent a million babies her way, she'd probably find a way to care for them. She understands that sacrificial love is one of the most powerful weapons in the Christian's arsenal of grace.

Prophets come in all sizes and shapes, and I imagine the prophet Elijah, for example, would have used stronger words than Mother Teresa in denouncing moral injustices. Yet I cannot help thinking that of all the words on abortion President Clinton has heard while in office, Mother Teresa's sank in deepest.

My second conclusion may appear to contradict the first: commitment to a style of grace does not mean Christians will live in perfect harmony with the government. As Kenneth Kaunda, the former President of Zambia, has written, "what a nation needs more than anything else is not a Christian ruler in the palace but a Christian prophet within earshot."

From the very beginning Christianity—whose founder, after all, the state executed—has lived in tension with government. Jesus warned his disciples that the world would hate them as it had hated him, and in Jesus' case it was the powerful who conspired against him. As the church spread throughout the Roman empire, its followers took up the slogan "Christ is Lord," a direct affront to Roman authorities who required all citizens to take the oath "Caesar [the state] is Lord." An immovable object had met an irresistible force.

Early Christians hammered out rules to govern their duties to the state. They forbade certain professions: the actor who had to play the part of pagan gods, the teacher forced to teach pagan mythology in public schools, the gladiator who took human life for sport, the soldier who killed, the policeman and the judge. Justin, who would become a martyr, spelled out the limits of obedience to Rome: "To God alone we render worship, but in other things we gladly serve you, acknowledging you as kings and rulers of men, and praying that with your kingly power you be found to possess also sound judgment."

As the centuries unfolded, some rulers showed sound judgment and others did not. When conflict came, brave Christians stood up against the state, appealing to a higher authority. Thomas à Becket told the English king, "We fear no threats, because the Court from which we come is accustomed to give orders to emperors and kings."

Missionaries who carried the gospel to other cultures saw the need to challenge certain practices, bringing them into direct conflict with the state. In India they attacked the caste system, child marriage, bride burning, and the immolation of widows. In South America they banned human sacrifice. In Africa they opposed polygamy and slavery. Christians understood that their faith was not merely private and devotional, but had implications for all of society.

It was no accident that Christians pioneered in the antislavery movement, for example, because of its theological underpinnings. Philosophers like David Hume considered blacks inferior, and business leaders viewed them as a cheap source of labor. Some courageous Christians saw beyond the slaves' utility to their essential worth as human beings created by God and led the way to their emancipation.

For all its flaws the church at times has, fitfully and imperfectly to be sure, dispensed Jesus' message of grace to the world. It was Christianity, and only Christianity, that brought an end to slavery, and Christianity that inspired the first hospitals and hospices to treat the sick. The same energy drove the early labor movement, women's suffrage, prohibition, human rights campaigns, and civil rights.

As for America, Robert Bellah says that "there has not been a major issue in the history of the United States on which religious bodies did not speak out, publicly and vociferously." In recent history, the main leaders of the civil rights movement (Martin Luther King Jr., Ralph Abernathy, Jesse Jackson, Andrew Young) were clergy, and their stirring speeches showed it. Churches black and white provided the buildings, the networks, the ideology, the volunteers, and the theology to sustain the movement.

Martin Luther King Jr. later broadened his crusade to encompass the issues of poverty and opposition to the war in Vietnam. Only recently, as political activism has shifted to conservative causes, has Christian involvement in politics caused alarm. As Stephen Carter suggests in *The Culture of Disbelief*, that alarm may simply betray the fact that those in power dislike the positions of the new activists.

Stephen Carter offers good counsel about political activism: To be effective, "gracious" Christians must be wise in the issues they choose to support or oppose. Historically, Christians have tended to go off on tangents. Yes, we have led the way in abolition and civil rights. But Protestants have also veered off on frenzied campaigns against Catholics, against immigration, against Freemasons. Much of society's present concern over Christian activism traces back to those ill-conceived campaigns.

What about today? Are we choosing our battles wisely? Obviously, abortion, sexual issues, and the definitions of life and death are issues worthy of our attention. Yet when I read the literature produced by evangelicals in politics I also read about gun rights, abolishing the Department of Education, the NAFTA trade agreements, the Panama Canal treaty, and term limits for Congress. A few years back I heard the president of the National Association of Evangelicals include in his list of top ten concerns, "Repeal of the capital gains tax." Too often the agenda of conservative religious groups matches line for line the agenda of conservative politics and does not base its priorities on a transcendent source. Like everyone else, evangelicals have a right to present arguments on all the issues, but the moment we present them as part of some "Christian" platform we abandon our moral high ground.

When the civil rights movement, the great moral crusade of our time, emerged in the mid-sixties, evangelicals mostly sat on the sidelines. Many Southern churches, like my own, fiercely resisted the change. Gradually, spokesmen such as Billy Graham and Oral Roberts followed in step. Only now are evangelical denominations such as the Pentecostal Fellowship of North America and Southern Baptists seeking unity with black churches. Only now are grassroots movements such as the Promise Keepers making racial reconciliation a priority.

To our shame, Ralph Reed admits that the spark for the recent surge of evangelicals in politics was not lit by concern over abortion, injustice in South Africa, or any other compelling moral issue. No, the Carter administration kindled the new activism when it ordered the Internal Revenue Service to investigate private schools, requiring them to prove they were not established to preserve segregation. Up in arms over this breach of the church-state barrier, evangelicals took to the streets.

All too often in their forays into politics Christians have proved "wise as doves" and "harmless as serpents"—exactly the opposite of Jesus' precept. If we expect society to take seriously our contribution, then we must show more wisdom in our choices.

My third conclusion about church-state relations is a principle I borrow from G. K. Chesterton: a coziness between church and state is good for the state and bad for the church.

I have warned against the church becoming "moral exterminators" for the world. Actually, the state needs moral exterminators and may welcome them whenever the church obliges. President Eisenhower told the nation in 1954, "Our government makes no sense unless it is founded on a deeply felt religious faith—and I don't care what it is." I used to laugh at Eisenhower's statement until one weekend I got caught in a situation that showed me the plain truth behind it.

I was participating in a forum with ten Christians, ten Jews, and ten Muslims in New Orleans, coinciding with the heart of Mardi Gras season. We stayed at a Catholic retreat center far removed from the revelry downtown, but one evening several of us wandered over to the French Quarter to watch one of the Carnival parades. It was a frightening scene.

Thousands of people jammed the streets so tightly that we were swept along in a human wave, unable to break loose. Young women hung over the balconies yelling, "Breasts for beads!" In exchange for a gaudy plastic necklace they would pull up their T-shirts and bare themselves. For an elaborate necklace they would strip naked. I saw drunken men pick a teenage girl from the crowd and yell at her "Show your tits!" When she refused, they stripped off her top, hoisted her to their shoulders, and pawed at her as she screamed in protest. In their drunkenness, lust, and even violence, the revelers at Mardi Gras were demonstrating what happens when human desires are allowed to run unchecked.

The next morning, back at the retreat center, we compared accounts of the evening. Some of the women, ardent feminists, were badly shaken. We realized that each of our religions had something to contribute to overall society. Muslim, Christian, or Jew, we all helped society comprehend why such animal behavior was not merely unacceptable but also evil. Religion defines evil and gives people the moral strength to resist. As "the conscience of the state," we help inform the world about justice and righteousness.

In that civic sense, Eisenhower was right: society needs religion, and it matters little what kind. The Nation of Islam helps clean up the ghetto; the Mormon church makes Utah a low-crime, family-friendly state. Founders of the United States recognized that a democracy especially, dependent less on imposed order and more on the virtue of free citizens, needs a religious foundation.

A few years ago, philosopher Glenn Tinder wrote a widely discussed article for *The Atlantic Monthly* titled "Can We Be Good Without God?" His meticulously argued conclusion was, in a word, no. Human beings inevitably drift toward hedonism and selfishness unless something transcendent—*agape* love, Tinder argued—causes them to care about someone other than themselves. With ironic timing, the article appeared one month after the Iron Curtain fell, an event that dashed the idealism of those who had tried to build a just society without God.

We dare not, however, forget the last part of Chesterton's aphorism: while a coziness between church and state may be good for the state, it is bad for the church. Herein lies the chief danger to grace: the state, which runs by the rules of ungrace, gradually drowns out the church's sublime message of grace.

Insatiable for power, the state may well decide that the church could prove even more useful if the state controlled it. This happened most dramatically in Nazi Germany when, ominously, evangelical Christians were attracted to Hitler's promise to restore morality to government and society. Many Protestant leaders initially thanked God for the rise of the Nazis, who seemed the only alternative to communism. According to Karl Barth, the church "almost unanimously welcomed the Hitler regime, with real confidence, indeed with the highest hopes." Too late did they learn that once again the church had been seduced by the power of the state.

The church works best as a force of resistance, a counterbalance to the consuming power of the state. The cozier it gets with government, the more watered-down its message becomes. The gospel itself changes as it devolves into civil religion. Aristotle's lofty ethics, Alasdair MacIntyre reminds us, had no place for a good man showing love to a bad man—in other words, had no place for a gospel of grace.

In sum, the state must always water down the absolute quality of Jesus' commands and turn them into a form of external morality—precisely the opposite of the gospel of grace. Jacques Ellul goes so far as to say the New Testament teaches no such thing as a "Judeo-Christian ethic." It commands conversion and then this, "Be perfect . . . as your heavenly Father is perfect." Read the Sermon on the Mount and try to imagine any government enacting that set of laws.

A state government can shut down stores and theaters on Sunday, but it cannot compel worship. It can arrest and punish KKK murderers but cannot cure their hatred, much less teach them love. It can pass laws making divorce more difficult but cannot force husbands to love their wives and wives their husbands. It can give subsidies to the poor but cannot force the rich to show them compassion and justice. It can ban adultery but not lust, theft but not covetousness, cheating but not pride. It can encourage virtue but not holiness.

The abdication of Belief
Makes the Behavior small.

EMILY DICKINSON

NINETEEN

Patches of Green

During the volcanic eruption of Mt. St. Helens, intense heat melted away the soil, leaving bare rock coated with a thick mantle of ash. Naturalists of the Forest Service wondered how much time must pass before any living thing could grow there. Then one day a park employee stumbled across a lush patch of wildflowers, ferns, and grasses rooted tenaciously to a strip of the desolation. It took a few seconds for him to notice an eerie fact: this patch of vegetation formed the shape of an elk. Plants had sprouted from the organic material that lay where an elk had been buried by ash. From then on, the naturalists looked for such patches of luxuriance as an aid in calculating the loss of wildlife.

Long after a society begins to decay, signs of its former life continue to assert themselves. Without knowing why, people cling to moral customs of the past, the "habits of the heart" in Robert Bellah's phrase. Properly seeded, like the animal shapes dotting the blank sides of Mt. St. Helens, these bring life to an otherwise barren landscape.

Victorian England offers one example of a place where patches of green sprang to life, a place where a group of dedicated Christians graced all of society. It was a somber time of history, marked by slavery in the colonies, child labor in the factories, and squalor in the cities. Change came from below, as it usually does, rather than being imposed from above.

Nearly five hundred British charitable organizations formed during the nineteenth century, at least three-quarters of them evangelical in their approach. The Clapham Sect, a small group of committed Christians, including Charles Simeon and William Wilberforce, got five of its members elected to Parliament. While Wilberforce devoted his entire career to the abolition of slavery, others took up the cause of debtor's prisons, resulting in the release of fourteen thousand prisoners. Still others led crusades in favor of education, housing for the poor, and help for the disabled while opposing child labor, public immorality, and drunkenness. Opponents mocked "the saints," a label which the Clapham Sect wore proudly.

During this same era William Booth used to stroll through the slums of London's East End as his wife taught a Bible class. He noticed that every fifth building was a pub, where men would loiter all day, drinking away their families' livelihood. Many pubs even provided steps at the counter so that small children could climb up and order gin. Appalled at these conditions, William Booth opened the "Christian Mission" in 1865, serving the "down and outers" ignored by others, and out of that vision grew the Salvation Army. (Imagine an organization forming today with that name!) When traditional denominations frowned on the clientele Booth was attracting, he had to form his own church to accommodate these "trophies of grace."

Many people do not know that the Salvation Army operates as a local church as well as a charity. Yet no charitable organization attracts more financial support, and the Salvation Army ranks at the top on any survey of effectiveness: they feed the hungry, shelter the homeless, treat addicts and alcoholics, and show up first at disaster scenes. The movement has continued to grow so that today these soldiers of grace number a million—one of the world's largest standing armies—and serve in a hundred countries. William Booth's lump of yeast now leavens societies around the world.

The reforms undertaken by William Booth and by the Clapham Sect eventually became public policy. And Victorian qualities of honesty, hard work, purity, and charity spread throughout society, helping to spare England the violent disruptions of other nations.

Europe and the United States continue to draw on the moral capital of Christian faith, the overflow of grace. Yet polls reveal that a majority of Americans are anxious about the future (Gallup polls say eighty-three percent of Americans believe the nation is in moral decline). Historian Barbara Tuchman, who has won two Pulitzer prizes for her writing and surely does not represent the alarmism of the religious right, worries about moral bankruptcy. She told Bill Moyers of her concern over

> the loss of a moral sense, of knowing the difference between right and wrong, and of being governed by it. We see it all the time. We open any morning paper and some official has been indicted for embezzlement or corruption. People go around shooting their colleagues or killing people. . . . I ask myself, have nations ever declined from a loss of moral sense rather than from physical reasons or the pressure of barbarians? I think that they have.

Once a Christian consensus has faded, once religious faith has been stripped away from society, what happens then? We need not speculate, for our century has provided case-study answers to that very question. Consider Russia.

The Communist government attacked Russia's heritage with an antireligious fury unprecedented in human history. They razed churches, mosques, and synagogues, banned religious instruction to children, shuttered seminaries and monasteries, imprisoned and killed priests. We all know what happened, of course. After tens of millions of deaths and after experiencing social and moral chaos, the Russian people finally awoke. As usual, the artists spoke first. Alexander Solzhenitsyn said:

> Over half a century ago, while I was still a child, I recall hearing a number of older people offer the following explanation for the great disasters that had befallen Russia: "Men have forgotten God; that's why all this has happened." Since then I have spent well-nigh fifty years working on the history of our revolution; in the process I have read hundreds of books, collected hundreds of personal testimonies, and have already contributed eight volumes of my own toward the effort of clearing away the rubble left by that upheaval. But if I were asked today to formulate as concisely as possible the main cause of the ruinous revolution that swallowed up some sixty million of our people, I could not

put it more accurately than to repeat: "Men have forgotten God; that's why all this has happened."

He spoke those words in 1983, when the USSR was still a superpower and Solzhenitsyn was being widely assailed. Less than a decade later, though, the leaders of Russia were quoting his words with approval, as I heard in person when I visited Russia in 1991.

I saw in Russia a people starved for grace. The economy, indeed the entire society, was in a state of free fall, and everyone had someone to blame. Reformers blamed the Communists, die-hard Communists blamed the Americans, foreigners blamed the Mafia and the Russians' lousy work ethic. Recriminations abounded. I noted that ordinary Russian citizens had the demeanor of battered children: lowered heads, halting speech, eyes darting this way and that. Whom could they trust? Just as a battered child finds it hard to believe in order and love, these people were finding it hard to believe in a God who sovereignly controls the universe and who passionately loves them. They find it hard to believe in grace. Yet without grace, what will end the cycle of ungrace in Russia?

I left Russia overwhelmed at the necessary changes ahead of them, and yet I also left with a sense of grim hope. Even on a moral landscape stripped bare, I saw signs of life, patches of vegetation softening the barrenness, growing in the shape of what had been killed.

I heard from ordinary citizens who now relished their freedom to worship. Most had learned about the faith from a *babushka*, an old grandmother. When the state cracked down on the church, it ignored this group: let the old women sweep the floors and sell the candles and cling to the traditions until they all die off, they reasoned. The aged hands of the *babushki*, though, rocked the cradles. Young churchgoers today often say they first learned about God in childhood through the hymns and stories Grandma would whisper as they drifted off to sleep.

I will never forget a meeting in which Moscow journalists wept—I had never before seen journalists weep—as Ron Nikkel of Prison Fellowship International told of the underground churches that were now thriving in Russia's penal colonies. For seventy years prisons had been the repository of truth, the one place where you could safely speak the name of God. It was in prison, not church, that people such as Solzhenitsyn found God.

Ron Nikkel also told me of his conversation with a general who headed the Ministry of Internal Affairs. The general had heard of the Bible from the old believers and had admired it, but as a museum piece, not something to be believed. Recent events, though, had made him reconsider. In late 1991 when Boris Yeltsin ordered the closing of all national, regional, and local Communist Party offices, his ministry policed the dismantling. "Not one party official," said the general, "not one person directly affected by the closings protested." He contrasted that to the seventy-year campaign to destroy the church and stamp out belief in God. "The Christians' faith outlasted any ideology. The church is now resurging in a way unlike anything I have witnessed."

In 1983 a group of Youth With a Mission daredevils unfolded a banner on Easter Sunday morning in Red Square: "Christ is Risen!" it read in Russian. Some older Russians fell to their knees and wept. Soldiers soon surrounded the hymn-singing troublemakers, tore up their banner, and hustled them off to jail. Less than a decade after that act of civil disobedience, all over Red Square on Easter Sunday people were greeting each other in the traditional way, "Christ is risen!" . . . "He is risen indeed!"

On the long airplane flight from Moscow to Chicago, I had much time to reflect on what I had seen in Russia. While there, I felt like Alice in Wonderland. The cash-strapped government was nevertheless setting aside billions of rubles to help restore churches damaged or destroyed by the Communist regime. We prayed with the Supreme Soviet and with the KGB. We saw Bibles for sale in the Russian government buildings. The editors of *Pravda* asked if one of us could write a religious column for the front page of their newspaper. Educators invited us to submit a curriculum based on the Ten Commandments.

I had the distinct impression that God was moving—not in the spiritualized sense of that phrase but quite literally packing up and moving. Western Europe now pays God little heed, the United States is pushing

God to the margins, and perhaps the future of God's kingdom belongs to places like Korea, China, Africa, and Russia. The kingdom of God thrives where its subjects follow the desires of the King—does that describe the United States of America today?

As an American, the prospect of such a "move" makes me sad. At the same time, however, I understand more clearly than ever before that my ultimate loyalty lies with the kingdom of God, not the United States. The original followers of Jesus watched their beloved Jerusalem burn to the ground, and I am certain they looked back through tears as they moved on to Rome and Spain and Ethiopia. Augustine, who wrote his *City of God* to help explain the dual citizenship of a Christian, lived through the collapse of Rome, and watched from his deathbed as flames devoured his home city of Hippo in northern Africa.

Not long ago I had a conversation with an elderly missionary who had spent his early career in China. He had been among the six thousand missionaries expelled after the Communists took over. As in Russia, these Communists too strove mightily to destroy the church, which until then had been a showcase of the missionary movement. The government forbade house churches, made it illegal for parents to give religious education to their children, imprisoned and tortured pastors and Bible teachers.

Meanwhile, the exiled missionaries sat on the sidelines and wrung their hands. How would the church in China fare without them? Without their seminaries and Bible colleges, their literature and curricula, without even the ability to print Bibles, could the church survive? For forty years these missionaries heard rumors, some discouraging and some encouraging, about what was happening in China, but no one knew for sure until the country began opening up in the 1980s.

I asked this elderly missionary, now a renowned China expert, what had happened in the intervening forty years. "Conservatively, I would estimate there were 750,000 Christians when I left China. And now? You hear all sorts of numbers, but I think a safe figure would be 35 million believers." Apparently, the church and the Holy Spirit fared quite well on their own. The church in China now constitutes the second largest evangelical community in the world; only the United States exceeds it.

One China expert estimates that the revival in China represents the greatest numerical revival in the history of the church. In an odd way, the government hostility ultimately worked to the church's advantage. Shut out of the power structures, Chinese Christians devoted themselves to worship and evangelism, the original mission of the church, and did not much concern themselves with politics. They concentrated on changing lives, not changing laws.

I returned from Russia less concerned about what might happen inside the marble and granite walls of the U.S. Capitol and Supreme Court buildings, and more concerned about what might happen inside the frame walls of churches scattered throughout America. A renewal of spirituality in the United States will not descend from the top down; if it occurs at all, it will start at the grass roots and grow from the bottom up.

I must admit that my return to the United States gave me little reason to hope that Russia and the world might learn grace from Christians here. Randall Terry was pronouncing on National Public Radio that the Midwest floods, which caused thousands of farmers to lose their lands, houses, and livestock, had come as God's judgment against America's failure to support his anti-abortion crusade. The next year, 1992, proved to be one of the most fractious election years, as the religious right flexed its muscle for the first time on a national scale. Christians seemed more interested in power than in grace.

Shortly after the 1992 election I shared a panel with Lucinda Robb, granddaughter of President Lyndon Johnson and daughter of Senator Chuck and Lynda Robb. Her family had just gone through a bruising campaign against Oliver North, in which right-wing Christians picketed their every appearance. "I thought we were Christians," Lucinda told me. "We grew up with Billy Graham as a frequent visitor, and we have always been active in church. We truly believe. But these demonstrators treated us like we were demons from hell."

The panel we shared addressed the topic "Culture Wars" before a large gathering that tilted toward the liberal Democratic persuasion and included a strong Jewish minority. I had been selected as the token evangelical Christian. In addition to Lucinda Robb, the panel included the presidents of the Disney Channel and Warner Brothers, as well as the president of Wellesley College and Anita Hill's personal attorney.

To prepare for my talk, I went through the Gospels for guidance, only to be reminded how unpolitical Jesus was. In the words of P. T. Forsyth, "The largest and deepest reference of the Gospel is not to the world or its social problems, but to Eternity and its social obligations." Today, each time an election rolls around Christians debate whether this or that candidate is "God's man" for the White House. Projecting myself back into Jesus' time, I had difficulty imagining him pondering whether Tiberius, Octavius, or Julius Caesar was "God's man" for the empire.

When my turn came to speak, I said that the man I follow, a Palestinian Jew from the first century, had also been involved in a culture war. He went up against a rigid religious establishment and a pagan empire. The two powers, often at odds, conspired together to eliminate him. His response? Not to fight, but to give his life for these his enemies, and to point to that gift as proof of his love. Among the last words he spoke before death were these: "Father, forgive them, for they do not know what they are doing."

After the panel, a television celebrity came up to me whose name every reader would recognize. "I've got to tell you, what you said stabbed me right in the heart," he said. "I was prepared to dislike you because I dislike all right-wing Christians and I assumed you were one. You can't imagine the mail I get from right-wingers. I don't follow Jesus—I'm a Jew. But when you told about Jesus forgiving his enemies, I realized how far from that spirit I am. I fight my enemies, especially the right-wingers. I don't forgive them. I have much to learn from the spirit of Jesus."

In that celebrity's life, the slow, steady undertow of grace was at work.

Jesus' images portray the kingdom as a kind of secret force. Sheep among wolves, treasure hidden in a field, the tiniest seed in the garden, wheat growing among weeds, a pinch of yeast worked into bread dough, a sprinkling of salt on meat—all these hint at a movement that works within society, changing it from the inside out. You do not need a shovelful of salt to preserve a slab of ham; a dusting will suffice.

Jesus did not leave an organized host of followers, for he knew that a handful of salt would gradually work its way through the mightiest empire in the world. Against all odds, the great institutions of Rome—the law code, libraries, the Senate, Roman legions, roads, aqueducts, public monuments—gradually crumbled, but the little band to whom Jesus gave these images prevailed and continues on today.

Søren Kierkegaard described himself as a spy, and indeed Christians behave like spies, living in one world while our deepest allegiance belongs to another. We are resident aliens, or *sojourners*, to use a biblical phrase. My visits to totalitarian states have filled that phrase with new meaning.

For many years dissidents in Eastern Europe met in secret, used code words, avoided public telephones, and published pseudonymous essays in underground papers. In the mid-1970s, however, these dissidents began to realize that their double lives had cost them dearly. By working in secret, always with a nervous glance over the shoulder, they had succumbed to fear, the goal of their Communist opponents all along. They made a conscious decision to change tactics. "We will act as if we are free, at all costs," Polish and Czech dissidents decided. They began holding public meetings, often in church buildings, despite the presence of known informers. They signed articles, sometimes adding an address and phone number, and distributed newspapers openly on the street corners.

In effect, the dissidents started acting in the way they thought society should act. If you want freedom of speech, speak freely. If you love the truth, tell the truth. The authorities did not know how to respond. Sometimes they cracked down—nearly all the dissidents spent time in prison—and sometimes they watched with a frustration bordering on rage. Meanwhile the dissidents' brazen tactics made it far easier for them to connect with one another and the West, and a kind of "freedom archipelago" took shape, a bright counterpart to the darkling "Gulag archipelago."

Remarkably, we have lived to see these dissidents triumph. An alternative kingdom of ragged subjects, of prisoners, poets, and priests, who conveyed their words in the scrawl of hand-copied *samizdat*, toppled what seemed an impregnable fortress. In each nation the church operated as a counterforce, sometimes quietly and sometimes loudly insisting on a truth that transcended, and often contradicted, official propaganda. In Poland the Catholics marched past government buildings shouting, "We forgive you!" In East Germany, Christians lit candles, prayed, and marched in the streets until one night the Berlin Wall collapsed like a rotten dam.

Early on, Stalin built a village in Poland called Nowa Huta, or "New Town," to demonstrate the promise of communism. He could not change the entire country at once, he said, but he could construct one new town with a shiny steel factory, spacious apartments, plentiful parks, and broad streets as a token of what would follow. Later, Nowa Huta became one of the hotbeds of Solidarity, demonstrating instead the failure of communism to make just one town work.

What if Christians used that same approach in secular society and succeeded? "In the world the Christians are a colony of the true home," said Bonhoeffer. Perhaps Christians should work harder toward establishing colonies of the kingdom that point to our true home. All too often the church holds up a mirror reflecting back the society around it, rather than a window revealing a different way.

If the world despises a notorious sinner, the church will love her. If the world cuts off aid to the poor and the suffering, the church will offer food and healing. If the world oppresses, the church will raise up the oppressed. If the world shames a social outcast, the church will proclaim God's reconciling love. If the world seeks profit and self-fulfillment, the church seeks sacrifice and service. If the world demands retribution, the church dispenses grace. If the world splinters into factions, the church joins together in unity. If the world destroys its enemies, the church loves them.

That, at least, is the vision of the church in the New Testament: a colony of heaven in a hostile world. Dwight L. Moody said, "Of one hundred men, one will read the Bible; the ninety-nine will read the Christian."

Like the dissidents in Communist countries, Christians live by a different set of rules. We are a "peculiar" people, wrote Bonhoeffer, which he defined as extraordinary, unusual, that which is not a matter of course. Jesus was not crucified for being a good citizen, for being just a little nicer than everyone else. The powers of his day correctly saw him and his followers as subversives because they took orders from a higher power than Rome or Jerusalem.

What would a subversive church look like in the modern United States? Some observers have called the United States the most religious nation on earth. If true, that fact leads to a bracing question, as articulated by Dallas Willard: Shouldn't a quarter pound of salt be having more effect on a pound of meat?

Surely a peculiar people should demonstrate a higher standard of personal ethics than the surrounding world. Yet, to take just one example, pollster George Barna discovered that born-again Christians in modern America actually have a higher rate of divorce (twenty-seven percent) than nonbelievers (twenty-three percent); those who describe themselves as fundamentalists have the highest percentage of all (thirty percent). Indeed, four of the six states with the highest divorce rates fall in the region known as the Bible Belt. Far from being peculiar, modern Christians tend to look just like everyone else, only more so. Unless our personal ethics rise above the level around us, we can hardly hope to act as a moral preservative.

Even if Christians demonstrated the highest standard of ethics, however, that alone would not fulfill the gospel. After all, the Pharisees had impeccable ethics. Rather, Jesus reduced the mark of a Christian to one word. "By this all men will know that you are my disciples," he said: "if you *love* one another." The most subversive act the church can take is consistently to obey that one command.

Perhaps the reason politics has proved such a snare for the church is that power rarely coexists with love. People in power draw up lists of friends and enemies, then reward their friends and punish their enemies. Christians are commanded to love even their enemies. Chuck Colson, who perfected the art of power politics under the Nixon Administration, now says he has little faith in politics to solve the social problems of today. Our best efforts at changing society will fall short unless the church can teach the world how to love.

Colson cites a poignant example of a Christian who obeyed the command of love rather than the rules of power. After President Nixon resigned in disgrace, he retreated to his San Clemente compound to live in virtual isolation. Because politicians did not want to sully their own reputations by being seen with him, Nixon had few visitors at first. One exception was Mark Hatfield, an outspoken Christian who had often opposed Nixon in the U.S. Senate. Colson asked why he risked the trips to San Clemente. "To let Mr. Nixon know that someone loved him," Hatfield replied.

I know something of the abuse Billy Graham received for meeting with Bill and Hillary Clinton and for praying at Clinton's inaugurations. Graham too believes the command to love transcends political differences, and for this reason he has ministered to every president since Harry Truman, regardless of politics. In a private interview, I asked Reverend Graham which president he had spent the most time with. To my surprise, he named Lyndon Johnson, a man with whom he had deep political differences. Yet Johnson had a fear of death and "he always seemed to want a pastor around." For Graham, the person was more important than the policy.

During the Brezhnev era at the height of the Cold War, Billy Graham visited Russia and met with government and church leaders. Conservatives back home reproached him for treating the Russians with such courtesy and respect. He should have taken a more prophetic role, they said, by condemning the abuses of human rights and religious liberty. One of his critics accused him of setting the church back fifty years. Graham listened, lowered his head, and replied, "I am deeply ashamed. I have been trying very hard to set the church back two thousand years."

Politics draws lines between people; in contrast, Jesus' love cuts across those lines and dispenses grace. That does not mean, of course, that Christians should not involve themselves in politics. It simply means that as we do so we must not let the rules of power displace the command to love.

Ron Sider has said,

> Think of the impact if the first thing radical feminists thought of when the conversation turned to evangelical men was that they had the best reputation for keeping their marriage vows and serving their wives in the costly fashion of Jesus at the cross. Think of the impact if the first thing the homosexual community thought of when someone mentioned evangelicals was that they were the people who lovingly ran the AIDS shelters and tenderly cared for them down to the last gasp. A little consistent wholesome modeling and costly servanthood are worth millions of true words harshly spoken.

A friend of mine worked at a pregnancy counseling center. A committed Catholic, she counseled clients to choose against abortion and let her find adoptive parents for their babies. Because of its location close to a major university, pro-choice demonstrators often picketed the center. One cold, snowy Michigan day, my friend sent out for doughnuts and coffee, ordering enough for all the demonstrators opposing her center. When the food arrived, she went out in person to offer it to her "enemies."

"I know we disagree on this issue," she told them. "But I still respect you as people, and I know it must be cold standing out here all day. I thought you might want some nourishment."

The pickets were shocked speechless. They mumbled thanks and stared at the coffee, though most refused to drink it (had she laced it with poison?).

Christians may choose to enter an arena of power, but when we do so we dare not leave love behind. "Power without love is reckless and abusive," said Martin Luther King Jr. "Power at its best is love implementing the demands of justice."

Friedrich Nietzsche accused the Christian church as having "taken the side of everything weak, base, ill-constituted." He scorned a religion of pity that thwarted the law of evolution and its rules favoring power and competition. Nietzsche put his finger on the scandal of grace, a scandal that he traced back to "God on the cross."

Nietzsche was right. In Jesus' parables, the rich and healthy never seem to make it to the wedding feast, while the poor and the weak come running. And through the ages, Christian saints have chosen the most un-Darwinian objects for their love. Mother Teresa's nuns lavish care on homeless wretches who have mere days if not hours left to live. Jean Vanier, founder of the l'Arche movement, lives in a home that employs seventeen assistants to work with ten mentally handicapped men and women, none of whom will ever be able to speak or coordinate their hand movements. Dorothy Day of the Catholic Worker Movement admitted to the folly of her soup kitchen: "What a delightful thing it is," she said, "to be boldly profligate, to ignore the price of coffee and go on serving the long line of destituted men who come to us, good coffee and the finest of bread."

The Christian knows to serve the weak not because they deserve it but because God extended his love to us when we deserved the opposite. Christ came *down* from heaven, and whenever his disciples entertained dreams of prestige and power he reminded them that the greatest is the one who serves. The ladder of power reaches up, the ladder of grace reaches down.

As a journalist, I have had the privilege of seeing many wonderful examples of Christians who dispense grace. Unlike political activists, this group does not often make the newspapers. Faithfully they serve, seasoning our culture with the preservative of the gospel. I tremble to imagine what the modern United States would look like without the "salt of the earth" in its midst.

"Never underestimate the power of a minority who cherish the vision of a just and gentle world," said Robert Bellah. These are the people I wish would come to mind when I ask my airplane seatmates, "What does an evangelical Christian look like?"

I know the hospice movement well, for my wife works in one as a chaplain. I once interviewed Dame Cicely Saunders, founder of the modern hospice movement, at St. Christopher's Hospice in London. A social worker and nurse, she was appalled at the way medical staff treated people who were about to die—in essence, ignoring them, as tokens of failure. This attitude offended Saunders as a Christian, for care of the dying has traditionally been one of the church's seven works of mercy. Since no one would listen to a nurse, she returned to medical school and became a doctor before founding a place where people could come to die with dignity and without pain. Now, hospices exist in forty countries including two thousand in the United States alone—about half of which have a Christian base. Dame Cicely believed from the beginning that Christians offer the best combination of physical, emotional, and spiritual care for people facing death. She holds up hospice care as a glowing alternative to Dr. Kevorkian and his "right to die" movement.

I think of the thousands of chapters based on the twelve-step program that meet in church basements, VFW halls, and living rooms all across the nation, any night of the week. The Christians who founded Alcoholics Anonymous faced a choice: whether to make it a restrictively Christian organization or to found it on Christian principles and then set it free. They chose the latter option, and now millions of people in America look to their program—based on dependence on a "Higher Power" and on a supportive community—as a remedy for addictions to alcohol, drugs, sex, and food.

I think of Millard Fuller, a millionaire entrepreneur from Alabama who still speaks with a cotton-field twang. Rich but miserable, his marriage on the rocks, he headed to Americus, Georgia, where he fell under the spell of Clarence Jordan and the Koinonia Community. Before long, Fuller gave away his personal fortune and founded an organization on the simple premise that every person on the planet deserves a decent place to live. Today Habitat for Humanity enlists thousands of volunteers to build houses all over the world. I once heard Fuller explain his work to a skeptical Jewish woman, "Ma'am, we don't try to evangelize. You don't have to be a Christian to live in one of our houses or to help us build one. But the fact is, the reason I do what I do, and so many of our volunteers do what they do, is that we're being obedient to Jesus."

I think of Chuck Colson, imprisoned for his role in Watergate, who emerged with a desire to climb not up, but down. He founded Prison Fellowship, which today operates in almost eighty countries. Families of more than two million U.S. prisoners have received Christmas presents thanks to Colson's Angel Tree project. Overseas, church members bring pots of stew and loaves of fresh-baked bread to prisoners who would otherwise starve. The Brazilian government even allows Prison Fellowship to oversee a prison run by the Christian inmates themselves. Humaita Prison employs only two staff members and yet has no problems with riots or escapees and has a repeat offender rate of four percent compared to seventy-five percent in the rest of Brazil.

I think of Bill Magee, a plastic surgeon who was shocked to find that in Third World countries many children go through life with cleft palates that never get treated. They cannot smile, and their lips curl open in a constant sneer, making them the object of ridicule. Magee and his wife organized a program called Operation Smile: planeloads of doctors and support personnel travel to places like Vietnam, the Philippines, Kenya, Russia, and the Middle East in order to repair facial deformities. So far, they have operated on more than thirty-six thousand children, leaving behind a legacy of children's smiles.

I think of medical missionaries I have known in India, especially those who work with leprosy patients. On the scale of ungrace, there is no more abused group of people on earth than leprosy victims who come from the Untouchable caste. You cannot descend any lower. Most of the major advances in the treatment of leprosy have come from Christian missionaries, because they were the only people willing to touch and care for leprosy victims. Thanks largely to the work of these faithful servants, the disease is now fully controllable by drugs, and the chance of contagion is minimal.

I think of Bread for the World, an agency founded by Christians who believed they could best help the hungry not by starting a competitor to World Vision but by lobbying Congress on behalf of the world's poor. Or of Joseph's House, a home for AIDS patients in Washington, D.C. Or of Pat Robertson's Operation Blessing that runs inner-city programs in thirty-five large cities, or of Jerry Falwell's "Save a Baby Homes" where pregnant women can go to a loving home for support if they choose to carry their babies to term rather than abort—programs that get far less attention than do their founders' political views.

Rousseau said the church set up an irresolvable loyalty dilemma. How can Christians be good citizens of this world if they are primarily concerned about the next world? The people I have mentioned, and many millions like them, disprove his argument. As C. S. Lewis has noted, those most conscious of another world have made the most effective Christians in this one.

Man is born broken. He lives by mending.
The grace of God is glue.

EUGENE O'NEILL

TWENTY

Gravity and Grace

Simone Weil's life flamed like a bright candle before she died at the age of thirty-three. A French intellectual, she chose to work on farms and in factories in order to identify with the working class. When Hitler's armies rolled into France, she escaped to join the Free French in London, and there she died, her tuberculosis complicated by malnourishment when she refused to eat more than the rations of her countrymen suffering Nazi occupation. As her only legacy, this Jew who followed Christ left in scattered notes and journals a dense record of her pilgrimage toward God.

Weil concluded that two great forces rule the universe: gravity and grace. Gravity causes one body to attract other bodies so that it continually enlarges by absorbing more and more of the universe into itself. Something like this same force operates in human beings. We too want to expand, to acquire, to swell in significance. The desire to "be as gods," after all, led Adam and Eve to rebel.

Emotionally, Weil concluded, we humans operate by laws as fixed as Newton's. "All the *natural* movements of the soul are controlled by laws analogous to those of physical gravity. Grace is the only exception." Most of us remain trapped in the gravitational field of self-love, and thus we "fill up all the fissures through which grace might pass."

About the same time Weil was writing, another refugee from the Nazis, Karl Barth, made the comment that Jesus' gift of forgiveness, of grace, was to him more astonishing than Jesus' miracles. Miracles broke the physical laws of the universe; forgiveness broke the moral rules. "The beginning of good is perceived in the midst of bad. . . . The simplicity and comprehensiveness of grace—who shall measure it?"

Who shall measure it indeed? I have merely walked the perimeter of grace, as one walks around a cathedral far too large and grand to behold at one glance. Having begun with questions—What's so amazing about grace and why don't Christians show more of it?—I now end with a final question: What does a grace-full Christian look like?

Perhaps I should rephrase the question, How does a grace-full Christian *look*? The Christian life, I believe, does not primarily center on ethics or rules but rather involves a new way of seeing. I escape the force of spiritual "gravity" when I begin to see myself as a sinner who cannot please God by any method of self-improvement or self-enlargement. Only then can I turn to God for outside help—for grace—and to my amazement I learn that a holy God already loves me despite my defects. I escape the force of gravity again when I recognize my neighbors also as sinners, loved by God. A grace-full Christian is one who looks at the world through "grace-tinted lenses."

A pastor friend of mine was studying the assigned text for the day from Matthew 7 in which Jesus said, rather fiercely, "Many will say to me on that day, 'Lord, Lord, did we not prophesy in your name, and in your name drive out demons and perform many miracles?' Then I will tell them plainly, 'I never knew you. Away from me, you evildoers!'"

The phrase "I never knew you" leaped out from the page. Pointedly, Jesus did not say "*You* never knew *me*," or "You never knew the Father." It struck my friend that one of our main tasks, perhaps the main task, is to make ourselves known to God. Good works are not enough—"did we not prophesy in your name?"—any relationship with God must be based on full disclosure. The masks must come off.

"We cannot find Him unless we know we need Him," wrote Thomas Merton. For someone raised in a strong church background, that awareness may not come easily. My own church tended toward perfectionism, which tempted us all to follow the example of Ananias and Sapphira in misrepresenting ourselves spiritually. On Sundays well-scrubbed families emerged from their cars with smiles on their faces even though, as we later found out, they had been fighting abusively all week long.

As a child, I put on my best behavior on Sunday mornings, dressing up for God and for the Christians around me. It never occurred to me that church was a place to be honest. Now, though, as I seek to look at the world through the lens of grace, I realize that imperfection is the prerequisite for grace. Light only gets in through the cracks.

My pride still tempts me to put on the best front, to clean up appearances. "It is easy to acknowledge," said C. S. Lewis, "but almost impossible to realise for long, that we are mirrors whose brightness, if we are bright, is wholly derived from the sun that shines upon us. Surely we must have a little—however little—native luminosity? Surely we can't be *quite* creatures." He goes on, "Grace substitutes a full, childlike and delighted acceptance of our Need, a joy in total dependence. We become 'jolly beggars.'"

We creatures, we jolly beggars, give glory to God by our dependence. Our wounds and defects are the very fissures through which grace might pass. It is our human destiny on earth to be imperfect, incomplete, weak, and mortal, and only by accepting that destiny can we escape the force of gravity and receive grace. Only then can we grow close to God.

Strangely, God is closer to sinners than to "saints." (By saints I mean those people renowned for their piety—true saints never lose sight of their sinfulness.) As one lecturer in spirituality explains it, "God in heaven holds each person by a string. When you sin, you cut the string. Then God ties it up again, making a knot—and thereby bringing you a little closer to him. Again and again your sins cut the string—and with each further knot God keeps drawing you closer and closer."

Once my view of myself changed, I began to see the church in a different light too: as a community of people thirsty for grace. Like alcoholics on the path to recovery, we share a mutually acknowledged weakness. Gravity tempts us to believe we can make it on our own; grace corrects that error.

I think back one more time to the prostitute's comment at the beginning of this book: "Church! Why would I ever go there? I was already feeling terrible about myself. They would just make me feel worse." Church should be a haven for people who feel terrible about themselves—theologically, that is our ticket for entry. God needs humble people (which usually means humbled people) to accomplish his work. Whatever makes us feel superior to other people, whatever tempts us to convey a sense of superiority, that is gravity, not grace.

Readers of the Gospels marvel at Jesus' ability to move with ease among the sinners and outcasts. Having spent time around "sinners" and also around purported "saints," I have a hunch why Jesus spent so much time with the former group: I think he preferred their company. Because the sinners were honest about themselves and had no pretense, Jesus could deal with them. In contrast, the saints put on airs, judged him, and sought to catch him in a moral trap. In the end it was the saints, not the sinners, who arrested Jesus.

Recall the story of Jesus' dinner at the home of Simon the Pharisee, in which a woman not so different from the prostitute in Chicago poured perfume on Jesus and provocatively wiped his feet with her hair. Simon was repulsed—such a woman did not even deserve to enter his house! Here is how Jesus responded in that tense atmosphere:

> Then he turned toward the woman and said to Simon, "Do you see this woman? I came into your house. You did not give me any water for my feet, but she wet my feet with her tears and wiped them with her hair. You did not give me a kiss, but this woman, from the time I entered, has not stopped kissing my feet. You did not put oil on my head, but she has poured perfume on my feet. Therefore, I tell you, her many sins have been forgiven—for she loved much. But he who has been forgiven little loves little."

Why is it, I ask myself, that the church sometimes conveys the spirit of Simon the Pharisee rather than that of the forgiven woman? Why is it that I often do?

A novel published a century ago, *The Damnation of Theron Ware*, gave me a lasting image of what the church should be. A skeptical doctor speaking to a fundamentalist pastor and a Catholic priest said, "If you don't mind my saying so—of course I view you all impartially from the outside—but it seems logical to me that a church should exist for those who need its help, and not for those who by their own profession are so good already that it is they who help the church." The skeptic then described church as a place that should keep grace on tap. "Some come every day, some only once a year, some perhaps never between their baptism and their funeral. But they all have a right here, the professional burglar every whit as much as the speckless saint. The only stipulation is that they oughtn't to come under false pretences. . . ."

That image of church dispensing grace "on tap" has special poignancy for me because of an AA group that met in the basement of my church in Chicago. Alcoholics Anonymous can't get many churches to loan their facilities, for a very practical reason: their groups tend to make a mess. AA members fight off the demons of addiction to drugs and alcohol by relying on lesser demons of cigarettes and coffee, and few churches want to put up with the stains on floors and tables and the smoke damage to walls and drapes. The church I attended decided to open their doors to AA regardless.

I sometimes attended AA as an act of solidarity with a recovering alcoholic friend. The first time I accompanied him I was overwhelmed by what I found, for in many ways it resembled the New Testament church. A well-known television broadcaster and several prominent millionaires mixed freely with unemployed dropouts and kids who wore Band-Aids to hide the needle marks on their arms. The "sharing time" was like a textbook small group, marked by compassionate listening, warm responses, and many hugs. Introductions went like this: "Hi, I'm Tom, and I'm an alcoholic and a drug addict." Instantly everyone shouted out in unison, like a Greek chorus, "Hi, Tom!" Each person attending gave a personal progress report on his or her battle with addiction.

Over time I saw that AA runs on two principles: radical honesty and radical dependence. These are the very same principles expressed in the Lord's Prayer, Jesus' capsule summary of living "one day at a time," and in fact many AA groups recite the Lord's Prayer together at each meeting.

AA would never allow a person to say, "Hi, I'm Tom, I used to be an alcoholic but now I'm cured." Even if Tom has not had a drink for thirty years, he still must identify himself as an alcoholic—by denying his weakness he would make himself its victim. Also, Tom could never say, "I may be an alcoholic, but I'm not as bad as Betty there. She's a cocaine addict." In AA the ground is level.

As Lewis Meyer puts it,

> It is the only place I know where status means nothing. Nobody fools anybody else. Everyone is here because he or she made a slobbering mess of his or her life and is trying to put the pieces back together again. . . . I have attended thousands of church meetings, lodge meetings, brotherhood meetings—yet I have never found the kind of love I find at AA. For one small hour the high and mighty descend and the lowly rise. The leveling that results is what people mean when they use the word brotherhood.

For a "cure," the AA program demands of its members radical dependence on a Higher Power and on fellow strugglers. Most people in the groups I've attended substitute "God" for "Higher Power." They openly ask God for forgiveness and strength, and ask their friends around them for support. They come to AA because they believe that there, grace flows "on tap."

Sometimes as I went up and down the stairs connecting our church sanctuary to the basement, I thought of the upstairs/downstairs contrast between Sunday mornings and Tuesday evenings. Only a few of those who met on Tuesday evenings returned on Sundays. Though they appreciated the church's generosity in opening its basement to them, the AA members I talked with said they would not feel at ease in church. Upstairs people seemed to have it together, while they were just barely hanging on. They felt more comfortable in the swirl of blue smoke, slouched in metal chairs in jeans and a T-shirt, using swear words if they felt like it. That's where they belonged, not in a stained-glass sanctuary with straight-backed pews.

If only they realized, if only the church could realize, that in some of the most important lessons of spirituality, members of the basement group were our masters. They began with radical honesty and ended with radical dependence. Athirst, they came as "jolly beggars" every week because AA was the one place that offered grace on tap.

A few times at my church I preached the sermon, then assisted in the ceremony of communion. "I don't partake because I'm a good Catholic, holy and pious and sleek," writes Nancy Mairs about the Eucharist. "I partake because I'm a bad Catholic, riddled by doubt and anxiety and anger: fainting from severe hypoglycemia of the soul." After delivering the sermon, I helped nourish famished souls.

Those who desired to partake would come to the front, stand quietly in a semicircle, and wait for us to bring them the elements. "The body of Christ broken for you," I would say as I held out a loaf of bread for the person before me to break off. "The blood of Christ shed for you," the pastor behind me would say, holding out a common cup.

Because my wife worked for the church, and because I taught a class there for many years, I knew the stories of some of the people standing before me. I knew that Mabel, the woman with strawy hair and bent posture who came to the senior citizen's center, had been a prostitute. My wife worked with her for seven years before Mabel confessed the dark secret buried deep within. Fifty years ago she had sold her only child, a daughter. Her family had rejected her long before, the pregnancy had eliminated her source of income, and she knew she would make a terrible mother, and so she sold the baby to a couple in Michigan. She could never forgive herself, she said. Now she was standing at the communion rail, spots of rouge like paper discs pasted on her cheeks, her hands outstretched, waiting to receive the gift of grace. "The body of Christ broken for you, Mabel . . ."

Beside Mabel were Gus and Mildred, star players in the only wedding ceremony ever performed among the church's seniors. They lost $150 per month in Social Security benefits by marrying rather than living together, but Gus insisted. He said Mildred was the light of his life, and he didn't care if he lived in poverty as long as he lived it with her at his side. "The blood of Christ shed for you, Gus, and you, Mildred . . ."

Next came Adolphus, an angry young black man whose worst fears about the human race had been confirmed in Vietnam. Adolphus scared people away from our church. Once, in a class I was teaching on the book of Joshua, Adolphus raised his hand and pronounced, "I wish I had an M–16 rifle right now. I would kill all you white honkeys in this room." An elder in the church who was a doctor took him aside afterwards and talked to him, insisting that he take his medication before services on Sunday. The church put up with Adolphus because we knew he came not merely out of anger but out of hunger. If he missed the bus, and no one had offered him a ride, sometimes he walked five miles to get to church. "The body of Christ broken for you, Adolphus . . ."

I smiled at Christina and Reiner, an elegant German couple employed by the University of Chicago. Both were Ph.D.s, and they came from the same Pietist community in southern Germany. They had told us about the worldwide impact of the Moravian movement, which still influenced their church back home, but right now they were struggling with the very message they held dear. Their son had just left on a mission trip to India. He planned to live for a year in the worst slum in Calcutta. Christina and Reiner had always honored such personal sacrifice—but now that it was their son, everything looked different. They feared for his health and safety. Christina held her face in her hands, and tears dribbled through her fingers. "The blood of Christ shed for you, Christina, and you, Reiner . . ."

Then came Sarah, a turban covering her bare head, scarred from where doctors had removed a brain tumor. And Michael, who stuttered so badly he would physically cringe whenever anyone addressed him. And Maria, the wild and overweight Italian woman who had just married for the fourth time. "Thees one will be deeferent, I just know."

"The body of Christ . . . the blood of Christ . . ." What could we offer such people other than grace, on tap? What better can the church ever offer than "means of grace"? Grace here, among these shattered families and half-coping individuals? Yes, here. Maybe the upstairs church was not so different from the downstairs AA group after all.

Strangely enough, the lens of grace reveals those outside the church in the very same light. Like me, like everyone inside the church, they too are sinners loved by God. Lost children, some have strayed very far from home, but even so the Father stands ready to welcome them back with joy and celebration.

Diviners in a desert, modern artists and thinkers search in vain for alternate sources of grace. "What the world needs, I am ashamed to say, is Christian love," wrote Bertrand Russell. Not long before she died, the secular humanist and novelist Marghanita Laski told a television interviewer, "What I envy most about you Christians is your forgiveness. I have nobody to forgive me." And Douglas Coupland, who coined the term *Generation X*, concluded in his book *Life After God*, "My secret is that I need God—that I am sick and can no longer make it alone. I need God to help me give, because I no longer seem to be capable of giving; to help me be kind, as I no longer seem capable of kindness; to help me love, as I seem beyond being able to love."

I marvel at Jesus' tenderness in dealing with people who expressed such longings. John gives the account of Jesus' impromptu conversation with a woman at a well. In those days the husband initiated divorce: this Samaritan woman had been dumped by five different men. Jesus could have begun by pointing out what a mess the woman had made of her life. Yet he did not say, "Young woman, do you realize what an immoral thing you're doing, living with a man who is not your husband?" Rather he said, in effect, *I sense you are very thirsty.* Jesus went on to tell her that the water she was drinking would never satisfy and then offered her living water to quench her thirst forever.

I try to recall this spirit of Jesus when I encounter someone of whom I morally disapprove. *This must be a very thirsty person*, I tell myself. I once talked with the priest Henri Nouwen just after he had returned from San Francisco. He had visited various ministries to AIDS victims and was moved with compassion by their sad stories. "They want love so bad, it's literally killing them," he said. He saw them as thirsty people panting after the wrong kind of water.

When I am tempted to recoil in horror from sinners, from "different" people, I remember what it must have been like for Jesus to live on earth. Perfect, sinless, Jesus had every right to be repulsed by the behavior of those around them. Yet he treated notorious sinners with mercy and not judgment.

One who has been touched by grace will no longer look on those who stray as "those evil people" or "those poor people who need our help." Nor must we search for signs of "loveworthiness." Grace teaches us that God loves because of who God is, not because of who we are. Categories of worthiness do not apply. In his autobiography, the German philosopher Friedrich Nietzsche told of his ability to "smell" the inmost parts of every soul, especially the "abundant hidden dirt at the bottom of many a character." Nietzsche was a master of ungrace. We are called to do the opposite, to smell the residue of hidden worth.

In a scene from the movie *Ironweed*, the characters played by Jack Nicholson and Meryl Streep stumble across an old Eskimo woman lying in the snow, probably drunk. Besotted themselves, the two debate what they should do about her.

"Is she drunk or a bum?" asks Nicholson.

"Just a bum. Been one all her life."

"And before that?"

"She was a whore in Alaska."

"She hasn't been a whore all her life. Before that?"

"I dunno. Just a little kid, I guess."

"Well, a little kid's something. It's not a bum and it's not a whore. It's something. Let's take her in."

The two vagrants were seeing the Eskimo woman through the lens of grace. Where society saw only a bum and a whore, grace saw "a little kid," a person made in the image of God no matter how defaced that image had become.

Christianity has a principle, "Hate the sin but love the sinner," which is more easily preached than practiced. If Christians could simply recover that practice, modeled so exquisitely by Jesus, we would go a long way toward fulfilling our calling as dispensers of God's grace. For a long time, C. S. Lewis reports, he could never understand the hairsplitting distinction between hating a person's sin and hating the sinner. How could you hate what a man did and not hate the man?

> But years later it occurred to me that there was one man to whom I had been doing this all my life—namely myself. However much I might dislike my own cowardice or conceit or greed, I went on loving myself. There had never been the slightest difficulty about it. In fact the very reason why I hated the things was that I loved the man. Just because I loved myself, I was sorry to find that I was the sort of man who did those things.

Christians should not compromise in hating sin, says Lewis. Rather we should hate the sins in others in the same way we hate them in ourselves: being sorry the person has done such things and hoping that somehow, sometime, somewhere, that person will be cured.

Bill Moyers' documentary film on the hymn "Amazing Grace" includes a scene filmed in Wembley Stadium in London. Various musical groups, mostly rock bands, had gathered together in celebration of the changes in South Africa, and for some reason the promoters scheduled an opera singer, Jessye Norman, as the closing act.

The film cuts back and forth between scenes of the unruly crowd in the stadium and Jessye Norman being interviewed. For twelve hours groups like Guns 'n' Roses have blasted the crowd through banks of speakers, riling up fans already high on booze and dope. The crowd yells for more curtain calls, and the rock groups oblige. Meanwhile, Jessye Norman sits in her dressing room discussing "Amazing Grace" with Moyers.

The hymn was written, of course, by John Newton, a coarse, cruel slave trader. He first called out to God in the midst of a storm that nearly threw him overboard. Newton came to see the light only gradually, continuing to ply his trade even after his conversion. He wrote the song "How Sweet the Name of Jesus Sounds" while waiting in an African harbor for a shipment of slaves. Later, though, he renounced his profession, became a minister, and joined William Wilberforce in the fight against slavery. John Newton never lost sight of the depths from which he had been lifted. He never lost sight of grace. When he wrote " . . . That saved a wretch like me," he meant those words with all his heart.

In the film, Jessye Norman tells Bill Moyers that Newton may have borrowed an old tune sung by the slaves themselves, redeeming the song, just as he had been redeemed.

Finally, the time comes for her to sing. A single circle of light follows Norman, a majestic African-American woman wearing a flowing African dashiki, as she strolls onstage. No backup band, no musical instruments, just Jessye. The crowd stirs, restless. Few recognize the opera diva. A voice yells for more Guns 'n' Roses. Others take up the cry. The scene is getting ugly.

Alone, *a capella*, Jessye Norman begins to sing, very slowly:

Amazing grace, how sweet the sound
    That saved a wretch like me!
I once was lost but now am found—
    Was blind, but now I see.

A remarkable thing happens in Wembley Stadium that night. Seventy thousand raucous fans fall silent before her aria of grace.

By the time Norman reaches the second verse, "'Twas grace that taught my heart to fear, And grace my fears relieved . . . ," the soprano has the crowd in her hands.

By the time she reaches the third verse, "'Tis grace has brought me safe this far, And grace will lead me home," several thousand fans are singing along, digging far back in nearly lost memories for words they heard long ago.

When we've been there ten thousand years,
    Bright shining as the sun,
We've no less days to sing God's praise
    Than when we first begun.

Jessye Norman later confessed she had no idea what power descended on Wembley Stadium that night. I think I know. The world thirsts for grace. When grace descends, the world falls silent before it.

Sources

Chapter 1: The Last Best Word

13: *Niebuhr*: Quoted in D. Ivan Dykstra, *Who Am I? and Other Sermons.* Holland, Mich.: Hope College, 1983, p. 104.

14: *Bernanos*: Georges Bernanos, *The Diary of a Country Priest.* Garden City, N.Y.: Doubleday/Image, 1974, p. 233.

15: *Seamands*: David Seamands, "Perfectionism: Fraught with Fruits of Self-Destruction," in *Christianity Today*, April 10, 1981, pp. 24–25.

15: *MacDonald*: From a private conversation.

15: "*Growing Up Fundamentalist*": Stefan Ulstein, *Growing up Fundamentalist.* Downers Grove, Ill.: InterVarsity Press, 1995, p. 72.

Chapter 2: Babette's Feast: A Story

19: *Babette's Feast*: Short story included in Isak Dinesen, *Anecdotes of Destiny and Ehrengard.* New York: Random House/Vintage, 1993.

Chapter 3: A World Without Grace

29: *Herbert*: George Herbert, "The Church Militant," in *The English Poems of George Herbert.* Totowa, N.J.: Rowman and Littlefield, 1975, p. 196.

29: "*For the law*": John 1:17.

31: "*proverbs of ashes*": Job 13:12.

31: *Tournier*: Paul Tournier, *Guilt and Grace.* New York: Harper & Row, 1962, p. 23.

32: *Bombeck*: Erma Bombeck, *At Wit's End.* N. p.: Thorndike Large Print Edition, 1984, p. 63.

32: *James*: William James, *The Varieties of Religious Experience.* New York: The Modern Library, 1936, p. 297.

33: *St. John*: St. John of the Cross, *Dark Night of the Soul.* Garden City, N.Y.: Doubleday/Image, 1959.

33: *Hecht*: Anthony Hecht, "Galatians," in *Incarnation*, ed. Alfred Corn. New York: Viking, 1990, p. 158.

34: *Franklin*: Benjamin Franklin, *Autobiography*. New York: Buccaneer Books, 1984, pp. 103, 114.

35: "*Apology Sound-Off Line*": Jeanne McDowell, "True Confessions by Telephone," in *Time*, October 3, 1988, p. 85.

36: *Smedes*: Lewis B. Smedes, *Shame and Grace*. San Francisco: HarperCollins, 1993, pp. 80, 31.

37: *Times*: Nicholas D. Kristof, "Japanese Say No to Crime: Tough Methods, at a Price," in *The New York Times*, March 14, 1995, p. 1.

37: *Hemingway*: Ernest Hemingway, "The Capitol of the World," in *The Short Stories of Ernest Hemingway*. New York: Scribner, 1953, p. 38.

38: "*Every child that is born*": Quoted in Paul Johnson, *Intellectuals*. New York: Harper & Row, 1988, p. 145.

40: *Greave*: Peter Greave, *The Second Miracle*. New York: Henry Holt and Company, 1955.

41: "*a compassionate and gracious God*": Psalm 86:15.

Chapter 4: Lovesick Father

45: *Lewis*: Cited in Scott Hoezee, *The Riddle of Grace*. Grand Rapids: Eerdmans, 1996, p. 42.

52: "*This my son*": Luke 15:24, Revised Standard Version.

52: "*But while*": Luke 15:20.

53: "*In the same way*": Luke 15:10.

53: *Nouwen*: Henri J. M. Nouwen, *The Return of the Prodigal Son*. New York: Doubleday/Image, 1994, p. 114.

54: "*God, have mercy*": Luke 18:13.

54: "*There will be more*": Luke 15:7.

55: "*Jesus, remember*": Luke 23:42–43.

55: *Kierkegaard*: Søren Kierkegaard, *Training in Christianity*. Princeton: Princeton University Press, 1947, p. 20.

56: "*This my son was dead*": Luke 15:32.

Chapter 5: The New Math of Grace

59: *Luke*: Luke 15:3–7.

59: *John*: John 12:3–8.

60: *Mark*: Mark 12:41–44.

60: *Matthew*: Matthew 20:1–16.

61: "*Friend, I am*": Matthew 20:13–15.

62: *Buechner*: Frederick Buechner, *Telling the Truth*. San Francisco: Harper & Row, 1977, p. 70.

63: "*How many times*": Matthew 18:21–22.

63: "*Pay back*": Matthew 18:28.

64: *Lewis*: C. S. Lewis, "On Forgiveness," in *The Weight of Glory and Other Addresses*. New York: Collier Books/Macmillan, 1980, p. 125.

64: *Lewis Himself*: C. S. Lewis and Don Giovanni Calabria, *Letters*. Ann Arbor, Mich.: Servant Books, 1988, p. 67.

64: *Volf*: Miroslav Volf, *Exclusion and Embrace*. Nashville: Abingdon Press, 1996, p. 85.

65: "*For my thoughts*": Isaiah 55:8–9.

65: "*You do not stay*": Micah 7:18.

65: "*Swords will flash*": Hosea 11:6–9.

66: "*Go, show your love*": Hosea 3:1.

66: "*But where sin increased*": Romans 5:20.

66: *Buechner*: Frederick Buechner, *The Longing for Home*. San Francisco: HarperCollins, 1996, p. 175.

67: *Sayers*: Dorothy L. Sayers, *Christian Letters to a Post-Christian World*. Grand Rapids: Eerdmans, 1969, p. 45.

68: *Dr. Bob Smith*: Story recounted in Ernest Kurtz, *The Spirituality of Imperfection*. New York: Bantam, 1994, pp. 105–6.

69: *Donne*: John Donne, *John Donne's Sermons on the Psalms and the Gospels*. Berkeley: University of California Press, 1963, p. 22.

70: "*God of all grace*": 1 Peter 5:10.

Chapter 6: Unbroken Chain: A Story

80: "*lost coin, lost sheep*": Luke 15:20.

80: *Missionary in Lebanon*: Kenneth E. Bailey, *Poet & Peasant*. Grand Rapids: Eerdmans, 1976, pp. 161–64, 181.

Chapter 7: An Unnatural Act

85: *Tolstoy*: William L. Shirer, *Love and Hatred: The Stormy Marriage of Leo and Sonya Tolstoy*. New York: Simon & Schuster, 1994, pp. 26, 65–67.

86: *Auden*: W. H. Auden, "September 1, 1939," in *Selected Poems*. New York: Vintage Books/Random House, 1979, p. 86.

86: *O'Connor*: Elizabeth O'Connor, *Cry Pain, Cry Hope*. Waco, Tex.: Word Books, 1987, p. 167.

87: "*Forgive us*": Matthew 6:12, King James Version.

87: *Williams*: Charles Williams, *The Forgiveness of Sins*. Grand Rapids: Eerdmans, 1984, p. 66.

87: "*If you do not*": Matthew 6:15.

87: *Dryden*: Louis I. Bredvold, ed., *The Best of Dryden*. New York: T. Nelson and Sons, 1933, p. 20.

88: "*Therefore, if you are offering*": Matthew 5:23–24.

88: "*This is how*": Matthew 18:35.

88: *Jones (footnote)*: Gregory Jones, *Embodying Forgiveness: A Theological Analysis*. Grand Rapids: Eerdmans, 1995, p. 195.

89: "*that you may be sons*": Matthew 5:44–47.

89: *Bonhoeffer*: Dietrich Bonhoeffer, *The Cost of Discipleship*. New York: Macmillan, 1959, pp. 134–35.

91: *Thielicke*: Helmut Thielicke, *Waiting*, op. cit., p. 112.

92: *Nouwen*: Henri Nouwen, *Return*, op. cit., pp. 129–30.

93: "*Do not take revenge*": Romans 12:19.

Chapter 8: Why Forgive?

97: *Luther*: Quoted in "Colorful Sayings of Colorful Luther," in *Christian History*, vol. 34, p. 27.

97: *Márquez*: Gabriel García Márquez, *Love in the Time of Cholera*. New York: Alfred A. Knopf, 1988, pp. 28–30.

98: *Mauriac*: François Mauriac, *Knot of Vipers*. London: Metheun, 1984.

98: *Karr*: Mary Karr, *The Liar's Club*. New York: Viking, 1995.

99: *Smedes*: Lewis B. Smedes, *Shame*, op. cit., pp. 136, 141.

101: *Trapp*: Kathryn Watterson, *Not by the Sword*. New York: Simon & Schuster, 1995.

101: *Hugo*: Victor Hugo, *Les Misérables*. New York: Penguin, 1976, p. 111.

102: *Smedes*: Lewis B. Smedes, "Forgiveness: the Power to Change the Past," in *Christianity Today*, January 7, 1983, p. 24.

104: *Weil*: Simone Weil, *Gravity and Grace*. New York: Routledge, 1972, p. 9.

106: "*We do not have*": Hebrews 4:15.

107: "*God made him*": 2 Corinthians 5:21.

107: "*If it is possible*": Matthew 26:39.

107: "*forgive them*": Luke 23:34.

Chapter 9: Getting Even

109: *Wiesenthal*: Simon Wiesenthal, *The Sunflower*. New York: Schocken, 1976.

113: *Klausner*: Joseph Klausner, *Jesus of Nazareth: His Life, Times, and Teaching*. London: George Allen & Unwin, 1925, p. 393.

115: *Smedes*: Lewis B. Smedes, *Forgive and Forget*. San Francisco: Harper & Row, 1984, p. 130.

116: *Guardini*: Romano Guardini, *The Lord*. Chicago: Regnery Gateway, 1954, p. 302.

117: *Thielicke*: Helmut Thielicke, *Waiting*, op. cit., p. 62.

117: *Wilson*: Mark Noll, "Belfast: Tense with Peace" in *Books & Culture*, November/December 1995, p. 12.

118: *O'Connor*: Elizabeth O'Connor, *Cry Pain*, op. cit., p. 50.

119: *Time*: Lance Morrow, "I Spoke . . . As a Brother," in *Time*, January 9, 1984, pp. 27–33.

119: "*for they do*": Luke 23:34.

Chapter 10: The Arsenal of Grace

123: *Wink*: Walter Wink, *Engaging the Powers*. Minneapolis: Fortress, 1992, p. 275.

123: *The Wages of Guilt*: Ian Buruma, *The Wages of Guilt: Memories of War in Germany and Japan*. New York: Farrar, Straus and Giroux, 1994.

124: "*We, the first*": Quoted in *Response*, a publication of the Simon Wiesenthal Center in Los Angeles.

134: *Trueblood*: Elton Trueblood, *The Yoke of Christ*. Waco, Tex.: Word, 1958, p. 37.

136: *Wink*: Walter Wink, *Engaging*, op. cit., p. 191.

137: *Tutu*: Michael Henderson, *The Forgiveness Factor*. Salem, Ore.: Grosvenor Books USA, 1996, p. xix.

137: *King*: David Garrow, *Bearing the Cross*. New York: William Morrow, 1986, pp. 81, 500, 532.

138: *van der Post*: Laurens van der Post, *The Prisoner and the Bomb*. New York: William Morrow and Company, 1971, p. 133.

Chapter 11: A Home for Bastards: A Story

142: *Campbell*: Will D. Campbell, *Brother to a Dragonfly*. New York: The Seabury, 1977, pp. 220–24.

145: "*while we were*": Romans 5:8, italics added.

Chapter 12: No Oddballs Allowed

148: *"You are to"*: Leviticus 11:11.

149: "*I am the Lord*": Leviticus 11:44.

149: *Wouk*: Herman Wouk, *This Is My God*. New York: Little, Brown and Company, 1987, p. 111.

149: *Douglas*: Quoted in Sheldon Isenberg and Dennis E. Owen, "Bodies, Natural and Contrived: the Work of Mary Douglas" in *Religious Studies Review*, Vol. 3, No. 1, 1977, pp. 1–17.

150: *Neusner*: Jacob Neusner, *A Rabbi Talks with Jesus*. New York: Doubleday, 1993, p. 122.

151: "*For the generations*": Leviticus 21:17–20.

151: "*who hast not*": Quoted in John Timmer, "Owning Up to Baptism," in *The Reformed Journal*, May-June 1990, p. 14.

151. Volf, *Exclusion*, op. cit., p. 74.

153: "*in all Judea*": Acts 1:8.

153: "*began looking*": Mark 11:18.

153: "*the poor*": Luke 14:13.

155: "*There is neither*": Galatians 3:28.

156: "*Therefore, since we have*": Hebrews 4:14, 16.

156: "*since we have confidence*": Hebrews 10:19–21.

157: "*the Spirit himself*": Romans 8:26.

Chapter 13: Grace-Healed Eyes

171: "*All have sinned*": Romans 3:23.

171: *Tournier*: Paul Tournier, *The Person Reborn*. New York: Harper & Row, 1966, p. 71.

175: *Thielicke*: "Jesus gained . . ." from Helmut Thielicke, *How the World Began*. Philadelphia: Muhlenberg, 1961, p. 62.

175: *Thielicke*: "When Jesus loved . . ." from Helmut Thielicke, *Christ and the Meaning of Life*. Grand Rapids: Baker, 1975, p. 41.

175: *Dostoevsky*: Quoted in Helmut Thielicke, *Waiting*, op. cit., p. 81.

Chapter 14: Loopholes

177: *Hughes*: From radio interview, based on story in Robert Hughes, *The Fatal Shore*.

177: *Auden*: W. H. Auden, "For the Time Being," in *The Collected Poetry of W. H. Auden*. New York: Random House, 1945, p. 459.

178: *Lloyd-Jones*: Quoted in Stephen Brown, *When Being Good Isn't Good Enough*. Nashville: Nelson, 1990, p. 102.

178: "*Even though*": 1 Timothy 1:13–15, italics added.

180: *Lewis*: "St. Augustine" from C. S. Lewis, *Letters to an American Lady*. Grand Rapids: Eerdmans, 1967, p. 71.

180: *Lewis*: "To condone" from C. S. Lewis, *The Problem of Pain*. New York: Macmillan, 1962, p. 122.

181: *Heaney*: Quoted in Helen Vendler, "Books" in *The New Yorker*, March 13, 1989, p. 107.

182: *Tournier*: Paul Tournier, *Guilt*, op. cit., p. 112.

182: *Lewis*: C. S. Lewis, *Mere Christianity*. New York: Macmillan, 1960, p. 60.

183: "*For God*": John 3:17.

183: *Tournier*: Paul Tournier, *Guilt*, op cit., pp. 159–60.

184: "*change the grace*": Jude 4.

184: *Luther*: Quoted in Walter Kaufmann, *The Faith of a Heretic*. Garden City, N.Y.: Doubleday, 1961, pp. 231–32.

184: "*grow in grace*": 2 Peter 3:18.

184: *Trobisch*: Walter Trobisch, *Love Yourself*. Downers Grove, Ill.: Inter-Varsity Press, 1976, p. 26.

185: "*All have sinned*": Romans 3:23.

185: "*But where sin*": Romans 5:20.

185: "*What shall we*": Romans 6:1.

185: "*What then?*": Romans 6:15.

186: "*We died*": Romans 6:2.

186: "*Count yourselves*": Romans 6:11, italics added.

186: "*Do not let*": Romans 6:12.

188: *Mauriac*: François Mauriac, *God and Mammon*. London: Sheed & Ward, 1946, pp. 68–9.

190: *Bonhoeffer*: Quoted in Clifford Williams, *Singleness of Heart*. Grand Rapids: Eerdmans, 1994, p. 107.

190: "*teaches us*": Titus 2:12.

190: *Mairs*: Nancy Mairs, *Ordinary Time*. Boston: Beacon Press, 1993, p. 138.

191: *Augustine*: Quoted in Kathleen Norris, *The Cloister Walk*. New York: Riverhead, 1996, p. 346.

Chapter 15: Grace Avoidance

195: "*Snakes . . .*": Matthew 23:33, 16–18, 27.

196: "*You Pharisees*": Luke 11:39.

196: "*So when*": Matthew 6:2–6.

197: "*Love the Lord*": Matthew 22:37.

197: "*Be perfect*": Matthew 5:48.

197: *Tolstoy*: Leo Tolstoy, "An Afterword to 'The Kreutzer Sonata,'" in A. N. Wilson, *The Lion and the Honeycomb: The Religious Writings of Tolstoy*. San Francisco: Harper & Row, 1987, p. 69.

198: "*Woe to you*": Luke 11:46.

198: "*You shall not misuse*": Exodus 20:7.

199: "*Do not cook*": Exodus 23:19.

199: "*You shall not commit*": Exodus 20:14.

200: "*You give a tenth*": Matthew 23:23–24.

201: "*It was a great relief*": Quoted in Walter Wink, *Naming the Powers*. Philadelphia: Fortress, 1984, p. 116.

202: "*Be on your guard*": Luke 12:1, Matthew 23:3.

204: "*Everything they do*": Matthew 23:5–7.

205: "*filthy rags*": Isaiah 64:6.

205: *Nouwen*: Henri Nouwen, *Return*, op. cit., p. 71.

206: "*For I would not*": Romans 7:7–8.

206: *Küng*: Hans Küng, *On Being a Christian*. Garden City, N.Y.: Doubleday, 1976, p. 242.

207: *Luther*: Quoted in Karen Armstrong, *A History of God*. New York, Alfred A. Knopf, 1974, p. 276.

208: *Capon*: Robert Farrar Capon, *Between Noon and Three*. San Francisco: Harper & Row, 1982, p. 148.

209: "*For the kingdom*": Romans 14:17.

Chapter 17: Mixed Aroma

229: *New York Times*: "Government Is Not God's Work," in *New York Times*, August 29, 1993.

230: "*When the foundations*": Psalm 11:3.

230: "*The only way*": Quoted in Rodney Clapp, "Calling the Religious Right to Its Better Self," *Perspectives*, April 1994, p. 12.

231: *Terry*: Virginia Culver, "200 hear Terry hit 'baby killers'," in *The Denver Post*, July 30 1993, p. 4B.

231: *Reed*: Quoted in Jim Wallis, *Who Speaks for God?* New York: Delacorte, 1996, p. 161.

232: *Willimon*: William H. Willimon, "Been there, preached that," in *Leadership*, Fall 1995, p. 76.

233: *Jefferson*: Quoted in Robert Booth Fowler, *Religion and Politics in America*. Metuchen, N.J.: Scarecrow, 1985, p. 234.

234: *Manchester*: William Manchester, *A World Lit Only by Fire*. Boston: Little, Brown and Company, 1993, p. 191.

234: *Johnson*: Paul Johnson, *A History of Christianity*. New York: Atheneum, 1976, p. 263.

234: *Newbigin*: Lesslie Newbigin, *Foolishness to the Greeks*. Grand Rapids: Eerdmans, 1986, p. 117.

235: "*We're tired*": Quoted in Walter Wink, *Engaging*, op. cit., 263.

235: "*police department*": Quoted in Rodney Clapp, *Perspectives*, op. cit., p. 12.

235: "*Code of Connecticut*": Quoted in Brennan Manning, *Abba's Child.* Colorado Springs: NavPress, 1994, p. 82.

Chapter 18: Serpent Wisdom

239: *"undertaken, for"*: Quoted by Paul Johnson, "God and the Americans," a lecture delivered in 1994 at the Pierpont Morgan Library in New York.

239: "*Our constitution*": Quoted in John R. Howe Jr., *The Changing Political Thought of John Adams*. Princeton: Princeton University Press, 1966, p. 185.

239: "*We are a Christian*": Quoted in Richard John Neuhaus, *The Naked Public Square*. Grand Rapids: Eerdmans, 1986, p. 80.

239: "*I believe*": Speech by Earl Warren reported in "Breakfast at Washington," in *Time*, February 14, 1954, p. 49.

241: *Dobson*: James Dobson, "Why I Use 'Fighting Words,'" in *Christianity Today*, June 19, 1995, p. 28.

242: "*Love your enemies*": Matthew 5:44.

244: *Reed*: Ralph Reed, *Active Faith*. New York: The Free Press, 1996, pp. 120, 65.

246: *Kaunda*: Quoted in Tom Sine, *Cease Fire*. Grand Rapids: Eerdmans, 1995, p. 284.

246: "*Christ is Lord*": Christoph Schönborn, "The Hope of Heaven, The Hope of Earth," in *First Things*, April 1995, p. 34.

246: "*To God alone*": Quoted in Robert E. Webber, *The Church in the World: Opposition, Tension, or Transformation?* Grand Rapids: Zondervan, 1986.

246: *Becket*: Quoted in Jacques Maritain, *The Things That Are Not Caesar's*. London: Sheed & Ward, 1930, p. 16.

247: *Bellah*: Robert N. Bellah, et al., *The Good Society*. New York: Vintage, 1992, p. 180.

249: *Eisenhower*: Quoted in Paul Johnson, *The Quest for God.* New York: HarperCollins, 1996, p. 35.

250: *Barth*: Quoted in Paul Johnson, *History*, op. cit., p. 483.

251: "*Be perfect*": Matthew 5:48.

Chapter 19: Patches of Green

255: *Tuchman*: Quoted in *Bill Moyers: A World of Ideas*, ed. Betty Sue Flowers. New York: Doubleday, 1989, p. 5.

255: *Solzhenitsyn*: Excerpt from his Templeton Prize acceptance address in 1993.

260: *Forsyth*: Quoted in Donald Bloesch, *The Crisis of Piety*. Colorado Springs: Helmers and Howard, 1988, p. 116.

260: "*Father, forgive*": Luke 23:34.

263: *Bonhoeffer*: Dietrich Bonhoeffer, *Cost*, op. cit., p. 136.

263: "*By this*": John 13:35, italics added.

265: *Sider*: Quoted in Bob Briner, *Deadly Detours*. Grand Rapids: Zondervan, 1996, p. 95.

265: *Nietzsche*: Friedrich Nietzsche, *The Anti-Christ*. New York: Penguin, 1968, pp. 115–18.

266: *Day*: Dorothy Day, *The Long Loneliness*. San Francisco: HarperCollins, 1981, p. 235.

266: *Bellah*: Quoted in speech by John Stott.

Chapter 20: Gravity and Grace

271: *Weil*: Simone Weil, *Gravity*, op. cit., pp. 1, 16.

271: *Barth*: Karl Barth, *The Word of God and the Word of Man*. New York: Harper & Row, 1957, p. 92.

272: *Merton*: Thomas Merton, *No Man Is an Island*. New York: Harcourt, Brace and Company, 1955, p. 235.

273: *Lewis*: C. S. Lewis, *The Four Loves*. London: Geoffrey Bles, 1960, p. 149.

273: "*God in heaven*": Quoted in Ernest Kurtz, *Spirituality*, op. cit., p. 29.

274: "*Then he turned*": Luke 7:44–47.

274: *Damnation*: Harold Frederic, *The Damnation of Theron Ware*. New York: Penguin, 1956, pp. 75–76.

276: *Meyer*: Quoted in Brennan Manning, *The Gentle Revolutionaries*. Denville, N.J.: Dimension, 1976, p. 66.

277: *Mairs*: Nancy Mairs, *Ordinary Time*, op. cit., p. 89.

280: *Nietzsche*: Quoted in Williams, *Singleness*, op. cit., p. 126.

281: *Lewis*: C. S. Lewis, *Mere*, op. cit., pp. 105–6.

Other books by Philip Yancey

The Jesus I Never Knew
Disappointment with God
Where Is God When It Hurts?
Church: Why Bother?
Discovering God
Finding God in Unexpected Places
The Gift of Pain (with Dr. Paul Brand)
Fearfully and Wonderfully Made (with Dr. Paul Brand)
In His Image (with Dr. Paul Brand)
The Student Bible, NIV (with Tim Stafford)
The Jesus I Never Knew, Study Guide (with Brenda Quinn)

The Gift of Pain

The autobiography of Dr. Paul Brand follows his dramatic career in medicine across three continents.

Fearfully and Wonderfully Made

Philip Yancey teams with Dr. Paul Brand to offer insight into the marvelous details of the human body and draw analogies to the relationship expressed by New Testament writers in the metaphor of the body of Christ.

In His Image

The companion to *Fearfully and Wonderfully Made* unfolds spiritual truths through a physician's knowledge of the blood, the head, the spirit, and pain.

We want to hear from you. Please send your comments about this book to us in care of the address below. Thank you.

ZondervanPublishingHouse
Grand Rapids, Michigan 49530
http://www.zondervan.com